THE INDIANS OF ILLINOIS

by

Helen Cox Tregillis

HERITAGE BOOKS
2012

HERITAGE BOOKS
AN IMPRINT OF HERITAGE BOOKS, INC.

Books, CDs, and more—Worldwide

For our listing of thousands of titles see our website
at
www.HeritageBooks.com

Published 2012 by
HERITAGE BOOKS, INC.
Publishing Division
100 Railroad Ave. #104
Westminster, Maryland 21157

Copyright © 1983, 1991 Helen Cox Tregillis

Other books by the author:

*Ancestors: A Teaching Story Using the Families of Cox, Hayes, Hulse,
Range, Worley and Others with Suggested Lessons*

Central Illinois Chronicles, Volumes 1-3

Illinois, the 14th Colony: French Period

Indians of Illinois

People and Rural Schools of Shelby County, Illinois

River Roads to Freedom: Fugitive Slave Notices and Sheriff Notices Found in Illinois Sources

The Native Tribes of Ohio

The front cover illustration is of Chief Shabbona

All rights reserved. No part of this book may be reproduced or transmitted in any form or by any means, electronic or mechanical, including photocopying, recording or by any information storage and retrieval system without written permission from the author, except for the inclusion of brief quotations in a review.

International Standard Book Numbers
Paperbound: 978-1-55613-502-6
Clothbound: 978-0-7884-9427-7

Contributions from the Woodland
    Native Americans

- Corn and other foods
- Place names
- Attitude toward life and nature
- Love of freedom
- Arrival of babies spaced
- Literature and art
- Peacemakers and peacekeepers
- Medical skills
- Idea of democracy and influence on early colonists as evidenced by quotation from Benjamin Franklin in the 1750's

"It would be a very strange thing, if six Nations of ignorant Savages should be capable of forming a scheme for such a Union, and be able to execute it in such a manner, as that it has subsisted ages, and appears indissoluble, and yet that a like Union should be impracticable for ten or a dozen English colonies, to whom it is more necessary, and must be more advantageious; and who cannot be supposed to want an equal understanding of their interests."

An Indian at His Father's Grave
by James Stelle
Published in SOUTHERN ILLINOISAN (Shawneetown)
September 2, 1853

Stop! whiteman stop! This mound you see
  Is where my father's ashes lay;
'Tis dearer far than life to me--
  Oh! do not force his child away.
This mossy earth is where he trod,
  A noble warrior good and brave,
But now his spirit is with God!
  And I am left to watch his grave.

Those mighty woods belonged to him,
  Now he has gave them all to me.
For when his eyes in death grew dim,
  He said, "'Tis thine, go and be free."
Go hunt the game, young warrior go.
  Meet every danger face to face,
And let no base perfidious foe
  Pollute your father's resting place.

It was the Mighty Spirit's will
  To make thee wiser far than we,
To teach thee better how to kill,
  Then hear thy brother's prayer to thee;
I cannot fight with thee--I'm done,
  And in thy power to kill or save;
But do not force a forest son
  From his departed father's grave!

They heed me not!--they force me back;
  They plow my father's hillock rends,
And on the earth his bones they stack,
  Regardless of his praying friends;
Regardless of the tears that flow,
  Or blood that poured out day by day--
Oh! Father Spirit, mercy show,
  The whitemen forced your son away!

TABLE OF CONTENTS

Contributions from the Woodland Native Americans ..Preface
An Indian at His Father's Grave........................Preface
Introduction.. 1
In the Beginning--Early Ancestors of the Illinois.... 3
The Illinois--Descendants of the Mound Builders...... 14
Other Indians of Illinois............................. 27
Selected Biographies of Early Native Americans
    Aptakisic... 36
    Beaubien Family................................... 37
    Big Foot.. 38
    Black Hawk.. 39
    Black Partridge................................... 42
    Bourbonnais....................................... 44
    Billy Caldwell.................................... 45
    Naw Kaw Caromaine................................. 46
    Chicagou.. 47
    Christmas Dagney.................................. 49
    Jean Baptiste Ducoigne............................ 50
    Jean Baptiste Pointe Du Sable..................... 51
    Gomo.. 52
    Hononegah... 53
    Jeneir.. 54
    Kannekuk.. 55
    Keokuk.. 56
    La Framboise Family............................... 58
    Mamantouensa...................................... 59
    Metea... 61
    Joseph Ogee....................................... 62
    Antoine Ouilmette................................. 63
    Pakoisheecan...................................... 64
    Baptiste Peoria................................... 65
    Pontiac... 66
    Alexander Robinson or Chechepinqua................ 68
    Shaubenee... 69
    Shick Shack or Shakah............................. 71
    Tecumseh.. 72
    Topennebee.. 74
    Wabunsee or Wauponehsee........................... 75
    Wakieshiek.. 76
    Winnemac.. 77
Anecdotal Stories of Early Indians of Illinois
    and Early Newspaper Accounts...................... 78
Alphabetical Listing of Indian and Indian-related
    Individuals Found on Various Documents and
    Records... 102

Bibliography   145
Index   151

LIST OF ILLUSTRATIONS

Animal tracks	6
Archange Ouilmette	101
Arrowheads	2,62,63,65,68
Ball sticks	53
Black Hawk	39
Black Partridge medal	43
Bonefish hook	21
Buffalo hunt	26
Burial vases	19,41,46
Cahokia mound artifact	32
Celt or ungrooved axe	57,84
Ceremonial stone	81,83,84
Copper axe	77
Copper ear buttons	77
Designs	35
Detroit of 1705	89
Discoids	60
Dwellings	91
Eagle on copper plate	28
Flint spade	65
Flint tool	83
French missionaries to Indians	87
Frontier fort	98
Gorget, mound	37
Grafton, Illinois pictograph	21
Grooved hammer stone	67
Grooved stone axe	57,58
Ground flint battle axe	58
Hafted spade	67
Hafted weapon	49
Illinois counties	78
Illinois territory of 1765	24
Illinois totem	14
Illinois villages of 1680	12
Indian letter on birch bark	48
Indian picture writing	51
Indian tribes east of Mississippi	54
Indian tribes of 1700	13
Indian village	25
Iroquois dwelling	86
Joliet's map of 1673-74	94
LaSalle's explorations	85
LaSalle map of 1684	17
Madison Co., Illinois mound	68
Marshno, Mr. Josephine	70
Medicine bag	82
Moccasins	20
Mound skull	50

Contd.

Northwest territory	90
Notched hoe	68
Papoose	80
Pendants	75
Piasa figure	96
Pictograph	10
Pipes	74
Portages	93
Prehistoric sites of Illinois	4
Quah, Modwe	70
Revolutionary war in the west	95
Shabbona	70
Shell beads	38
Shells, mound	64
Spear head	65
Sphynx pipe	79
Stone gouge	49
Tecumseh	73
United States in 1783	92
Wampum	86
War club	81
Warrior garb	34
White Cloud	76
Winnebago beaded dance pouch	30

INTRODUCTION

Anything said now about the Illinois who formerly lived in this territory can only be past history at best. Their glory, pride of their native ground is no more. A small trophy, indeed, to a great people's memory to have a state named after them. Ironic that the settler never hesitated to take from the Native American but yet never bothered to thank him for all that he had done.

Name loaning is one of the largest gifts from the Native American. Hence, the name Illinois graces the land where once these people lived and prospered. Originally the name meant "the most perfect man." How fitting! The early Illinois were indeed men who were proud of what they were--human beings. Many called them cowards because they did not fight. Their beliefs and trust in fellow man were so great, why should they be discredited for upholding their beliefs.

George Catlin, an American artist, merely preserved for us the portraits and beliefs of the Indian at **their** best, and worse as white men encroached on **their ways** of life.

> "I have seen him shrinking from civilized approach, which came with all its vices, like the dead of the night, upon him...seen him gaze and then retreat like the frightened deer....I have seen him shrinking from the soil and haunts of his boyhood, bursting the strongest ties which bound him to the earth and its pleasures. I have seen him set fire to his wigwam and smooth over the graves of his fathers...clap his hand in silence over his mouth, and take the last look over his fair hunting ground, and turn his face in saddness to the setting sun....
>
> I love a people who have always made me welcome to the best they had...who are honest without laws, who have no jails and no poor-houses...who never take the name of God in vain...who worship God without a Bible, and I believe God loves them also,...who are free from religious animosities...who have never raised a hand against me, or stolen my property, where there is no law to punish either,...who never fought a battle with white men except on their own ground...and Oh, how I love a people who don't live for the love of money!"
> (I HAVE SPOKEN)

Jean Baptiste Ducoigne stated to George Rogers Clark that the Illinois were descendants of the ancient Mound Builders. In truth, why not accept the man's statement for a fact.

As a creature of the land and nature, I do not find the Indian difficult to understand at all. The Illinois and all the others were caretakers of the land. They took only what they needed to survive and returned more than what they had borrowed. They understood as I that we--all men--are more a part of the universe, the natural order of things, then we oftentimes try to forget by possessing in selfish ownership that which is never ours to own since we are in reality the dust of the earth. We are merely trying to buy our own dust.
Eric Sloane in his SPIRITS OF '76 summarizes what I feel and can not express in words.

"Thankfulness happened to be an important tie to friendship with the American Indians who regarded gratitude above simple good manners: to them, ingratitude was the unpardonable sin and gratitude was godliness: their cermonies were full of thanksgivings. 'We are grateful for the land,' goes one common prayer of the Red Man, 'and for all the things upon the land which the Spirit has bestowed.' In the dust wherever modern progress has buried other cultures, we have buried much of the magic of earlier civilizations.

"I have often read about the American Indian's belief that God owns the earth and man is only a tenant upon it: the idea seems primitive and quaint to us nowadays. Yet the sooner we realize it is a basic truth, the better for civilization. America is proud of its cities and highways, all its developments and improvements, but in the eyes of Whoever or Whatever created the earth and its countryside, we might well hang our heads in shame."

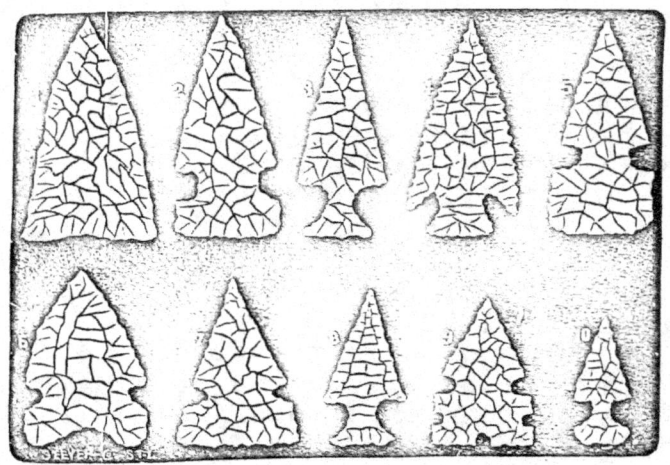

1893 Illinois State Exhibit
World's Columbian Exposition

In the Beginning--
Early Ancestors of the Illinois
Chapter 1

In the beginning the territory of Illinois was a paradise filled with game and an abundance of natural fruits. Before 10,000 B.C. early man came into the territory and settled along the fertile river valleys. Where he came from still poses debatable issues among present-day scholars. Whether he crossed the Bering Straits or came from the Mediterranean area is not important but that he was here, is.

That early man was an ancestor to natives encountered by later Europeans in the sixteenth and seventeenth centuries. The native here was not a short-timed resident. Indeed, if he could have, he could have traced his ancestry back for 500 generations. If he had, then his race would have been the longest in existence. The Indian remained a man of nature and in harmony with his gods--manitous who answered to the Great Spirit. The Winnebago--later residents of Illinois--perhaps summed it up well about his world:

> Pleasant it looked,
> This newly created world.
> Along the entire length and breadth
> Of the earth, our grandmother,
> Extended the green reflection
> Of her covering
> And the escaping odors
> Were pleasant to inhale.
>   (THE WORLD OF THE AMERICAN INDIAN)

Thus the Indian did not worship nature. He appealed to it because through him and nature flowed the "permeating occult force which is vaguely and fearfully apprehended." (A STUDY OF SIOUAN CULTS)

10,000 to 8000 B.C. Paleo or Clovis Indian

Long before Columbus made his voyage in 1492, early man in the Illinois country was hunting game, birthing children, and burying his dead. The Illinois River valley served as the fertile provider just as the Nile had for the Egyptians. The early man here was more than a hunter. He was a man of nature and he used what nature provided. Remains of these early inhabitants have been recently studied in the past few years. Strange that after centuries of being unknown, that this early man now comes to the surface.

It has just been since May 1979 that archaeology has uncovered existence of this early man in the Illinois River valleys. During most of the native's lifetime, he was a hunter

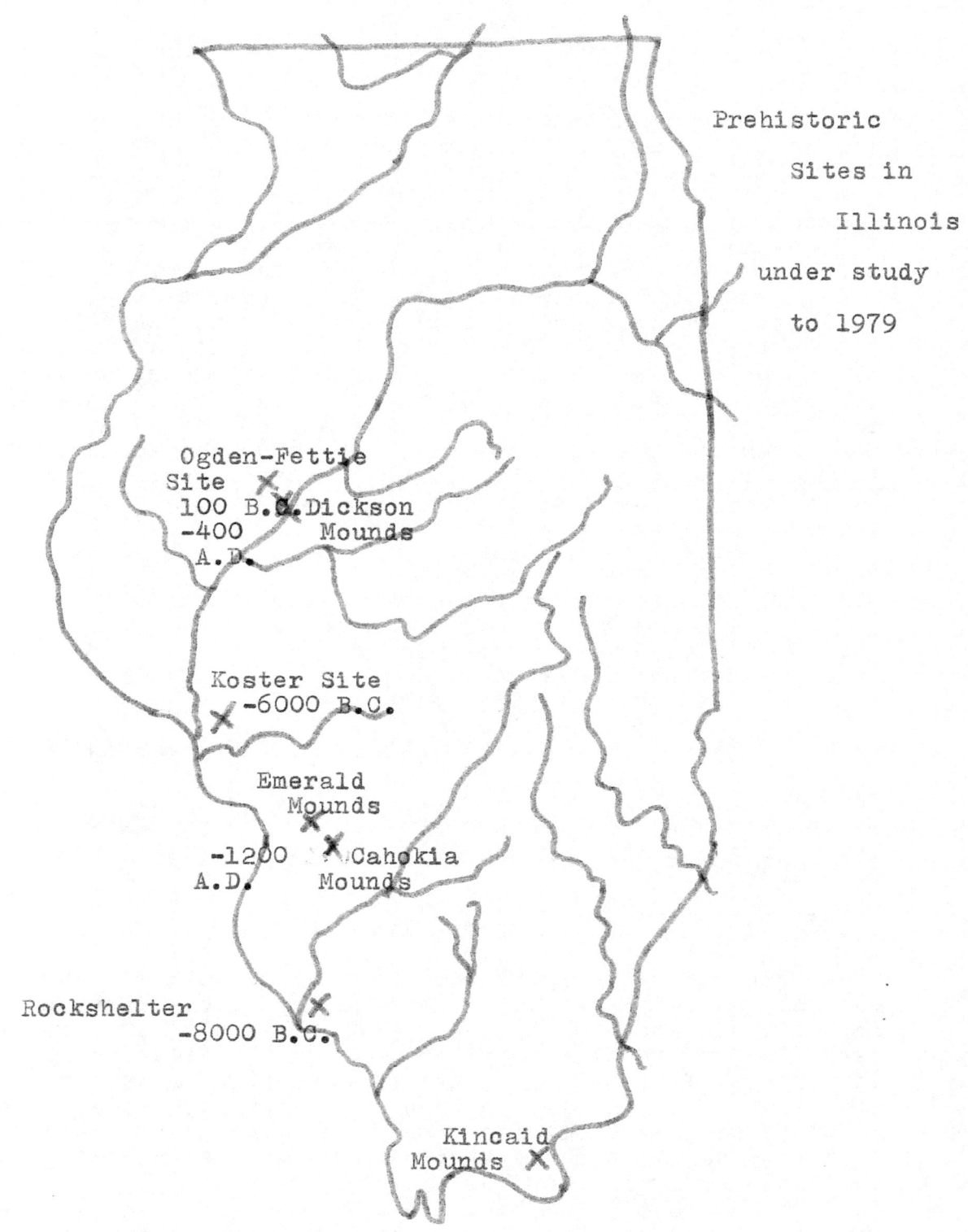

and forager for food. They used rock cliffs or caves for shelters. They did use tools--flint or other stone--for projectile points. The process they used is described later in this chapter.

This early man was believed to be the first here and the first ancestor of the Indian. Recently--1979--Clovis man's remains have been found south of St. Louis. By all indications, this early man hunted mammoths, mastodons, bison, horses and camels. The points he used were four to six inches long at the end of a wooden shaft.

During the summers these people probably lived on the edge of the waterways where they were close to fish, mussels and other water animals. In colder weather, the people probably moved into protected areas under bluffs in wooded areas. They travelled extensively from place to place, according to the game.

For clothing they more than likely used animal skins, either scrapped or with fur intact. And they probably also knew the use of fire. Game, natural-food stores were plentiful. In fact, it has been estimated that in the lower Illinois valley six thousand years ago, a year's yield would be "180,000 bushels of walnuts and hickory nuts, 50,000 bushels of acorns, 100 deer, 10,000 squirrels, 200 turkeys, and even five black bear" from a ten-square-mile area. (THE WORLD OF THE AMERICAN INDIAN)

To fell the larger game--the seven or eight foot tall bison, mastodon, or mammoth--, several male hunters would surround or drive the animal to a mud pit or a fall. When the animal was down, they would stab, jab, or stone until the animal would stop bellowing. The Indian hunter used this fall-kill method effectively until the 19th century.

8000 to 6000 B.C. Archaic Indian

The most interesting of the recent discoveries has been that at Koster Sites in Calhoun County, Illinois. A farmer by the name of Harlin Helton showed Stuart Struever the place where he had always found many artifacts in the lower Illinois valley. The next summer, Struever, an associate professor of archeology at the Northwestern University, returned to the area with a team of students. They made a few test sites and were successful. The result has been one of the most important finds thus far in North American archaeology.

Here the Indians built a modest village, fortified it. The houses were "rude"--posts supporting woven stick walls and thatch roofs. And they had learned how to dig terraces. They selected sites by natural springs, some of which are still running today. Physically the Indians were in good shape, not the small primitive weaklings pictured by many. Evidence has revealed that "they were a remarkable hearty breed. There's no reason to assume they were poor, underpriviledged Indians. Actually, they had it quite good." (Jane Buikstra, Northwestern anthropodogist)

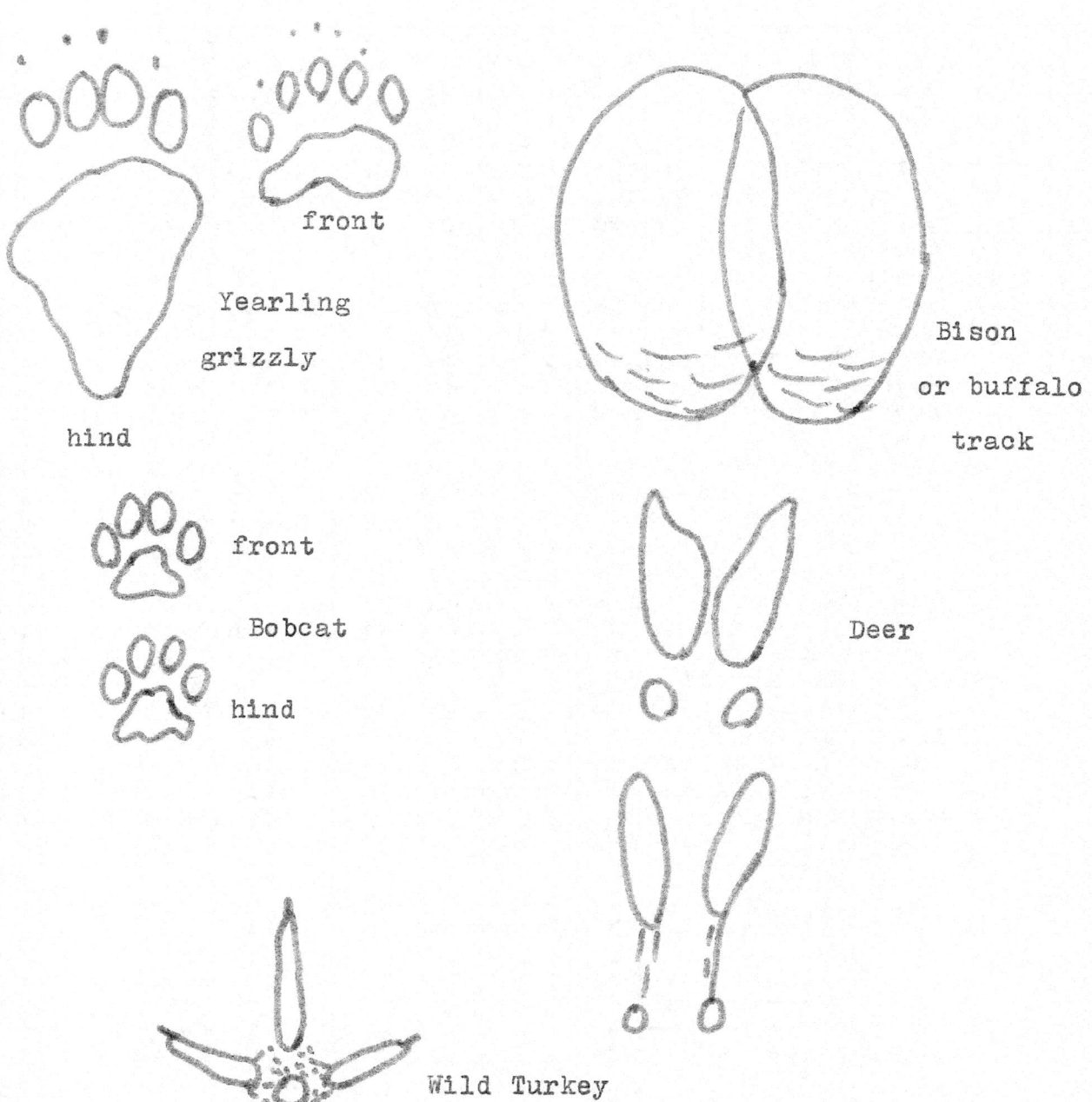

The early Indian of Illinois tracked such animals. A FIELD GUIDE TO ANIMAL TRACKS by Claus J. Murie.

Most of the Indians lived to their forties or fifties, suffered no malnutrition, little tooth decay, and suffered no epidemic diseases. Men averaged six feet in height.

Thus, the early inhabitants in the Illinois country were not roamers but permanent settlers in a village life for a number of years until supplies became too low or garbage became too great. Imagine the scene with a people routinely awaking each day. The women gathered fruits, fished, worked on skins and pottery. The men hunted with spears, tools of their own making. Sometimes the women planted a few seeds for squash and gourds which dried for winter eating. They also domesticated small animals, dogs, for pets and in some cases, buried them with ceremony after the animal died. Some of the villages would cover four or five acres in area and at others, villages would be rather sizable with 500 individuals or more. They seldom fought with others in the area. There was no need since there was plenty for all. They certainly knew the advantage of the location at Koster since the area was well protected from floods and it was convenient to food and spring water sources. In the forest, game was plentiful with black bear, mountain lion, elk, coyote, wolves, prairie chickens, and wild turkey. The waters of the Illinois provided all sorts of fish, including shell. Imagine, if you will, that for nearly 500 generations, these people prospered, multiplied and lived in peace. During this time, they also participated in a trading ring--"that spanned much of the continent." (Peter Gorner, CHICAGO TRIBUNE)

Indeed, Barry Fell in his AMERICA, B.C. and his supporters theorize that ancient people of Mediterranean origin provided much of the trade traffic for the area with copper, ores, shells, pottery, etc. Artifacts within the burial mounds substantiate the existence of the early trading.

Tool making also became manifest very early. The first was a spear. The bow and arrow did not appear until around 1000 A.D. Early Indians became quite skilled in creating tools from stone--particularly flint which can have an edge sharper than the modern day steel scalpel. The tool maker would first take a large flint nodule and a small hammerstone. He would rest the nodule on his knee or leg for support and hit the flint with the hammerstone. Small shallow flakes or chips would fly from the larger piece. He would constantly turn the nodule around and chip along the edges of both sides. After a short time and much patience, a useful tool or point would result. These tools or points are still found today.

6000 to 2000 B.C. Later Archaic Indians

Today three locations of these ancient people provide study for modern-day man. The first already mentioned being at Koster Sites--between the joining of the Illinois and Mississippi Rivers. The other location is in Randolph County where the Kaskaskia River flows in the Mississippi. It was at the latter location that the Cahokia Indians created their large mounds of dirt. Another area is the Dickson Mounds in Fulton County on the Illinois River.

Stuart Struever at Koster Sites discovered that the people occupying the area the longest used large roasting pits to cook their meats. Quite possibly the meat would have been bear or buffalo which came later. From other remains of dwellings, he concluded the houses were permanent not the "mythical tent" created by later romantics. Struever further indicated that "We've dug up vanished(civilizations) and found artifacts they had collected from cultures who died thousands of years before them..." "Scientists from a host of disciplines were able to re-create the daily life of surprisingly sophisicated peoples who lived in peace and extracted a good living from their environment by working perhaps 20 hours a week....And they didn't start killing each other until...1200 A.D." (Peter Gorner) All this has showed up in the remains of the mounds. Disease developed among the early man and many bodies showed violent deaths, indicated by the arrowheads stuck within the skeleton structures.

1000 B.C. to 450 A.D. Hopewell Indian

The lower Illinois valley still remained the location for many of the Indians. Their development by this time was somewhat more complex as they were later known as the Hopewell. Here the Hopewells grew their crops and domesticated animals. At one location there is strong evidence that the site was a trade center where many other tribal individuals met to barter goods. Their villages were organized by social status and cemetery plots were nearby.

The Hopewell were the ones who buried precious artifacts with the dead. Most counties along the river bottoms have such village sites. In 1969 such a site was investigated by the University of Illinois study team before completion of the Lake Shelbyville dam in Shelby County, Illinois. On that particular site, three villages had existed at different time periods. The villages had trenches or stockades. Pole-holes were dug to support houses. Fire pits and food storage pits were also found. These people also developed a monetary system using a particular flint type called "Hornstone" or "dongola." Piles of these discs have been found in leaders' graves. They did raise a few crops but mostly maintained themselves by hunting. However, it was quite possible that during this period that the human population increased. During the 1920's in a Shelbyville, Illinois gravel pit, a skeleton of a tall man was found in a stone-lined grave. With his skeleton were some artifacts, especially a beautifully carved calument or pipe.

450 to 1000 A.D. The Mississippian Indians

These early people had by this time made use of metal.

Copper engravings have been found in the mound or burial remains. Also corn began to be cultivated more extensively as a stable food crop. Squash, beans, and melons had already been grown. A water tradeway developed up and down the Mississippi between the people here and those in Mexico. The bow was beginning to appear in the north but the major tools still remained the mace, knife, spear and spear thrower. Also more prevalent now was clan ownership of an area. The individual did not possess for himself but for others. The later Illinois encountered by the French still professed the community laws. The French were more tolerant of the Indian's belief than the English, Spanish, and later "white" Americans. As William Brandon well stated, "On the one hand the communal outlook produced attitudes toward cooperation and group identity that were reflected in some measure in every gesture of Indian existence, from practical jokery to religion. On the other hand the ingrained custom of personal acquisition at the expense of one's neighbors, of striving in constant competition against each other, colored every aspect of European life and thought." Indeed, the Indian already lived the Golden Rule and loved his neighbor. No wonder he was often perplexed by the "Bible toting" preachers. To the Indian the Great Spirit owned the land and it was a gift from Him for man to use, not possess.

The trade networks became more extended--obsidian from the Rockies, tobacco from Virginia to the St. Lawrence, copper from the present Canadian border to North Carolina, flint and salt and pipestone everywhere. Also by this time, a primitive confederacy developed among the Illinois tribes.

1000 to 1200 A.D. Later Mississippian Indians

This period became a turning point in the Indians' development. Stronger fortifications on higher ground became a necessity. Larger numbers huddled together for mutual protection and moral support. Warning signs in huge pictographs--such as the "Piasa" described by Marquette-- along the river bluff walls. The name Piasa was given to the picture later. Indians who desired to protect their areas painted the warnings in order to frighten would-be invaders away. Such invaders might well have been the Aztecs from the south, wanting to have a few victims for human sacrifice. Fantastic stories of seagoing monsters who inhabited the waterways were passed by word of mouth to discourage travellers along the river.

A very interesting pictograph was created, carved rather, on the Illinois River bluff in Pike County. The outline strongly resembles the border of the United States or the North American continent. The superinposed figure of an archer within a solemn face, points toward the East or the European area. Was the pictograph drawn by its artist to descry the coming of Europeans during the sixteenth or seventeenth centuries or was it drawn much earlier to indicate the origin of early man here? A representation of this pictograph was on display in the 1893 World's Columbian Exposition, Illinois Exhibit at Chicago.

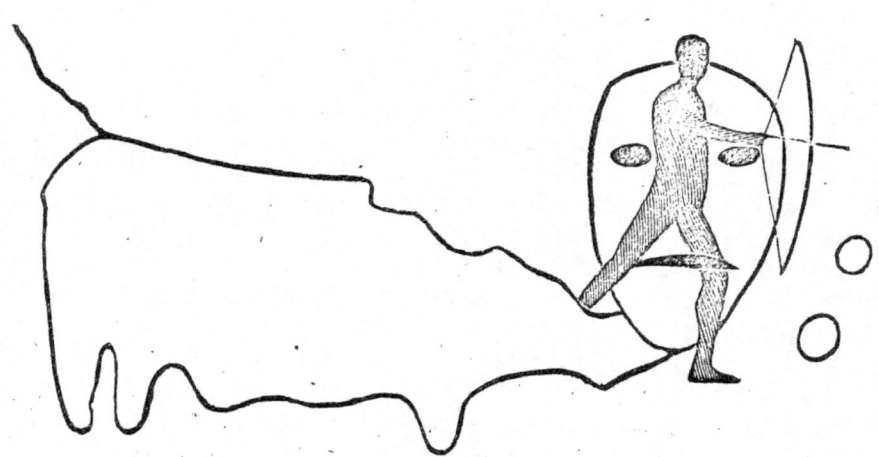

An Ancient Pictograph Carved on Rock of the Illinois River Bluff in Pike County.

900 to 1400 A.D. Late Woodland, Mound Builders

These Cahokian mound builders or mound building people created a "bustling, gigantic Indian city of 30 to 40,000 people--a capital city which was the center of religion, trade, economics, government, and social activity for a tremendous area....There were probably several small villages in the area. They built pit houses for each family. The floors were two to four feet below the surface and vertical posts set in the perimeter formed the walls, which were covered with layers of thatch or reed mats. The roofs were likewise thatched....Agriculture became the major and stable food base as improved and more productive varieties of corn were grown, as well as beans, squash, pumpkins, sunflower, etc...." (William Iseminger)

The Indian farmers would girdle trees with stone axes, then burn the stumps and underbrush to clear an area. Often the dead stumps would remain. As then as now the planter would mix bean seeds with the corn so the beans would vine on the stalks. Holes would merely be poked with a stick or stone hoe. Melons would also often be planted among the corn hills. The plots would be close to the village area and selected individuals had the tasks of acting human "scarecrows." Later colonists were taught by the Indian to include a small fish in the corn hill for fertilizer. These methods of farming were often ridiculed by the colonists but the colonists did not hesitate to destroy the Indian cornfields in order to starve them out. Official government publications reveal that the Indian settlements in the Northeast and Illinois territories were supported by the food products from extensive fields. However, the colonists did borrow the Indians' ideas of corncribs, husking pins, clambakes and husking bees.

Jean Baptiste de Coigne, last chief of the Kaskaskians, indicated to General George Rogers Clark that the earth mounds were used for palaces and fortifications. Again studies are proving this to be true. These dirt mounds took years to build since it has been surmised that the individuals would dig with a shell and wooden implement to fill a 50 to 60 pound basket. Then it would be humanly-carried to the mound and dumped. Around these mounds, developed a well-organized community with a definite social structure. Even the area was organized with open plaza spaces, market places, residential sections, and cemetery plots. Divisions of labor even became evident as different craftsmen created their wares to be traded and sold in the market areas. Again, the dwellings were permanent structures built in rectangular shapes, and arranged in rows along streets. Some of the mounds were built for temples or ceremonial purposes. The largest mound in the Cahokia area is called Monk's Mound which covers an area of over 14 acres at the base and rises to a height over 100 feet. On the top has been discovered the ruins of an "enormous temple over 100 feet long, 48 feet wide, and possibly 50 to 60 feet high." (Iseminger) Other mounds were used for burial purposes.

The Mound Builders were extensive tradesmen and went to the Great Lakes area for copper, to southern Wisconsin for lead ore, and to the Ohio River area in southern Illinois for salt and flint. For good fortune in their life, they were also followers of astrology and astronomy as evidenced by the remains of the "American Woodhenge" which is a "large circle (up to 480 feet in diameter) of tall wooden posts and a central observation post...used to calculate, observe and predict the movements of the sun (and possibly the moon), throughout the year--a form of a calendar and observatory 1,000 years old!" (Iseminger)

The ancient city of Cahokia lasted for several hundred years and existed as the center or hub for the area. The entire "hub" five square miles and its "downtown" covered more than seven hundred acres. These people were also the first to subsist mainly on food crops. Their large number demanded it.

What happened to this society?

Again it must not be overlooked that these early people lived in Illinois country for over 500 generations in peace. By 1200 A.D. the population could well have been 50,000. However, how be it, by pestilence, plague or invasion, the tribes suffered and perished in large numbers. The towns or communities were vacated and moved elsewhere. Quite possibly they turned to the forest or woodlands for protection. Either way the causes must have been drastic or else the people would not have left their stable homes and crops. A study of the Jesuit, French and Spanish documents could well provide answers or clues to early peoples here. When the French first encountered the Illinois, the Illinois told them of fleeing to land in the west beyond the big water (the Mississippi). That they had just returned to their homelands along the Illinois in the 1600's.

Location of Illinois villages around 1680

1400 to 1780 A.D. Historic Indians

By this time, the Indians lived in villages further up the Illinois River. More than likely, the earlier paradises in the convexes of the rivers were no longer paradises. Invaders from other tribes along the river must have been the danger since "taboo" signs were painted on the river cliffs. For years on end, the Indian families would come and go and quite possibly never would have encountered a stranger. But the trading that went on, belies that assumption. The ancient Mayans in the Popul Vuh called the early man here the people of the wood. "There are generations in the world, there are country people, whose face we do not see, who have no homes, they only wander through the small and large woodlands..." (William Brandon) Could they have been talking of the Indian here around 1200 A.D. when they left their villages?

The year 1540 also saw some changes. Hernando de Sota had led an expedition from Florida to the Mississippi, bringing measles and smallpox to the Indians along the way. The diseases spread, wiping out whole families and sometimes, tribes. The people scattered from their dwelling places along the Kaskaskia and Illinois, to avoid the scourge of disease.

Toward the end of the 17th century or 1690, the most numerous tribe was that of the Illinois. They comprised several different tribes: the Kaskaskias, Cahokias, Peorias, Tamarois, Mouingouenas, Mitchigamias (Weas and Piankaskaws). They also occupied the most territory as indicated on the map. After Marquette's exploration, the French encountered around 11,000 Illinois in one area.

Location of various tribes by 1700

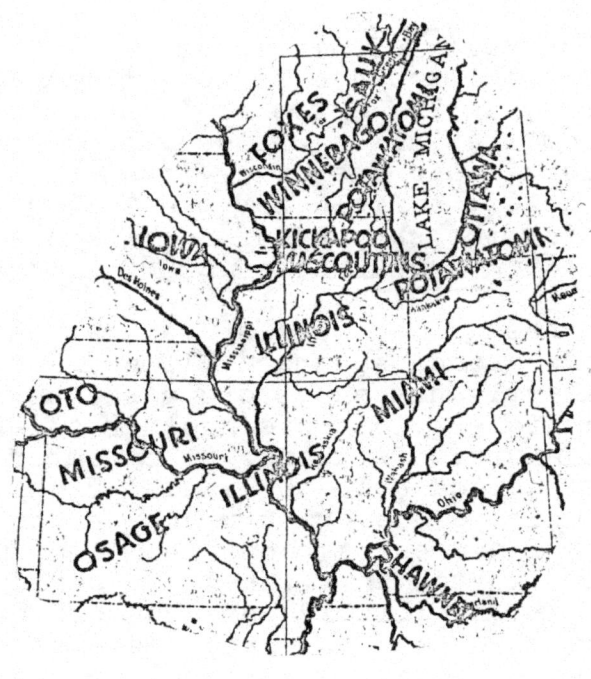

The Illinois:
Descendants of the Mound Builders
Chapter 2

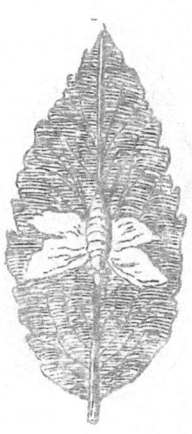

Totem of the Illinois

August 13, 1803: Treaty of Vincennes
The Illinois tribe ceded to the United States all their rights for 8,608,167 acres in Illinois territory. Their payment from the United States was 350 acres near the town of Kaskaskia and one other tract of 1280 acres; a house for the chief; a field for the tribe; $100 annually for seven years for the support of a priest; $300 to assist the tribe in building a church; and $580 in needed articles.

One of the last Kaskaskian Chiefs Jean Baptiste de Coigne stated that the mounds around southern Illinois were built by his ancestors. Apparently his ancestors used the mounds for palaces and fortifications. To quote another chieftain--Tamenund--who was an ancient Delaware: "I remember that when I was a laughing boy I stood upon the sands of the great sea shore and saw a big white canoe, with wings whiter than the swan's and wider than many eagles, come from the rising sun. In the canoe were many white men....Then the children of the Lenape (Linneway, ininiwek, Illini) were masters of the world. The salt lake gave us fish, the woodlands gave us deer, and air gave us many birds. We took wives who bore us children;

we worshiped the Great Spirit, and we kept the enemy beyond the sound of our hunting grounds." (Northey. THE AMERICAN INDIAN) Hiram Beckwith further substantiated the origin or importance of the Illinois. "The name Ill-i-mouek, Ill-i-ne-wek, Len-i-wek, and Ill-i-ni was applied only to the Illinois confederation....This people who had dominated over surrounding tribes, claiming for themselves the name of Illini or Lenneway, to distinguish their superior manhood, have disappeared from the earth." (ILLINOIS AND INDIANA INDIANS)

Much material describing the early Illinois for being non-fighters does not take in account that for many centuries there was no need for fighting since there were no enemies. C.B. Walker in his MISSISSIPPI VALLEY of 1878 stated, "The good sense of these primitive men was apparently as sharp and clear to the advantages of situation and value of soils as the many-sided intelligence of a more enlightened people. It is also another proof that they selected freely; that they were not troubled, for the most part with enemies. They settled on the best lands, and evidently did not need to fear the vicinity of the natural highways--the rivers-- which the Indians of later times commonly avoided with great care, as places of residences, because it would likely bring enemies to the sudden ruin of their towns...."

Somehow or another when Walker began his second part of the book, he ignored the early accounts from the French of the Illinois Indian. According to Walker, the Indians found by the Europeans were merely small wandering bands who were always fighting and never spent much constructive time doing anything. On the contrary, the Illinois Indians who lived along the Illinois River were peaceful farmers first and foremost, and hunters, second. Walker had heard of the story of a great people existing in the Mississippi valley but they were driven out by northeastern and eastern raiding tribes. He had no way to prove or disprove the story. An interesting note added by Walker was that the Lenni-Lenapes (Illini,ininiwek) were said to be the "original stock" of the later Algonquins. The Delaware shared much in common with the early Illinois.

Late in the seventeenth century when the Jesuits and the French entered the Illinois territory, they found that the Illinois believed in a Great Spirit--Manitou--creator of all living things and for most purposes they did believe in an after world. There was no priest or for the most part a head religious person but there were medicine men or seers. Thus, the Indian's belief was not much different from the later American naturalist or transcendentalist--man is but a small part of a vast universe but that he--man--plays a very vital role.

Most of the Illinois' dress was simple at the best. The men wore breechcloths, with an added cloak or cape during visits and inclement weather. The dress of the women was described "modest" by the early Jesuit missionaries. "They adore the head with feathers of many colors, of which they make garlands and crowns which they arrange very becomingly;

above all things, they are careful to paint the face with different colors, but especially with vermilion. They wear collars and ear rings made of little stones which they cut like precious stones: some are blue, some red and some white as alabaster: to these must be added a flat piece of porcelain which finishes the collar." (Thwaites, JESUIT RELATIONS, 67:163-175.)

In 1673, Pierre Marquette found the Illinois to be very friendly. To his surprise many of them in places had already encountered Europeans because the chiefs were wearing cloth, and some warriors were carrying guns, knives, hatchets and gunpowder in small thick bottles of glass. These earlier Europeans were likely the <u>coureur de bois</u>, runner of the bush, or trappers who forged ahead in the wilderness for their own profits as early as the 1640's. In 1699 the French government passed laws to limit the freedom of the coureur de bois.

Marquette and his men found the village or town of the Illinois to be in a choice location along the valley of the Illinois River, in low broad meadows. At this same location nearly the whole Illinois population was comprised of eleven tribes; at other locations, only two tribes. The meadows around the village "were extensively cultivated, yielding large crops, chiefly of Indian corn....The village graveyard appears to have been on a rising ground, near the river immediately in front of the town of (present day) Utica." (Parkman)

Other tribes Marquette discovered had already been trading with the Illinois for their earthenware, beads, and other wares. Corn was another trade commodity. LaSalle, another French explorer, later reported in 1682 that the Illinois numbered 20,000 around his Ft. St. Louis on the upper Illinois River.

LaSalle had earlier learned that prior to 1670 the Illinois had left their homes and fled to west of the Mississippi after being forced there by raiding Iroquois and Fox. The Illinois had tried for a number of years (1655-1667) to stop the Iroquois from moving into the territory. However, the Iroquois later aided by the Sioux were too much for them. By the time LaSalle explored the Illinois River and Illinois country, the Illinois were returning to their homes.

Fortunately a Frenchman by the name of Sieur Deliette who was a nephew of Henri de Tonti, an officer in LaSalle's group, preserved for us a description of the early Illinois. Translations of Deliette's French account have been printed by the Illinois State Historical Society.

During the 1680's Sieur Deliette lived with the Illinois for a number of years. Deliette found the Illinois who called themselves in-ini-wek (men) to be no finer looking people of average height (tall compared to the French), "faces as beautiful as white milk," and full of life.

Mary Hartwell Catherwood in 1899 further described the Illinois to be "a nimble, well-formed people, skillful with bow and arrow....Oftentimes a chief," she added, "would wear a scarf or belt of fur crossing his left shoulder, encircling his waist and hanging in fringe. Arm and leg bands ornamented him, and he also had knee rattles of deer hoofs..."

A hundred years later after Deliette, a William Biggs, who was a captive, described his captors the Kickapoos as "very white skinned Indians." Natalie Maree Belting, a present day authority at the University of Illinois, declared that the early Indian of Illinois were fairer skinned than the French who came here.

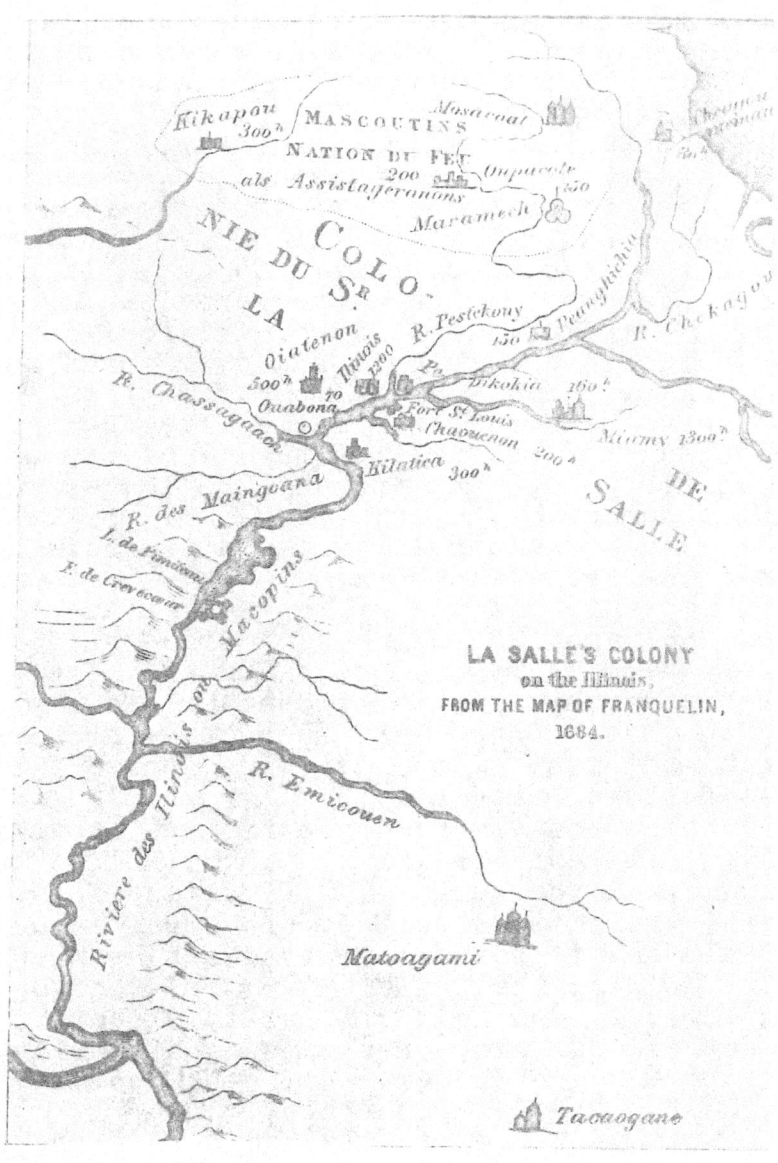

This map shows the location of the early Illinois villages as LaSalle drew them in 1684. The numbers followed by an "h" indicate the number of huts at the various locations.

According to the eyewitness, Deliette described the Illinois country as the most beautiful country he had ever seen. In some places he found it necessary to empty his canoe and carry it because of rapids or low water. Deliette talked with fellow Indian comrades before he started for the Illinois country. He listened to the Illinois and Miami stories about the "deluge" and how a ship was built to save all mankind. That the ship overturned and turned into the earth. Deliette was further told that the language of the Illinois and the Miami was the same and he later found it to be true. He discovered that the accent of the Illinois was very short compared to the long accent of the Miami; the former pronounced the "h" and the latter, the "f".

In 1688 Deliette persuaded his uncle Henri de Tonti to let him join a group of Illinois on a buffalo hunt for five weeks. The Illinois at that time inhabited most of the country along the Illinois River.

When Deliette finally made it to the Illinois camp, he found that most of the young men were already gone on the buffalo hunt. The women and girls with axes were going to the woods to cut poles and peel bark for summer hunting cabins to set up on the edge of the prairie to catch the cool air. These summer lodges were shaped like very long rounded cover-wagons having a hole in the middle of the roof for smoke to escape. The women wove rush mats and overlapped them on the framework of poles. They would also put mats on the ground floor except down the middle where the fires were built. Each fire was used by two families who lived opposite in stalls made of blankets. The ends of the lodges were left open during the summer. The more permanent winter lodges were again large and rectangular with gable roofs but the walls were made of heavy elm bark.

As the women were setting up the summer hunting cabins, the young men who remained behind cut three poles and made a large tripod to hang a big kettle of water. The young men invited Deliette and his man to be seated. Soon two hunters arrived with two bucks which were butchered in short order. The old men and the rest of the men were served first and this procedure was followed with all the meals.

The main object of the summer hunt were the buffalo which still roamed the Illinois prairies. These killed buffalo would be skinned and the tongues would be the first meat cooked in camp. Deliette described his first encounter with the live buffalo and it scared him to death as the buffalo would be driven toward the hunters for the shooting. He, Deliette, immediately ran in the opposite direction at the first charge of the buffalo, thus causing his fellow Indian companions to have a good laugh. Deliette declared on that hunt, the Illinois killed 120 buffalo.

Most all the buffalo meat obtained during the summers would be cut into strips and dried. The Illinois would make a wooden crate, ten feet long, three feet wide, and four feet deep called a gris. Beneath the gris, they would keep a small

Burial Vases from Mounds in Illinois.

1893 Illinois State Exhibit
World's Columbian Exposition

fire continually burning for a week. The meat would be turned periodically so as to dry out the pieces thoroughly.

To Deliette's amazement, if some of the men failed in killing a buffalo, the others would share theirs. The Illinois were generous during their feasts and did not fail to invite strangers as Miami, Ottawa, Pottawatomi, Kickapoo and others who happened along. The first coureur de bois were treated just the same.

The Illinois women would later spin the buffalo hair into peltry sacks and garters. For decoration, the women would use porcupine quills from the Pottawatomi and Ottawa on their moccasins, dresses, vests, etc.

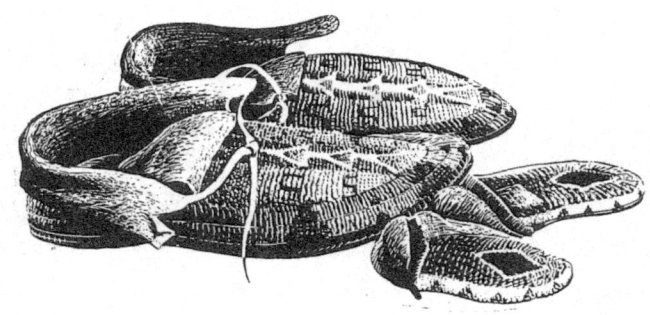

At one time, Deliette made the mistake of killing a buffalo calf since the Illinois told him later that the calf was useless because of no fat. The Illinois did make use of the calf Deliette killed and wasted no part of it. Shortly Deliette noticed two hunters about to broil their meat. They took two bits of wood from their quivers and kindled them against some reeds from the wood. In short order, they had a fire going. "One of the pieces of wood which they use to make a fire is of white cedar, which is the most combustible, a foot long more or less, according as they choose to make it, and as thick as two fingers. On one side, on the very edge, they make little holes, in which they make a notch. They put in this pit of wood some rotten wood or some grass, dry and very fine, after taking care to crush it thoroughly in their hands. The other piece of wood is as thick as the little finger; it is a bit of a wood that has a black berry, which we call morette. When this wood is green it is very soft, and it is proportionately hard when it is dry. They shape the end to the size of the holes in the other piece of wood, into one of which they insert it, and by turning it in their hands without ceasing, they produce a sort of powder from which, after a very short time, one sees smoke issue, which shortly is converted into flame." (Deliette)

The game the Illinois hunted was quite plentiful and consisted of bears, does, stags, bucks, turkeys, lynxes, and huge cats. Deliette was always impressed in watching the young men agilely run after the game. They could run as long as a half hour without tiring.

The Illinois also made use of the vegetation--nuts, blackberries, chestnuts, grapes, apples and plums. Marquette also noted that the Illinois made sugar from the maple trees. Deliette added that the women made fur garters from a creature similar to the muskrat. Deliette, however, did not think much of the Illinois' use of skunk fur.

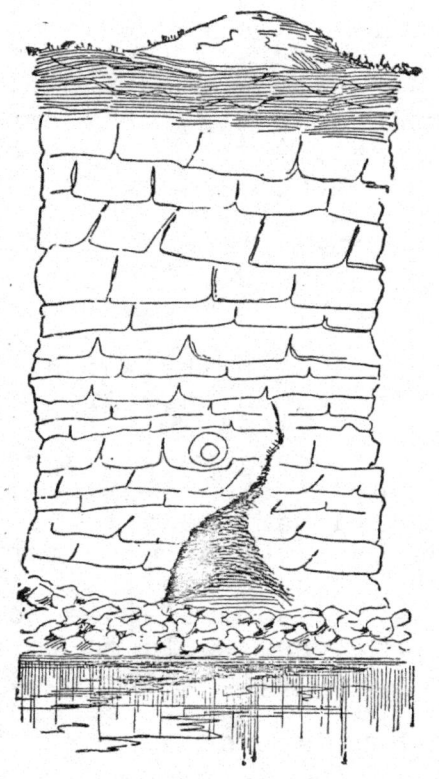

Grafton, with mound on top of bluff, and an old pictografic circle over the cave entrance.

1893 Illinois State Exhibit
World's Columbian Exposition

During the spring and summers, the women would work in the corn fields. Corn would be planted 3 to 4 grains in a hill and grow tall enough for men to lose their way in it. At the end of July, the women would mix or dry corn for winter storage. For daily meals, the women would cook the corn then dispose of the leftover since it'd soon spoil. If the corn

were to be dried, the women would let it set for two days
then store the grain in huge pots or holes in the ground.
The women's most important task with corn took place in August.
The women would husk the ears and spread them out to dry on
a huge skin. Each day the women would turn the ears to dry
in the sun. This they'd do for a week until all the moisture
would be removed. To shell the corn, the women would knock
off the kernals with sticks. It was during this time of
year, that the women also harvested the watermelons and
pumpkins. Deliette remarked that some of the pumpkins were
as big as water buckets. Marquette said in addition to maize,
"they also sow beans and melons, which are excellent, especially
those with a red seed. Their squashes are not of the best;
they dry them in the sun to eat in the winter and spring."
(Ethnology)

During some of Deliette's visit, it was nothing new to
have Iroquois and other intruders destroy the corn fields.
The intruders if caught were dealt with in short order.
Most of the time Deliette found the Illinois to be a very
congenial people. The women worked from morning to night.
The men hunted, butchered the game, did odd tasks, and entertained themselves. During the evenings, the men often played
a modified "shell game" with straws and beans. They also
played a form of la cross.

Deliette was quite impressed with the social habits of
the Illinois. He found that the women were treated well and
that the courtship ritual was a "patient wait" on the part
of the young male. The intended young woman herself and, her
brother if any, had the last say on the marriage match. In
some cases, the young woman would wait four to seven days
before she made her decision. For the already married,
disloyalty on either side was not tolerated.

Later in marriage when a pregnant wife was to be delivered,
she would not stay in her cabin. She would go to another one
which was especially prepared for childbirth. She would stay
there for three or four days then go home. Before her return
home, however, it was the husband's task to make the cabin
spotless.

Another marvel to Deliette was the healing practice of
the Illinois. He witnessed several serious wounds to be cleared
with poultices with no infection developing within the wounds.
A few healing men Deliette talked with were alarmed that the
French would amputate more often than not. Deliette remarked
that he saw no one with one arm or leg. They also had a way
with broken limbs which they would set and then the breaks
would heal in less than two months.

The loss of one in a family would bring gifts from others
to lessen the pain of loss. The relatives would pay four men
to bury the dead. A hollow grave somewhat larger than the
body would be dug and then lined with boards from a boat or
canoe. If the dead were a man, his hair and face would be
painted red and a white shirt would be put on him if the deceased
had one. A new breechcloth, new moccasins, and the best robe

would complete the corpse's demise to the new world. A small kettle or earthern pot with a small amount of corn, a calument or pipe with a pinch of tobacco, and bows and arrows would be buried with the man. The foot and head of the grave was merely marked with forked sticks. Deliette noted that the dead would be treated accordingly to what they liked in life.

Deliette remained with the Illinois at Ft. Pimitoui for seven years. There around the fort the Illinois had over 260 cabins which contained one to four fires each. This village was the largest with seven to eight thousand Illinois in 1680. These cabins comprised six different villages and there were two more Illinois villages at Cahokia with sixty cabins. During those days there were six divisions of the Illinois: Kaskaskia, Peoria, Moingwena, Coiracoentanen, Tamaroa, and Taporiara. It has been established there were altogether 30,000 to 40,000 Illinois before 1765.

Mary Hartwell Catherwood included a sketch of the totem of the Illinois. The totem represented or symbolized the tribe. From all appearances the leaf looked like one from an elm tree with a moth or butterfly on it. The Illinois did build their cabins from elm tree wood. Deliette did not indicate any idea about the Illinois' religion. In all likelihood they believed in Manito or a Great Spirit. The Great Spirit was the one who created all living things.

As early as 1680 La Salle was already establishing trading posts among the Illinois, specifically to increase the fur trade for the country of France. The main village of the Illinois had around four hundred huts covered with reed mats and no fortifications around them. The Illinois did not need fences around their fields since for many centuries there were no enemies. There were none until the northern and eastern tribes were pushed west and south because of decrease in game or the crowding of the white man. Years later, a chieftain admitted that fences were not needed around corn since it was not going anywhere.

In 1680-81 Iroquois instigated by the British invaded the Illinois to interrupt the French trade. Many Illinois were slaughtered and the remainder fled west across the Mississippi. Commandant Henri de Tonti of Ft. St. Louis at Starved Rock convinced the Illinois to come back again since the French decided to build a fort there. De Tonti built the fort large enough so the Illinois and others could go inside for safety during enemy attacks. The French and Illinois remained there for a few years but by 1691, the French were convinced that the fort had to be moved for the safety of everyone. Firewood was becoming scarce and water was not available during a seige. Thus in the winter of 1691 and 1692, a new fort was built at Lake Peoria often called Ft. Pimitoui or Ft. St. Louis.

At the beginning of the eighteenth century the Kaskaskia moved from northern Illinois to the mouth of the river which was named for them. The Kaskaskia enjoyed having the French for allies and at one time the tribes were afraid the French were going to abandon them. The French did leave Ft. St. Louis at Peoria but they convinced the Kaskaskia to settle there at the mouth of the river. There the Kaskaskia lived in their new location for a hundred years until they also had to move west.

During the early 1700's, Father Marest of the Kaskaskia settlement left a description of the Kaskaskia Illinois Indians. They are "very industrious and quite skillful in tilling the soil; they work with a plow, something I have not noticed anywhere else....Near their village there are three mills to grind the grain, to wit: one wind mill, which belongs to the Jesuits, which is chiefly patronized by the (French settlers); and two tread mills which are the property of the Illinois Indians....The Illinois Indians greatly delight in good eating and they often feast one another; their best dish is the meat of a dog or a small wolf, which they raise in their village. Most of the Illinois are Catholics. There is a good-sized church with baptismal font in their village....The men and women are modestly clothed when they come to church; they cover the body with a large skin, or they are dressed in a robe made of several skins sewed together."(J.H. Schlarman. FROM QUEBEC TO NEW ORLEANS)

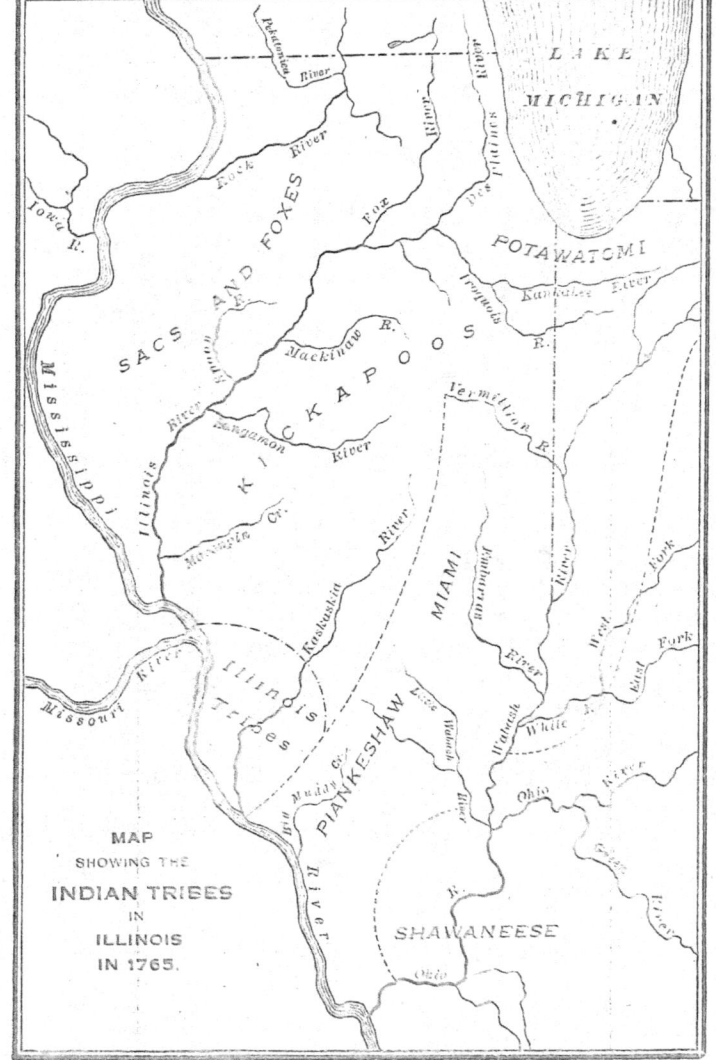

Map indicating small territory of the Illinois by 1765

Ruins of these Illinois towns are being studied today. In Randolph County, Illinois near the small town of Modoc, an Illinois village site has been discovered and it likewise is being excavated. This village site is much more recent in time and the Illinois probably lived there during the occupation of the French, 17th century. The village was not large but contained probably 100 to 200 people. Things found in the site were well-described two centuries earlier by the contemporary Frenchman Sieur Deliette.

Margaret Kimball Brown, a present-day writer and archeologist, gives the following verbal picture of the village as it was:

"A small village on a ridge in the midst of an open meadow, surrounded by a stockade for protection. Inside are a number of houses, mat and bark covered, with smoke rising through the tops from cooking fires within. Inside a cabin an Indian woman stirring sagamite (corn gruel) over the fire in her brass kettle, wearing a dress of tanned hides decorated across the top and bottom with white seed beads. Her moccasins have a row of shining brass tinkling cones, with tufts of red-dyed deer hair in them. On one side of the house a baby lying in a cradleboard plays with a large bell, amusing himself. The man with his flintlock gun is ready to leave for hunting, dressed only in his breechcloth and moccasins, and on the left side of his head two silver brooches are secured in a long lock of hair.

Outside other men are gathering for the hunting expedition, women are working at tanning hides for the traders, and children are running and playing." ("The Search for the Michigamea Indian Village")

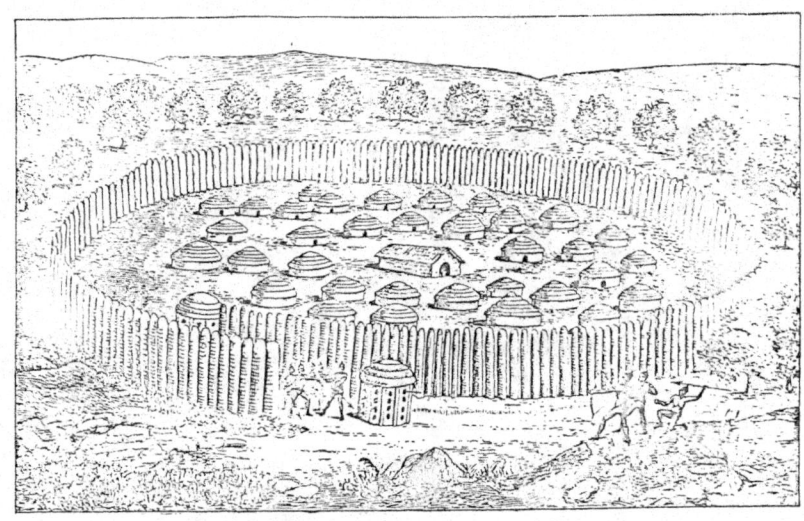

AN EARLY DRAWING OF AN INDIAN VILLAGE

In the latter part of this work there is included a list of tribal related people with some early French names who came to Ft. Pimitoui to work for two or three years. The settlement of Kaskaskia lasted until 1763 when the French lost the Illinois country. It was this same Kaskaskia that served as the first capital of the state of Illinois.

The Illinois by then had been reduced from thousands to just under one hundred individuals by the time Americans took the territory in the 1780's. The Illinois were slaughtered by other raiding tribes who were being pushed and instigated by the encroaching white man. During the late 17th century, the Illinois suffered two wars with the Iroquois. Scientists today are finding the mounds of those slaughtered Illinois.

INDIAN BUFFALO HUNT
[Reproduced from Le Page du Pratz, *Historie de la Louisiane*]

Other Indians of Illinois
Chapter 3

November 3, 1804: Sauk and Fox Conveyance: Treaty of
St. Louis. Gave the United States over 11 million
acres in Illinois territory. Payment by United States
was $1,000 first cost; immediate delivery of $2200
in goods and land for relocation west of the Mississippi.

Beside the Illinois there were the Sac (Sauk) and Fox who moved down from southern Wisconsin during the 1690's and made a permanent settlement on the Rock River. It was here in this settlement that one of the most famous Sac and Fox chiefs was born--Black Hawk. By the time Black Hawk was born in 1767, his people had farms, homes, a cemetery, and even some domesticated animals. These homes and farms were given up by Black Hawk's people in 1830 when the tribes were to move west to Iowa. Black Hawk's biography therein provides a verbal picture of the Sacs and Fox.

When the French discovered the Fox and Sacs, the villages had excellent black soil for growing corn. They would have a fort in the middle of their living area and the cabins around it would have thick bark. During some periods of time the Fox and Sac would barricade the fur trading routes along the rivers. The Foxes called themselves Mosk-wah (red) Ha-kee (earth) and their symbol was the fox. The Sacs called themselves Os-sa-wah (yellow) Ha-kee (earth). Another Sac or Sauk chief was Keokuk.

Father Claude Allouez came to the Fox village in 1670. To his surprise, the Fox were upset with the French trying to convert them to Christianity. To Allouez, their lodges seemed like harems since some of the chiefs had as many as eight wives. At one time he taught them the story of the cross and Emperor Constantine. They so enjoyed the story of the cross that they emblazoned their bull-hide shields with the cross.

By 1718 the Fox had gained a firm footing on the Rock River in Illinois. Because of the Fox in the territory, the Kaskaskia Illinois moved farther down on the Illinois River. The Fox remained at this location for many years. By 1809 nearly 6400 Sac and Fox lived in northern Illinois.

August 3, 1795: Treaty of Greenville. Miami Conveyance. Gave United States over 12,800 acres in Illinois territory. Payment by the United States was 150 bushels of salt. September 30, 1809 Treaty of Ft. Wayne gave United States over 282,000 acres in Illinois territory. Payment by United <u>States was</u> a $400 annuity.

The Miamis were another people that the French encountered in Illinois country. There were four different bands of the Miami who used the names: Miamis, Eel-rivers, Weas, and Piankeshaws. The Weas were settled around Chicago in the 1670's. Later the Miamis settled around the Wabash River and stayed there for nearly a century. Prior to the move, the Miamis had populous villages around the Starved Rock area, numbering at least 1500 in 1684. The later Miamis did not war with the white settlers. On the contrary, they appealed to General Washington to help protect them from the whites and the warring Kickapoos and Pottawatomies. Washington issued a proclamation forbidding the Miamis from being harmed by the white people. The Piankeshaw band between the Kaskaskia and Wabash became close to the French explorers and coureur de bois who appeared on the scene. Before the French had arrived, the Illinois and other tribes would marry at a later age, around 25 for the female and 30 for the male. But the French changed all that. Most of the young Indian women they married were very young. Much later around the 1820's Rev. Isaac McCoy, a Baptist missionary, declared that the Miamis were not a warlike people. However, the Miamis, likewise, had to move west to accommodate the land-hungry settlers. By the time all of the bands of the Miamis were in their new homes in Kansas, there were around only 500 left. They had also suffered great loss in numbers. The moving Miami tribe was lead west by Christmas Dagney who was French and Miami. His people had to leave behind their farms during the late fall and early winter. Transportation was by boat and by the time they arrived near Kansas City, many of them were sick, starved, and close to death. It was Baptiste Peoria who married Dagney's widow and later consolidated the Miamis and the Illinois Kaskaskias into the Confederated Tribes in 1867.

Eagle from a copper plate found by Major James Powell in a mound near Peoria, Illinois. AUTHENTIC INDIAN DESIGNS.

The early French settlers described the Miami as "polite, mild, and affable. They were good farmers and hunters." (ILLINOIS AND INDIANA INDIANS) Most of the men were of medium height, had round faces, and wore their hair long. Their houses were long or round, covered with reed mats.

The Miamis considered their chief as one of great authority. Often the chieftain would be attended night and day. The French would always be impressed with the demeanor of the Miami chiefs. In 1673 the Miami town was situated on a crown of a hill with the prairie stretched all round. In the middle of the town they had raised a tall wooden cross. The Miamis wore long locks of hair over each ear.

At one time the Miami were enemies of the Illinois. It was through no effort of their own but often because of actions taken against La Salle. La Salle finally managed to get the Miami and Illinois together.

Col. George Croghan representing the British surveyed the Miami territory in 1765. He described the land west of the future Danville between Vincennes and Vermilion Rivers. This was the Miami hunting grounds at the time. "We traveled through a prodigious large meadow called the (Miami's) hunting ground. Here is no wood to be seen, and the country appears like an ocean. The ground is exceedingly rich and partially overgrown with wild hemp. The land is well-watered and full of buffalo, deer, bears, and all kinds of wild game. ...then came to a high woodland, and arrived at Vermilion River, so called from a fine red earth found there by the Indians, with which they paint themselves...." (ILLINOIS AND INDIANA INDIANS)

August 25, 1828: Treaty of Green Bay. Winnebago conveyance. Gave United States over 750,000 acres in Illinois. Payment by United States was $20,000 in trade goods.

The Winnebago were another people who lived in northwestern Illinois next to the Sac and Pottawatomi territories. They became French allies and helped Pontiac, an Ottawa, in his efforts against the settler movement west. The meaning of the name Winnebago has several different interpretations. Most sources concur that the name originated from the salty water of the shores of their first home far to the west. They called themselves "people of the sea."

Prior to the War of 1812, the Winnebagoes were lead by Chief Naw-Kaw Caromaine. He later became one of Tecumseh's closest attendants. After the war, settlers or government officials feared that the Winnebagoes would unite with other tribes. Naw-Kaw managed to keep the peace and kept his braves from warring. He moved his tribe close to Kinzie's settlement at Dearborn or Chicago. Fifty years later, the Winnebagoes were to receive praise for their services in the Civil War. Close to one hundred of them left the Omaha

Winnebago beaded dance pouch made from the skin of an entire otter. AUTHENTIC INDIAN DESIGNS.

Reservation in Nebraska and enlisted in the Union. During the War of 1812 the Winnebago joined forces with the British against the Americans; they were a brave, good-natured lot who likewise gave their homes.

It was not until 1825 that peace was finally settled among the Winnebagoes, Sacs, Foxes and Pottawatomies. They had wrestled with the territory among each other for the previous two centuries and the Winnebago finally received the northwest corner of Illinois.

Another so-called war was the Winnebago War or scare of 1827. The main incident recorded by Illinois Governor Reynolds occurred during July of that year. Some boatmen north of Galena had kidnapped some Winnebago women for "corrupt and brutal purposes." (quoting Reynolds). The Winnebago husbands retaliated. That was the Winnebago War.

The Winnebago ceded all their lands to the United States finally in September 1832 at the Ft. Armstrong, Rock Island, Illinois for a reservation in Nebraska.

July 30, 1819: Treaty of Edwardsville. Kickapoo conveyance. Gave United States over 960,000 acres in Illinois. Payment by United was $2000 annually for 15 years. August 30, 1819: Treaty of Ft. Harrison. Gave United States over 2 million acres in Illinois. Payment by United States was $2000 for annuity in specie.

Around 1752 another people settled around Peoria called the Kickapoo which meant "he stands about." The Kickapoos along with the Sacs, Foxes, and Pottawatomies forced the Illinois away from the east and south of the Illinois River. The Kickapoo lived there for a number of years and then split into two bands: one at the Wabash and Vermilion Rivers and other along the Sangamon; another on the upper Kaskaskia or Okaw River. The Kickapoos were described later by a captive William Biggs in 1788 as being "very white skinned Indians." Because of his bravery and good looks, the Kickapoos liked Biggs and named him Moh-cos-se-a. They offered him a fair young woman for a wife but he protested saying that he was already married. It was she who waited on him when he first was brought to their village on the west bank of the Wabash in 1788. For his first meal, she fixed him hominy, and some dried meat sprinkled with sugar. Biggs later was treated by having his long, matted hair combed.

The Kickapoos did not have their villages close to other settlements so thus most of them escaped the demoralization of the trade with liquor. They were described as "industrious, intelligent, and cleanly in their habits, and were better armed and clothed. As a rule, the men were tall, sinewy, and active; the women lithe, and many of them by no means lacking in beauty." (ILLINOIS AND INDIANA INDIANS). Near the mouth of the Middle Fork of the Vermilion River, the Kickapoos had a populous city as evidenced by the extensive burial grounds. Here they stayed for a number of years.

The Kickapoos loved their homes and government officials had some difficulty convincing them to leave their homes. The Kickapoos had other villages on the Embarras near later Charleston, Illinois and on the Kaskaskia near later Shelbyville, Illinois. During the War of 1812 many of the Kickapoo villages were burned by Governor Edwards' forces. The band of Mac-ca-naw, Ka-an-a-kuck, and Pa-koi-shee-can were the last ones to migrate west in 1832-33. During their first year in Kansas they lost many of their people.

The Kickapoos had been noticed as early as 1612 by the French explorers. The Kickapoo were anything but friendly to the French during their occupation. By 1718 they had villages on the Rock River and in the area of Chicago. A few years later the Kickapoos had migrated farther south into Illinois but not without much bloodshed. In a treaty of 1819 the Kickappos asserted that they had occupied the territory for more than fifty years.

The biggest blood battle was to have taken place before 1750, twenty-five miles from Kaskaskia on the way to Shawneetown. Here many of the Illinois were slaughtered by the Kickapoo and Pottawatomi in a place called Battle Ground Creek.

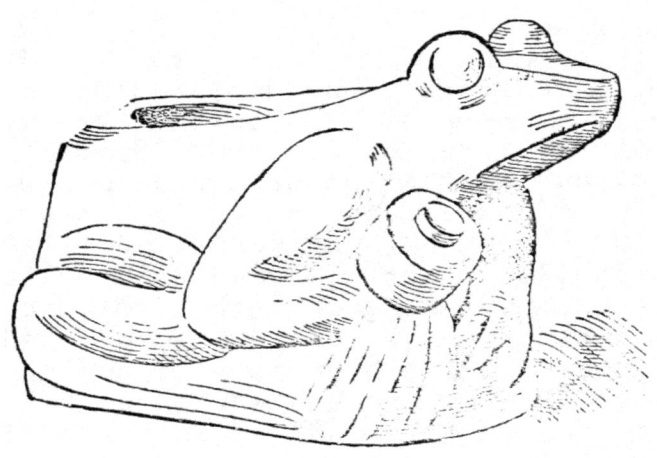

Found on a bluff east of Great Cahokia Mound. Illinois State Exhibit, World's Columbian Exposition of 1893.

October 12, 1832: Treaty of Tippecanoe River.
Pottawatomi conveyance. Gave United States over 560,000 acres in Illinois. Payment by United States was $32,000 in goods at once; $10,000 in goods in spring of 1833 and individual land grants. September 26, 1833: Treaty of Chicago. Gave United States over 1 million acres in Illinois. Payment by United States was $100,000 in trade goods; $280,000 in twenty annual payments of $14,000; $150,000 for erection of mills, houses, etc.

Among many of the tribes who moved into Illinois country were the Pottawatomi which meant simply "we are making a fire." The Pottawatomi were composed of the Ottawa, Chippewa, and Pottawatomi as they called themselves. Father Allouez in 1666 found them to be the "most docile and affectionate toward the French. Their wives and daughters are more reserved than those of other nations." (ILLINOIS AND INDIANA INDIANS). They moved south to northern Illinois in the 1680's.

Bacqueville de la Potherie, a French historian of the 17th and 18th centuries described the Pottawatomi thus: "...the behavior of these people is very affable and cordial, and they make great efforts to gain the good opinion of persons who come among them. They are very intelligent; they have an inclination for raillery; their physical appearance is good; and they are great talkers...." (Deale. HISTORY OF POTTAWATOMIES). Jean Claude Allouez found that the country inhabited by the Pottawatomi was "excellently adapted to raising corn, and they (had) fields covered with it, to which they are glad to have recourse, to avoid famine that is only too common is these regions...." (ILLINOIS AND INDIANA INDIANS).

By 1718 Father Marest recorded that the men were "well-clothed, like our domicilated Indians at Montreal....The old men often dance the medicine...The young men often dance in a circle, and strike posts. It is then they recount their achievements, and dance, at the same time, the war-dance; and whenever they act thus they are highly ornamented..." (ILLINOIS AND INDIANA INDIANS).

As common with most of the other tribes, the Pottawatomi women raised corn, beans, squashes, and melons. They made extensive use of vermilion for make-up and wore red or blue cloth dresses during the summer. George Catlin in later years observed the Pottawatomi play Bag-gat-i-way, a kind of la crosse during the summer. He discovered that "every player is dressed alike, that, divested of all dress except the girdle, etc. And in the desperate struggles for the ball when it is up, where hundreds are running together and leaping, actually over each others' head, and darting between their adversaries' legs, tripping and throwing and foiling each other in every possible manner, and every voice raised to the highest key, in shrill yelps and barks, there are rapid successions of feats and of incidents, that astonish and amaze far beyond the conception of any one who had not the singular good luck to witness them." (Catlin: LETTERS AND NOTES OF NORTH AMERICAN INDIANS).

The Pottawatomi were the last to leave Illinois in 1838. In some instances they were removed by force since they had lived with the white settlers in many years of peace. Thus the Indians of Illinois were no more.

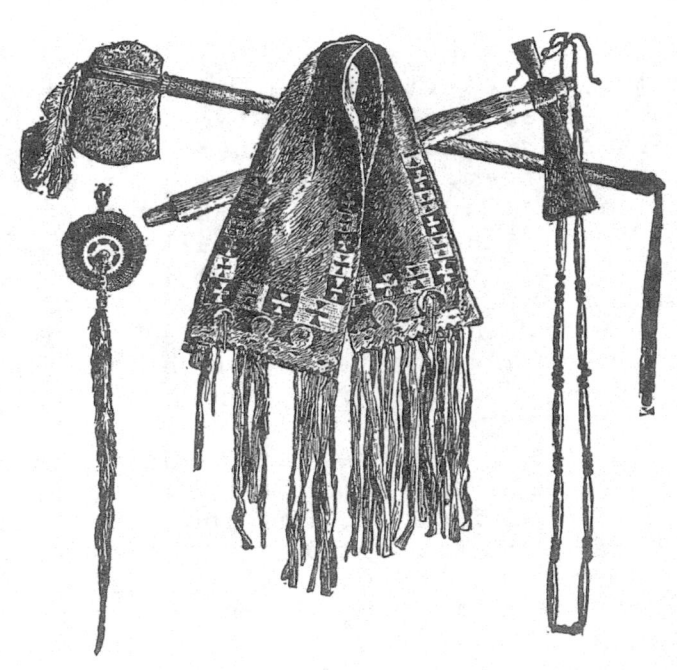

Selected Biographies of Early
Native Americans in the
Illinois Country
Chapter 4

On many occasions the author found sources which only mentioned a Native American by tribe name followed by man or woman. If there were any possibility that somewhere there would be a name given, the writer would delve into other materials. In some cases, the resulting biographies are rather short but at least there is an attempt to discuss human beings who actually existed and not refer to them obscurely as part of the whole.

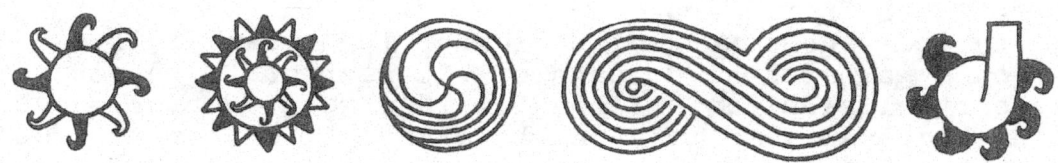

Aptakisic (c. 1790 - c. 1850)

Aptakisic was said to be an orator and the fact is fairly well substantiated since he signed several treaties representing a group of Potawatomies. His tribe when they were in Illinois lived in the area of Naperville, Du Page County. Their corn fields were on the Des Plaines River near the mouth of Indian Creek.

According to the recollections of Judge Henry W. Blodgett, Aptakisic and his people would frequently call on Blodgett's father who was a blacksmith to mend their traps and guns. Blodgett's family became well-acquainted with the old chief who was probably around 45 or 50 years old in the mid-1830's. Judge Blodgett became a good friend in his youth with a lad around the same age who was a son or grandson of the old chief. The chief "was a man of fine figure and presence, over six feet in height, straight, well proportioned, with clear bright eyes and a pleasant face and manner,.... He was good tempered, kind-hearted and generous, a good hunter and good provider for his family, and although an inveterate smoker, was very temperate, if not a total abstainer from the use of ardent spirits." (Blodgett).

After moving from Michigan territory in 1827, Aptakisic was one of many who signed for the Potawatomi giving up 565,000 acres in Illinois territory. In payment was $32,000 in goods; and $10,000 in goods the following spring. Aptakisic was not one of the chiefs who was reimbursed for a stolen horse. In this treaty he and his tribe were still permitted to hunt, fish and plant on any land which still belonged to the United States as long as they did not molest the settlers in the area.

By the second week of September 1833, many native Americans gathered at Chicago or Ft. Dearborn. This was to be the final session in Illinois. George B. Porter, governor of the Michigan territory and head negotiator, was the one who approached Aptakisic since he was spokesman for them. Porter explained that (President Jackson) the Great Father was dying and that he wanted to see his red children happy before he was buried with his fathers. Aptakisic acknowledged the concern of the Great Father for them. However, it was soon learned that not all the tribes there wanted to give up their land and move west of the Mississippi. It was Aptakisic who had to inform Porter of that fact. It was a few days after much confusion that the treaty was signed.

In the fall of 1837, Aptakisic and his people finally moved to a reservation on the west side of the Missouri River on the mouth of the Platt River then later to the Kansas territory south of the Kaw River.

Beaubien Family (c.1779-1863)

Jean Baptiste Beaubien was a French trader from around Detroit who visited Ft. Dearborn briefly in 1804. That same year he married Man-na-ben-a-qua, an Ottawa. Prior to 1812 Beubien moved back to Ft. Dearborn with his wife and a son Medart who was born around 1809. In the latter part of the year 1811 Man-na-ben-qua died and left Beaubien with two sons--the other one being Charles.

A few years later, Jean Baptiste Beaubien married Josette La Framboise, daughter of Francois La Framboise and his wife Shaw-we-no-qua. By 1819 Beaubien was a trader for the American Fur Company. From 1823 to 1839 Beaubien and his family occupied a two-story structure that had been abandoned by the government. A year before Beaubien and Josette moved there, they had a son--Alexander who was the first French-Indian child born at Ft. Dearborn.

Alexander's older half-brother Charles taught school at Ft. Dearborn in 1829. His other half-brother Medart went west with the Potawatomi in 1832.

During 1830-31 a debating society used to meet at the Beaubien residence since Beaubien was president. Two years earlier Beaubien had been appointed a justice of the peace. He performed six marriages during his term.

In 1839 Beaubien moved to his farm at Hardscrabble outside of the settlement. They lived there for a short time then moved again to Naperville. Jean Baptiste Beaubien died there in 1863.

Gorgets from Mounds.

1893 Illinois State Exhibit
World's Columbian Exposition

Big Foot (c. 1790-1845)

Big Foot or Maun-gee-zik was a Potawatomi chief who sympathezied with the Winnebagos. He was large-raw boned, big footed and dark visaged. His village was on the banks of Lake Geneva.

Big foot and his men were outside Chicago when many were gathered there for peace during 1827. Big Foot stood by while most of Ft. Dearborn burned during a lightening storm. Soon after he and his braves left, those inside the fort gathered and decided to send Shaubena and Billy Caldwell to talk to Big Foot.

Shaubena rode into Big Foot's village alone. Big Foot and Shaubena argued. Shaubena refused to help the Winnebagos take the Fort. Big Foot became enraged with Shaubena and almost killed him. Shaubena was thrown into a wigwam as a prisoner under guard. Caldwell helped Shaubena get released.

Finally the two convinced Big Foot to keep the peace. Big Foot signed three treaties in 1828, 1829, and 1833.

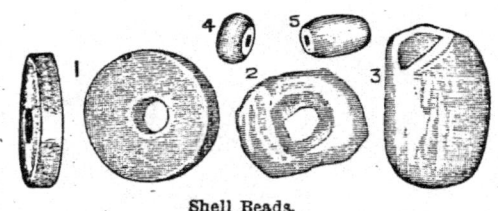

Shell Beads.

1893 Illinois State Exhibit
World's Columbian Exposition

Black Hawk (c.1767-1838)

Black Hawk or Ma-ka-tai-me-she-kia-kiak was born around 1767 on the Rock River, Illinois. His father was the Sac chief Pyesa. Black Hawk was one of the few who left his memoirs to those who followed him. For the last five years of his life, he told his story to Antoine Le Claire, a trader along the Des Moines River from 1833-1838.

George Catlin, a famous 19th century painter, described Black Hawk when the two met. "This man (Black Hawk), whose name has carried a sort of terror through the country where it has been sounded, has been distinguished as a speaker or counsellor rather than as a warrior; and I believe it has been pretty generally admitted, that 'Nah-pope' and the 'Prophet' were in fact, the instigators of the war (Black Hawk War of 1832); and either of them with much higher claims for the name of warrior than Black Hawk ever had. When I painted this chief, he was dressed in a plain suit of buckskin, with strings of wampum in his ears and on his neck, and held in his hand, his medicine-bag, which was the skin of a black hawk, from which he had taken his name, and the tail of which made him a fan, which he was almost constantly using."

BLACK HAWK.

Small sketch done by George Catlin

In 1804 Black Hawk seriously opposed the Treaty of St. Louis in which the Sac and Fox ceded all their lands east of the Mississippi to the United States. In later years Black Hawk would use that act as the beginning of the end of his race. He tried to enlist the aid of White Cloud to create a confederation of tribes which would counteract the flow of Americans west. His efforts failed.

"On June 27, 1831, Black Hawk made a treaty with General Gaines, and gave a reluctant consent to abandon his village and cornfields on the Rock River in Illinois and join Keokuk's band on their reservation in Iowa. General Gaines believed the trouble was ended, and so it probably would have been had the whites observed the provisions of the treaty. The Indians had been promised corn to supply the wants of their families in lieu of that which was left in their fields, but the amount was so meager that they began to suffer. In this emergency, a party of Sacs, to quote the language of Black Hawk, crossed the river, 'to steal corn from their own fields.' Moving with his band up Rock River, he was overtaken by a messenger from General Atkinson ordering him to return and recross the Mississippi. Black Hawk said he was not on the warpath, but going on a friendly visit to the village of White Cloud, the Winnebago Prophet, and continued on his journey. General Atkinson then sent imperative orders for him to return at once, or he would pursue him with his entire army and drive him back. In reply, Black Hawk said the general had no right to make the order so long as his band was peaceable, and that he intended to go on to the Prophet's village." (LIVES OF FAMOUS INDIAN CHIEFS.)

Black Hawk had nearly a thousand of his people with him; most were women and children with less than four hundred warriors. The Americans took it upon themselves to counteract the intentions. Volunteers were gathered and by July 21, 1832, most of the group of women and children in Black Hawk's band were slaughtered by fire from an armed boat on the Bad Axe River. A few weeks later Black Hawk and his sons were captured.

Black Hawk and his two sons, as well as his principal advisors and warriors, were brought to St. Louis, in chains, and Keokuk was appointed chief in his place. The prisoners were escorted through Eastern cities and Washington for display.

The following is Black Hawk's impression of being sent by steamboat to Jefferson Barracks, Missouri, shortly after his capture:

"On our way down, I surveyed the country that had cost us so much trouble, anxiety and blood, and that now caused me to be a prisoner of war. I reflected upon the ingratitude of the whites, when I saw their fine houses, rich harvests, and every thing desirable around them; and recollected that all this land had been ours, for which me and my people had never received a dollar, and that the whites were not satisfied until they took our village and our grave-yards from us, and removed us across the Mississippi....

We were now confined to the barracks, and forced to wear the BALL AND CHAIN! This was extremely mortifying, and altogether useless. Was the White Beaver (General Henry Atkinson) afraid that I would break out of his barracks, and run away? Or was he ordered to inflict this punishment upon me? If I had taken him prisoner on the field of battle, I would not have wounded his feelings so much, by such treatment--knowing that a brave war chief would prefer DEATH to DISHONOR! But I do not blame the White Beaver for the course he pursued--it is the custom among white soldiers, and, I suppose, was a part of his duty." ("Black Hawk as a Prisoner of War, 1832")

Black Hawk never attained his final rest. When he died on October of 1838, he was buried sitting-up in his blue uniform that was presented to him by the President of the United States. This was in McHenry County, Iowa and a few years later, his bones were dug up and put in the State Museum of Iowa which eventually burned.

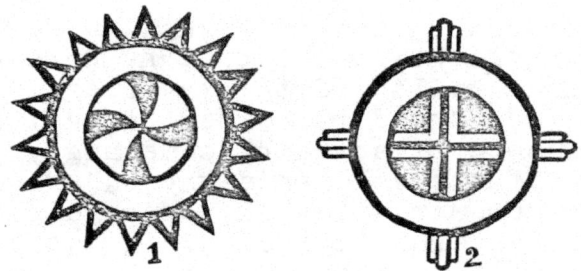

Figures on the Exterior of a Burial Vase.

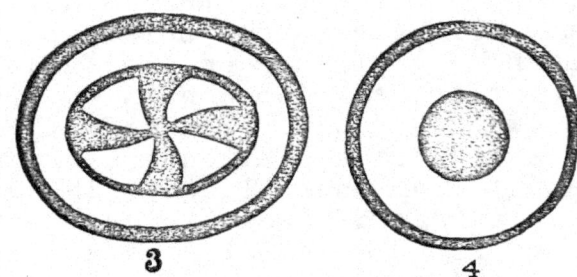

Figures on the exterior of a Burial Vase along the Mississippi.

1893 Illinois State Exhibit
World's Columbian Exposition

Black Partridge (c. 1780-c.1830)

Black Partridge was one of the Potawatomi chiefs located on Illinois River and around Lake Michigan in the early 1800's. His village was on the south side of the Illinois River, on the edge of the Peoria Lake. Often he made visits to Ft. Dearborn or Chicago. Black Partridge was well acquainted with Captain and Mrs. Heald who commanded Ft. Dearborn.

Early in 1806 Black Partridge and other Potawatomies had refused to join Tecumseh in a confederacy to slow the movement of the settlers going west. In 1810 at a council in St. Joseph, it was Chief Black Partridge and Chief Winnemac who again expressed their wishes against joining the confederacy.

When the United States declared war on England in 1812, Captain Heald was ordered to abandon Ft. Dearborn. Heald reportedly emptied the liquor supply in Lake Michigan and destroyed most of the ammunition. The Potawatomies became furious since they expected to receive most of the goods in gifts. Black Partridge warned the Captain about the young braves and that he could no longer control them for their actions.

It was on this famous occasion on August 14, 1812, that Black Partridge handed Heald his medal that he wore around his neck. Captain William Wells and thirty friendly Miamis escorted the Americans from the fort. They began their way to Detroit but they were attacked by some angry Potawatomi. Mrs. Linai T. Helm, one of the soldier's wives, was seized by a young warrior. In her words, "...A young Indian raised his tomahawk at me....I was dragged from his grasp by another and older Indian. The latter bore me struggling and resisting towards the lake....I soon perceived, however, that the object of my captor was not to drown me....I soon recognized, in spite of the paint with which he was disguised, the Black Partridge." She was taken to a place of safety till the firing ceased. Her husband Lieutenant Linai Helm was taken to a village on the Kankakee River and was held prisoner there for two months before Black Partridge discovered where he was. Black Partridge collected some money from a white trade stationed at Peoria and bought the Lieutenant from the village. The money was not enough so Black Partridge offered his own horse, his rifle, and his gold nose ring to satisfy the kidnappers. The Lieutenant was released and returned to his wife.

Unfortunately just a few months later that same year, Black Partridge's own village was destroyed by Governor Edwards' own men. On November 7, 1812, Governor Edwards reported: "...the ardor of the men could not be repressed, they abandoned their mired horses and pursued the savages on foot, through mud and water up to their waists every step, and many penetrated through to the bank of the river, a distance of three miles, where they found and burnt a Pottowatomy village, together with a great heap of corn & other property. Between 20 and 30 indians were killed and a number wounded, four prisoners taken; six american scalps, and some horses that had been lately stolen from St. Clair County were retaken. On our side four were wounded and only one of these dangerously."

MEDAL GIVEN TO BLACK PARTRIDGE BY THE AMERICANS.

Harper's Encycolopedia of United States History, Volume 1.

Bourbonnais (c. 1790-c.1850)

This French-Indian family was to contribute several members who were part of early Illinois history. Francois, senior, settled on the Kankakee River in 1828 and the area became known as Bulbona's Grove. Here he and his wife Calish, a Potawatomi, had some sons and daughters. The following is a story related by Percival Graham Rennick:

"As his name indicates, Bulbona was a Frenchman but his wife was a squaw. At the time mentioned, their daughter, Zeffa, had two lovers; one a fine looking young Indian from Indiantown and the other a French trader from Peoria. The mother's choice was the young Indian and the father's choice was the Frenchman. After a considerable period of rivalry, the two met at the home of Zeffa and the Frenchman entered into negotiations with the Indian and induced him to withdraw his offer of marriage to Zeffa for twenty-one blankets and fifty strings of beads. Soon after, the wedding was arranged and the Frenchman came up from Peoria with a priest stationed at this point. He also brought a Peoria fiddler along. Bulbona had invited all his friends in the surrounding territory, Frenchmen, Indians, and half-breeds. On the night of the wedding, Colonel Strowbridge, Dad Joe Smith and Henry Thomas, who had been at Peoria and were on their way home over the Peoria and Galena Trail, were passing Bulbona's place and were invited to stop and join in the wedding festivities. In addition to the other guests, some forty-five Indians were gathered outside of the house. When the white people ate and drank, the Indians ate and drank. When the white people danced, the Indians danced and squatted and yelled, but all in good nature. Sometimes the guests danced Indian dances and sometimes they danced French dances. While the ceremony was going on a pack of dogs heard another dog barking inside the cabin and rushed in and commenced barking at the priest. Bulbona kicked the dogs and this made them start fighting, and in the struggle the priest was thrown down, his robes torn and his face scratched. There was a good deal of swearing at the dogs, both in Indian dialect and French, and even the priest denounced them. Just at the beginning of the wedding ceremony, a light covered wagon drove up to the door and one of the occupants asked for shelter for the night. Bulbona told them that his house was full because of the wedding of his daughter, but on closer observation he saw that they were army officers and invited them to take a drink and to stay for the party. They accepted. The driver of the wagon was Mr. Kilgore of Peoria, and he related the story to N. Matson of Princeton, in 1872."

Francois and Calish also had two sons, Francois, Jr. and Washington. Both the mother and sons received lands in 1829 and 1832 as a result of some treaties. Francois, Jr., was the father of Mawteno for whom Manteno is named.

Billy Caldwell (Sauganash)
(c. 1781 -1841)

Caldwell was born around 1781 in Canada to an Irish officer Captain William Caldwell in the British army and a Potawatomi woman. Apparently they lived near Detroit since Caldwell learned from the Jesuit fathers there as a drowing boy. Thus he became fluent in French, English, and several different dialects. Later he married a daughter of Neescotnemeg who also had a son Minnemung known as Yellow Head. Early around 1800 he met the famous Tecumseh. Tecumseh and he travelled many miles together. Both of them fought in the War of 1812. During that war, Caldwell saved many prisoners in Chicago from the massacre.

Billy Caldwell had a strong, sinewy and straight physique. Often his fellow friends would call him "Straight Tree." From 1807 to 1812 he was Tecumseh's aide and secretary since the latter spoke little English.

In 1816 Caldwell using his rank of Captain wrote a commendation for Chamblee or Shaubenee for his service during the War of 1812.

By the 1820's Caldwell settled at Ft. Dearborn (Chicago). there he was well liked by the people and elected justice of the peace in 1826. In 1829 he received 2½ sections of land on the Chicago River adjoining the Indian tract of 1816. A few years later Caldwell and Shabona were effective in calming Big Foot to prevent a Winnebago uprising around Chicago.

Sometime in 1832 Caldwell had offered to buy books and clothing for all the tribal children if they would dress like Americans but they turned it down.

On October 20, 1832 Caldwell was to receive $600 a year through the treaty with the Potawatomi. The final treaty he participated in was the Chicago Treaty of 1833. It was Caldwell and Alexander Robinson who were asked to be the chief counselors in the tribes' business that September. Finally through several days of haggling, agreement was reached. The treaty was drawn up in five days by the two men plus Porter the government representative. The general council did not know what was done until it was presented to them. Through it, Caldwell was to receive $400 a year and $600 to each of his children. It was not long till the government built a frame house for Caldwell on the north branch of the Chicago River. The house was reported to be the first frame one for that area. Despite all this, Caldwell left Chicago in 1836 with his people for Council Bluffs, Iowa. He died there on September 28, 1841.

Naw Kaw Caromaine (c.1734-c.1838)

Naw Kaw or Wood was the principal chief of the Winnebagos in the late eighteenth century. He became one of Tecumseh's personal attendants during Tecumseh's height of power. Naw Kaw was with Tecumseh for around twenty years before Tecumseh was killed at the Battle of Thames. Naw Kaw repeated to Atwater an historian that Tecumseh "fell at the very first fire of the Kentucky dragoons, pierced by thirty bullets, and was carried four or five miles into the thick woods, and there buried by the warriors, who told the story of his fate." (ILLINOIS AND INDIANA INDIANS.) Atwater commented that Naw Kaw or Hootshoopkaw another attendant had never heard any of the other stories relating Tecumseh's death.

During the Black Hawk tragedy in 1832, Naw Kaw kept his policy of peace by not letting his Winnebago people aid Black Hawk. However, a few of them not under Naw Kaw's influence did join in the scrimishes.

Naw Kaw and the Winnebagos ceded their lands in 1828 and again in 1832 at Rock Island. They were moved from one reservation to another until they were finally settled near Omaha, Nebraska.

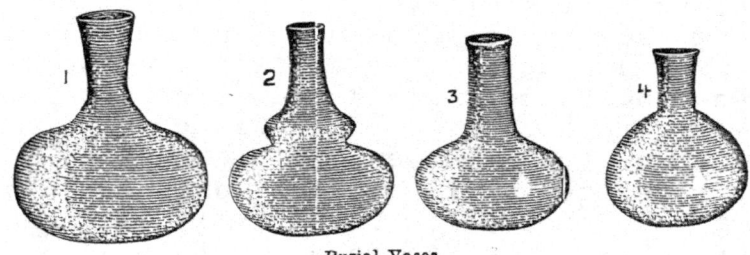

Burial Vases.

1893 Illinois State Exhibit
World's Columbian Exposition

Chicagou (c.1675-c.1740)

Chicagou was a chief of the Metchigama, a division of the Illinois nation. He was not a tribal chief but only a village chief according to the statements Chicagou often made.

However, La Salle reported in 1680 that he had seen three children of Chicagou's brother's baptized. Nicanape's children were Pierre, Joseph and Marie. In 1682 when La Salle once more visited Illinois country, Nicanape treated La Salle and his men to a feast.

In 1725 Chicagou was one of the delegates selected by the French authorities of the India Company to visit the country of France to see King Louis XV. It was reported that the chief was very well built phsically but he had been sick all the time that he was in France. There were six other tribal representatives who made the trip accompanied by Etienne Bourgmont acting for the India Company and Nicholas Ignace Beaubois, a Jesuit priest.

"The Indians arrived in France on September 20 and met with French officials the following week. The visit caused a sensation, and a description was printed in the popular journal Mercure de France. The article shows that members of the court regarded the Indian delegation as a novelty and not as representatives of a legitimate culture.... In return for pledges to support the French, the Indians were presented with extravagant gifts that were utterly useless in the wilderness. The Indians returned to America with tales of the strange and wonderful things they had seen in France, but their reports were met with disbelief. ..." ("An Indian Delegation in France, 1725".)

Chicagou was quite taken by all the extravagance of the French Court. Chicagou was the only one who did not dress in the clothes given by the French to the delegation. Of the ones there, he attracted more attention than any of the others. He usually stood before the French in his pentagonal cloth blanket with a silver border just above the edges. His loin cloth was made of a quarter-yard scarlet embellished with a silver band running around the inside of the edge. His moccasins were cloth--half red and half blue--held high by thongs tied to his belt.

On the experiences in France, Chicagou was most impressed when he had an audience with the Duchess of Orleans whose husband was next in line to the French throne if there were no male heirs born to Louis XV. Chicagou addressed her thus:

"I see with great joy that you are the beloved of the Great Spirit since, after making you the daughter of so many great chiefs, he gave you for a husband him who is himself a great Chief and the son of a great warrior. Your virtue gave the Great Spirit reasons for watching after you and loving you, just as your good heart makes all Frenchmen esteem and admire you. Always be as happy as you are now;

even more, be fruitful in producing warriors and great chiefs who will resemble the grandfathers of your husband and yourself. Finally live a long enough time so that the children of my children can one day come to see you as I have the good fortune of seeing you today." ("An Indian Delegation in France, 1725".)

As a gesture of her generosity, she allowed him to visit her own apartments. Chicagou received a magnificent snuffbox of black tortoise shell with a gold-embossed lid, having in its center a gold flower adorned with several precious gems. Chicagou still treasured this gift five years later and refused to part with it.

In 1918 A. Milo Bennet referred to Chicagou as the most famous of the Illinois. He also surmised that Chicago was named for the old chief.

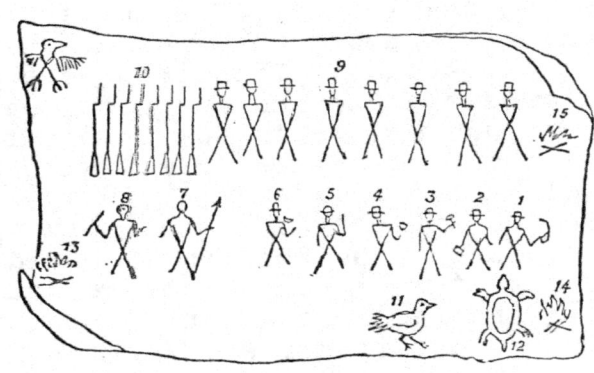

INDIAN LETTER ON BIRCH BARK   (FROM SCHOOLCRAFT.)

Christmas Dagney (1799-1848)

Dagney was born on Christmas day to Ambroise Dagney, a Frenchman of Kaskaskia and Me-chin-quam-e-sha, a Miami of the Wabash. His mother's name meant a beautiful shade tree. His uncle was Jocco the head chief of the village where his father Ambroise later settled.

Christmas and his sister Mary received a good education, learning both the French and English languages as well as several dialects of their mother's people. As a young man Christmas served many years at Fort Harrison and acted as an interpreter on many occasions.

On February 16, 1819 he married Mary Ann Isaacs who was a descendant of the Mohegan. He had met her at the Mission House when she was visiting near his home. His sister Mary Shields Cott later lived on a reservation west of Danville, Illinois. Their father Ambroise lived there near Danville until his death in 1848.

Christmas and his wife Mary had the unhappy task in 1846 to take the 350 related Miamis west to Lewisburg, Kansas. Most of them had to leave their good farms complete with homes. Years later Mary remarked: "that strong men would actually cry when they thought about their old homes in Indiana, to which many of them would make journeys barefooted, begging their way and submitting to the imprecations hurled upon them from the door of the white man as they asked for a crust of bread. I saw fathers and mothers give their little children away to others of the tribe for adoption, and then singing their funeral songs and joining in the solemn dance of death. Afterward go calmly away from the assemblage, never again to be seen alive." (ILLINOIS AND INDIANA INDIANS.) Nearly one-third of them died the first year in Kansas.

Ironically Christmas Dagney died a short time after moving to Kansas. He died the same year as his father in Illinois. His widow later married Baptiste Peoria.

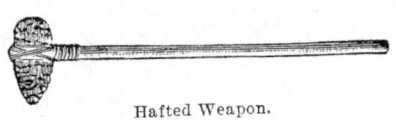

Hafted Weapon.

1893 Illinois State Exhibit
World's Columbian Exposition

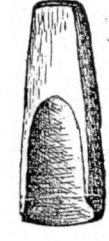

Stone Gouge.

Jean Baptiste Ducoigne (c.1770-1832)

Jean Baptiste Ducoigne was a French-Kaskaskia chief early in the 1800's near the Kaskaskia settlement of Illinois. Gen. William H. Harrison described Ducoigne as a gentlemanly man who wanted to live like a white man. Harrison wrote to the Secretary of War stating that "Ducoigne's long and well-proved friendship for the United States has gained him the hatred of all the other chiefs and ought to be an inducement with us to provide as well for his happiness, as for his safety." (HANDBOOK OF NORTH AMERICAN INDIANS.)

Ducoigne also assured Harrison that he or his people had never shed any blood of white men. Ducoigne was the signer in 1803 for the treaty of Vicennes and his son Louis signed in the treaty of Edwardsville in 1818. In the former Ducoigne received a hundred acres on which the United States agreed to build a house. He had two sons, Louis and Jefferson, and a daughter Ellen who married a settler. Apparently Ducoigne died before October, 1832 since a treaty of that date left a reserve to his daughter Ellen Ducoigne described as being heir to their late chief.

In earlier years when George Rogers Clark came to Kaskaskia, Ducoigne told him that the Cahokia Mounds were "palaces," surrounded by fortifications, and that they were the work of "his forefathers."

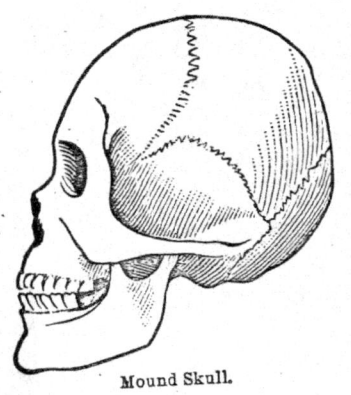
Mound Skull.

1893 Illinois State Exhibit World's Columbian Exposition

Jean Baptiste Pointe Du Sable
(1740-1818)

Jean Baptiste Pointe Du Sable was born possibly of a Frenchman and a Negro mother. At times he would say he was from Santo Domingo and at others he'd claim he was a Potawatomi chief.

After trapping for a number of years in the northwest territory, he finally built a cabin near the Chicago portage in 1779. There he operated a post for the British governor Patrick Sinclair. This was his second residence in Illinois country. His first was at Peoria in 1778. Sometime in the 1780's he was captured by the British and taken to Ft. Detroit and tried as a spy.

After release, he returned to his Chicago post where he stayed till 1796. Du Sable built a twenty by forty foot house of logs and bark. The furnishings which he bought in Detroit were very fine and included paintings. His wife was Catherine, a Potwatomi.

After ten years he made an extensive farm including two barns, a horse mill, a bakehouse, a dairy, a poultry house, and a smokehouse. He sold his trading post to Jean LaLime in 1796 who a few years later sold it to John Kinzie. Du Sale moved back to Peoria but by the time of his death August 28, 1818, he was in St. Charles, Missouri.

SAMPLES OF INDIAN PICTURE-WRITING

Writing by means of pictures preceded the alphabet which we now use. In this way the red man recorded his ideas on birch bark, wood, and the skins of animals.

Gomo (c. 1765-1815)

Gomo was a principal chief of the Illinois River band of the Potawatomi who by 1812 had a village on the left bank of the Illinois seventeen to twenty-one miles above Peoria.

In August of 1811 Gomo met several times with Captain Samuel Levering. These men contracted agreements since the Shawnee Prophet brother of Tecumseh was stirring up the tribes in Illinois. But Gomo was not impressed by the Phrophet. He agreed to contact the other chiefs and by the middle of the month, several met at Peoria to negotiate. So that fall the Illinois River valley was rather quiet. However, by that winter, game was scarce, and the crops had not been good for the tribes. The tribes resorted to stealing since the traders would not supply goods.

British interference was the scapegoat for the trouble between the Americans and the tribes. Gomo did not answer requests for return of stolen horses and he continued for some time to ignore the American's pleas. Early in 1812 Governor Edwards was desperate to make peace with the tribes. His efforts were dampened, however, when some settlers killed an Ottawa and captured two others on the mouth of the Illinois River.

A few days later Gomo assured Edwards that he too wanted peace. He did not believe Edward's statement that Americans did not want their land. Gomo promised not to aid the British but he would not turn some of his men over to Edwards. It was not long before Gomo's people began buying ammunition from the British traders.

Gov. Edwards took matters in hand and began to destroy villages along the Illinois River. In September of 1813 under command of Benjamin Howard, Gomo's village was destroyed. Howard described it thus:

"The General immediately made the necessary arrangements, and leaving the sick and a few who had lost their horses, we marched the next morning for Gomo's town. Here we found the enemy had taken water and ascended the Illinois. We burnt their village and two others in the neighborhood, and encamped on the ground two nights. The general, finding they had declined giving us a fight, marched back to Peoria." ("The Illinois River Potawatomi in War of 1812")

By September of that year, Gomo and others headed south. The tribes scattered and initiated no large attack against the settlers.

During the summer of 1814 Gomo and the others returned to the Illinois River area. Gomo, Black Partridge, and Pepper assured the Americans they wanted peace. In 1815 a treaty was signed but that same year, Gomo died.

Hononegah (c.1800-1847)

Hononegah was the Potawatomi wife of Stephen Mack, Sr. who settled near Rockton, Illinois in 1823. She was said to be intilligent, thrifty, industrious, and skillful with a needle. She always wore the dress of her people and only once wore the clothing of the settlers. She helped her husband run a trader station at or on Rock River.

On June 26th, 1832 Black Hawk and some of his warriors visited the trading post and while there a group of Winnebagos entertained them. Hononegah's husband stayed out of sight so as to alleviate any strain even though he was personally known to Black Hawk.

She and her husband had eleven children, nine of whom reached adult years. During those busy family years, she made sure that the children received a good education. She died in the town named for her husband where he had established a general mercantile business and built many houses for the residents.

On July 1, 1847 when she died, she left a year old child who later became Mrs. Carrie Mack Newberry of Pontiac, Michigan. Hononegah's brother-in-law Almon Mack of Rochester, Michigan took the little girl to raise.

Her husband died suddenly in April 1850. Both were buried with their son Henry in Phillip's Cemetery southwest of Macktown.

Stephen Mack, Jr. received $350 in the Treaty of 1833 and his heirs received $500 in trust. His sisters Rosa and Mary also received payment in that treaty.

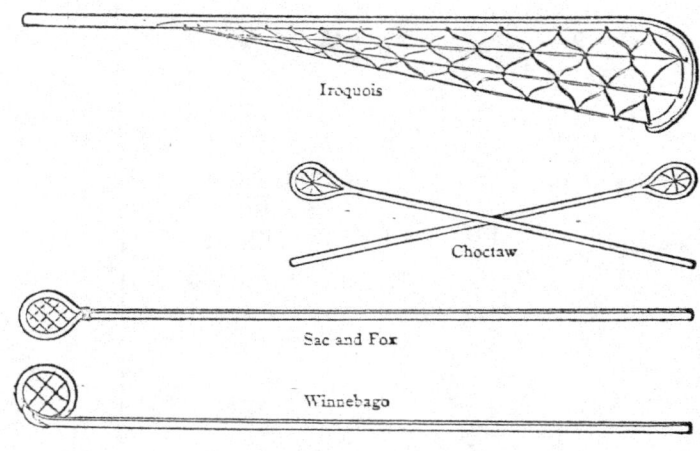

GROUP OF BALL STICKS

Jeneir (c.1780-c.1835)

Jeneir was the daughter of a Potawatomi chief and a member of Topennebee's band. She reportedly later married Moness or Isadore Momence a son of Pierre Moran, also a Potawatomi chief known as Peerish. Moran was a son of a Frenchman and a Potawatomi. Jeneir received a section of land in Kankakee County under a treaty signed in 1832.

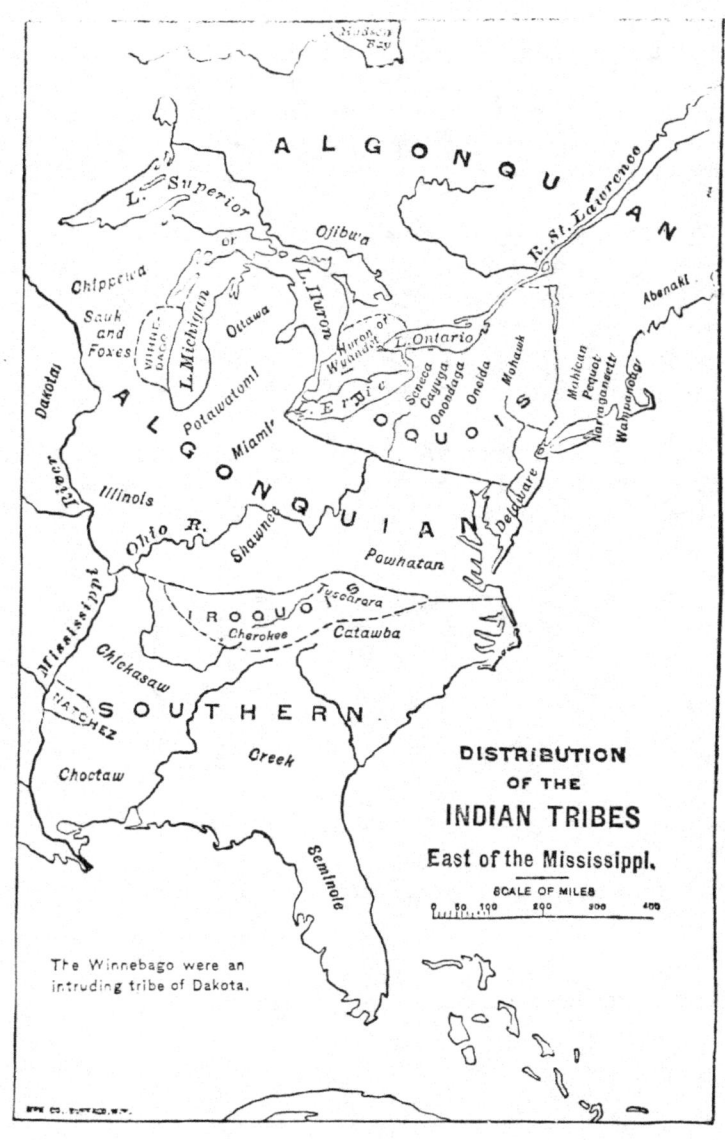

Kannekuk (c. 1797-1852)

Kannekuk was born around 1797 to a Kickapoo couple in Vermilion County near Danville, Illinois. At an early age Kannekuk began preaching after some conversion by Methodist missionaries. He often strived against liquor and its effects on his friends. He began his own church which was totally remarkable in that he could neither read, write or speak English.

By 1833 his tribe was removed to Kansas. There a Rev. Isaac McCoy, a Baptist missionary, described the Kickapoo Prophet's religious services in 1835:

"...Congregational worship is performed daily and lasts from one to three hours. It consists of a kind of prayer, expressed in broken sentences, often repeated in a monotonous sing-song tune, equalling about two measures of a common psalm tune. All in unison engage in this; and in order to preserve harmony in words each holds in his or her hand a small board, about an inch and a half broad and eight or ten inches long, upon which is engraved arbitrary characters, which they follow up with the finger until the prayer is completed...."("Kannekuk")

Kannekuk also invented prayer-sticks for use by his people.

Other successors continued the Kickapoo Prophet's church after his death from smallpox in 1852. He was buried near a village on the Missouri River in the north part of Leavenworth County, Kansas.

The Prophet was a tall, bony man, sharp black eyes, and an intelligent face. He had tremendous energy and a very persuasive manner which added to his influence. George Catlin painted his portrait in 1831.

During his lifetime Kannekuk signed the treaty of St. Louis on October 24, 1832. On September 30, 1833 the Prophet was paid $120 for two horses. It was later reported during his life that he had been married four times.

One of Kannekuk's sermons he made on July 17, 1831 near Danville has been preserved and is now available in print. The following is a part of that sermon:

"My fiends, where are your thoughts today? Where were they yesterday? Were they fixed upon doing good? Or were you drunk and tattling, or did anger rest in your hearts? If you have done any of these things your Great Father in Heaven knows it. His eye is upon you. He always sees you and will always see you. He knows all your deeds. He has knowledge of the smallest transactions of your lives."("Kannekuk".)

Keokuk (1780-1848)

Keokuk was a Sauk-Fox who lived in northern Illinois. He was reported to be a large and finely formed man. He had the ability to speak well and consequently had great influence over his followers. He was not chief until after 1833 when Black Hawk was captured. Keokuk had enough trust among the Americans and was appointed to take Black Hawk's place.

On November 30, 1832, Keokuk had sent the following letter to the Governor of Illinois:

"To the Great Chief of Illinois:

"My Father--I have been told by a trader that several of your village criers have been circulating bad news, informing the whites that the Indians were preparing for war, and that we are dissatisfied. My Father, you were present when the tomahawk was buried, and assisted me to place it so deep that will never again be raised against the white children of Illinois.

"My Father--Very few of that misguided band that entered Rock River last summer remain. You have humbled them by war, and have made them friendly by your generous conduct to them after they were defeated. Myself, and the greater part of the Sauks and Foxes, have firmly held you by the hand. We followed your advice, and did as you told us. My Father, I take pity on those of my nation that you forgave, and never mention the disasters of last summer. I wish them to be forgotten.

"I do not permit the criers of our village to proclaim any bad news against the whites, not even the truth. Last fall an old man, a Fox Indian, was hunting on an island, a short distance below Rock Island, for turkeys to carry to Fort Armstrong. He was killed by a white man. We passed it over--we have only spoken of it in whispers. Our agent has not heard of it. We wish to live in peace with the whites. If a white man comes to our camp or village, we give him a share of what we have to eat, a lodging if he wants it, and put him on the trail if he has lost it.

"My Father,--Advise the criers of your villages to tell the truth respecting us, and assist in strengthening the chain of friendship, that your children may treat us friendly when they meet us; and be assured that we are their friends, and that we have feelings as well as they have.

"My Father--This is all I have to say at present." (THE INDIAN TRIBES OF NORTH AMERICA.)

Keokuk repeatedly visited Washington and other Atlantic towns to let Americans know the peaceful intentions of his people. He was a proud man and he knew it. When George Catlin painted his portrait, Keokuk appeared with twenty of his most important men. He brought several items of his best wardrobe but selected the item which was purely of his people. He wore it for several days as he posed for his portrait. Keokuk insisted that he be painted sitting upon a horse and Catlin obliged.

Two years later after the painting of the portrait, Catlin was giving a lecture at Stuyvesant Institute in New York. Keokuk and several of his men were in the audience. One of the observers in the audience questioned the credibility of Keokuk sitting on such a fine horse. Catlin could not satisy the doubter so he called on Keokuk and his men to clarify the matter. Le Clair spoke up and told the audience that indeed it was the horse he sold to Keokuk for three hundred dollars. That settled the discussion.

Keokuk and his people moved to Iowa as did the other tribes. They were there for a few years then had to move to Kansas. Keokuk died there in 1848 but his body was moved back to Iowa and buried beneath his statue in the city named for him.

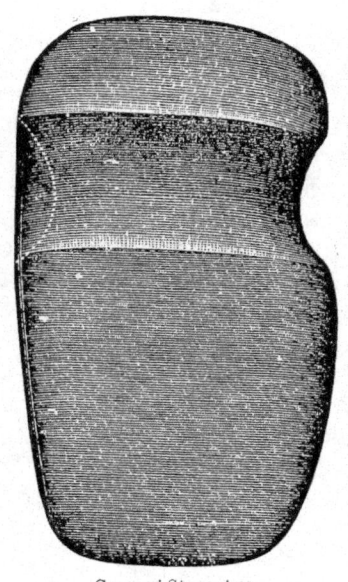
Grooved Stone Axe.

Celt, or ungrooved Axe.

1893 Illinois State Exhibit
World's Columbian Exposition

La Framboise Family (bef.1780-c.1907)

Francois La Framboise, Sr. was born around 1780. By the early 1800's he settled in Ft. Dearborn with his Ottawa wife Shaw-we-no-qua who was a daughter of a chief. Francois taught his wife how to read and write English and as a consequence she taught her own children and became the first school teacher there. They had five children: Claude, who married and had children; Joseph, who married Therese, a Potawatomi and had children; Alex, who married and had children; Josette, who married Jean Baptiste Beaubien and had children; and Francis, Jr. who died apparently before 1830.

In a later treaty with the Winnebago, Francois was reimbursed for two thousand dollars for a canoe load of merchandise he had lost to Chippewa and Ottawa in 1799 when the lake was frozen.

Francois, Sr. died on April 26, 1830. Administrator of his estate was his son-in-law Jean Baptiste Beaubien who was married to his daughter Josette. All the living children received one-fourth of the estate which amounted to around $250 each.

During the Black Hawk War, Claude and Joseph La Framboise enlisted. Joseph later became an advisor for the Michigan tribes in the treaty of Chicago in 1833. Joseph along with Billy Caldwell and Alexander Robinson received some annuities as a result of the treaty. Joseph apparently went to Kansas later since he signed the treaty in 1861 there as a chief.

Josette and Jean Baptiste Beaubien were the parents of the first mixed blood child who was recognized by the tribes close to Ft. Dearborn. Leather and beads were brought as presents for the mother and child. The Potawatomis danced all night in celebration that night of January 28, 1822. The son Alexander Beaubien lived to a good age and left his memoirs. He stated that he was probably the only one who could say:

"I saw my birth place grow from a settlement of half a hundred people to a metropolis of more than two million people." ("1822 Chicago, from TALES OF AN 1822 CHICAGOAN.")

Alexander Beaubien died in Chicago on March 25, 1907.

Ground Flint Battle Axe.

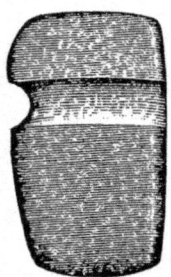
Grooved Stone Axe.

Mamantouensa (c.1660-c.1730)

Mamantouensa was chief of the Illinois Confederacy, and a member of the Kaskaskia tribe. The Confederacy consisted of the Cahokia, Kaskaskia, Michigamea, Moingwena, Peoria and Tamaroa tribes whose homes were along the Illinois River and at the mouth of Kaskaskia on the Mississippi. Mamantouensa was told to stay behind to lead his people when the French India Company selected delegates to visit France in 1725. Even though Mamantouensa did not accompany them to France, he did send a formal message which was read to King Louis. It read:

"Today, November 12, 1724, the aforesaid Mamantouensa accompanied by all the eminent people of his village paid a formal visit to M. de Boisbriant, first Lieutenant of the King and Commanding General of the province, and to M. du Tisné, Commandant among the Illinois. At that meeting, Mamantouensa entrusted the Reverand Father de Beaubois of of the Company of Jesus with a necklace to present to the King along with the following letter:

'Sir, My Father: I am nothing, and if I dare to speak to you, it is only in the name of my Nation, and particularly those whom I regard as my Chiefs. My Fathers, my Elders urge me on. In former times they heard your word and what I have to say to you, is, it seems to me, encouraged by your Father, your Grandfather and your Uncle. It is to them in particular that I have an obligation to speak clearly. My Father, I share your prayer, for the Black Robes have instructed me and all my Elders; My Father, it is up to you to fortify me in prayer. But I am so ashamed after having seen the Spanish Chapel at Pensacola, where I helped my father de Bienville in his capture of the place. Yes, my Father, I am ashamed, and it is this that makes me ask you frankly to be generous in our Houses of Prayer, in those of the Metchigamis, in those of the Kaokias and the Tamaroas, and in those of my own nation. Look more favorably on my nation than on any other since it has the advantage of already being attached to prayer. Send us more Black Robes and White Collars, for it was they who began to instruct us along with all my kinsmen, the Peorias, Tamaroas, Kaokias, Metchigamias, Moingonans, etc.

'I further beseech you, my Father, to confirm the promise made to me in your name by my father de Boisbriant. He promised me that no one would disturb me in my village, that no one would force me to make further moves in order to make room in it for Frenchmen, my brothers and your children, who are thus my kinsmen. I myself have retired from activity, but I still fear moving. Such moves disrupt the prayer, upset my young people, and even the Black Robe wearies of endlessly building anew and is thus not quick to follow us. Our wives and children suffer from it. It is for this reason that I wish to be the master of the Village and its land, for then no one would be so quick to speak of moving.

'I wish, my Father, that I could come to see you myself, but my fathers de Boisbriant and du Tisné, who manage your affairs here, told me to remain in order to maintain my village and to defend the Black Robes and the French village from the Fox, who are our mutual enemies.

'The Black Robe, the Great Chief of prayer, carries my necklace to you and it is he who will bring me your answer and lead back to me my Chiefs who will have the good fortune to see you. They will go, my Father, close to the sun, the lovely sun that makes our plants flourish. As for me, I remain as if in a shadow; I am small and cannot grow unless you make me conscious of your rays. I want to have this light upon me through having my Chiefs, who go to see you, return from this visit content, and also through having the Black Robe, Chief of Prayer, come back to relieve me of the shame I feel. I also want for all my Nation and its various villages to feel your protection more and more. I pray constantly to the Great Spirit for you and all your Cabin and for all those for whom you are the master. Live long; be, if you, a greater Chief than either your Father or your Grandfather, That is all; I, Mamantouensa, am your child and the brother of the French.'" ("An Indian Delegation to France, 1725".)

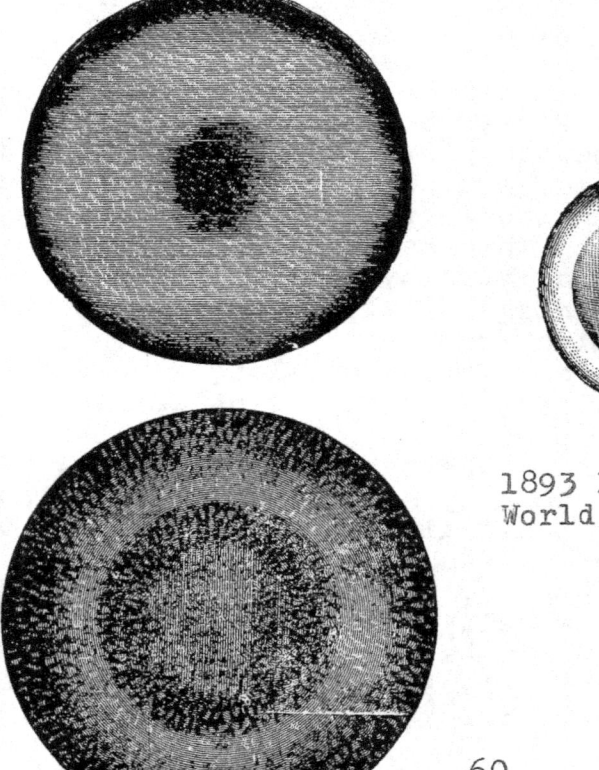

Discoids.

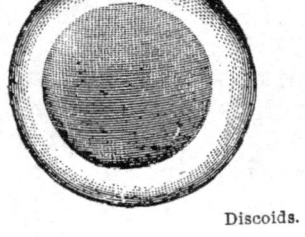 

Discoids.

1893 Illinois State Exhibit
World's Columbian Exposition

Metea (c.1760-1827)

Metea was presiding chief of Mus-qua Was-e-peo-tan near the joining of St. Joseph and the Maumee along the Wabash.

In 1821 August 14 Metea was one of the many chiefs who gathered at Chicago to sign a treaty. Gen. Cass was there again as authority for the government as he had done before with the Potawatomi in St. Mary's treaty of 1818 in Ohio. Metea had been there also.

Hon. Henry R. Schoolcraft was there during the conference and recorded the speeches. Cass of course spoke first to inform the group of what the government wanted. The delegation of Metea and others thought about the offer for a couple of days and returned. It was Metea who spoke first the second time. According to Schoolcraft, Metea stated:

"My Father--A long time has passed since we first came upon our lands; and our old people have all sunk into their graves. They had sense. We are all young and foolish, and do not wish to do anything that they would not approve, were they living. We are fearful we shall offend their spirits if we sell our lands; and we are fearful we shall offend you if we don't sell them. This has caused us great perplexity of thought, because we have counselled among ourselves, and do not know how we can part with the land. My Father-- Our country was given us by the Great Spirit, who gave it to us to hunt upon; to make our cornfields upon; to live upon; and to make down our beds upon when we die. And He would never forgive us, should we now bargain it away. When you first spoke to us for lands at St. Mary's, we said we had little, and agreed to sell you a piece of it; but we told you we could spare no more. Now you ask us again! You are never satisfied!

"My Father....We all shake hands with you. Behold our warriors, our women and children. Take pity on us and on our words." (THE ILLINOIS AND INDIANA INDIANS.)

Metea was not one without some physical wounds during his lifetime. In the fight around Ft. Wayne in 1812 his right arm was shattered. The arm never healed and hung limp at his side.

Metea did attend a last council in 1827 in Fort Wayne. Reportedly after the conference where he acted with diplomacy, he frolicked after the session. He supposedly became so drunk that he drank a bottle of AQUA FORTIS and died a half hour later.

Joseph Ogee (c.1800-c.1850)

Joseph Ogee was a French-Winnebago who lived at Peoria on Rock River. In 1830 John Dixon bought the ferry from Ogee that he had on the Rock River. Ogee then moved to Chicago. There he worked as a pilot and interpreter.

He served as an interpreter in the treaty with the Potawatomi in 1828. His wife was Madeline, a Potawatomi, who received a tract near the Fox River in 1829.

Joseph and Madeline separated after he sold the ferry to Dixon. They left behind their sons, one of which was John. The Dixons raised them for a time until they later joined their mother who had already returned to her Potawatomi family. The son John was dark complexioned with large round eyes.

A L.H. Ogee, a possible descendant, signed the treaty of 1861 in Kansas Territory.

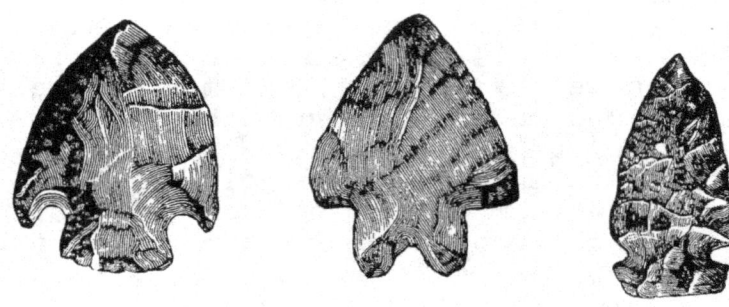

1893 Illinois State Exhibit
World's Columbian Exposition

Flint Drills.

Antoine Ouilmette (c.1760-1841)

Antoine Ouilmette was born near Montreal and quite possibly the son of French and native American parents. He later married Archange, a Potawatomi.

By 1790 he was working for the American Fur Company and moved to Ft. Dearborn, later Chicago. In 1796 he was working with Jean Baptiste Pointe Du Sable. His task was chiefly one of hauling boats and supplies across the Chicago portage. His cabin was not far from Du Sable's. During the Ft. Dearborn catastrophe, his family did not suffer as many of the others. After that, Alexander Robinson and he concentrated on attending the garrison garden.

According to records, in 1826, some of the Ouilmette children were students in the Carey Mission School which was a short distance from Ft. Dearborn. Those children were Louis, Mitchell and Lezett; also a son, Copah.

In July, 1829, through the treaty of Prairie du Chien, his wife and children received two sections north of Ft. Dearborn on Lake Michigan. It was not till 1835 that his family moved there. In 1838 the family joined the other Potawatomi going to Council Bluffs, Iowa. Seven of their children accompanied Archange. Archange died in 1840 and Antoine died a year later. Two of their daughters had married a Mann and a Welsh.

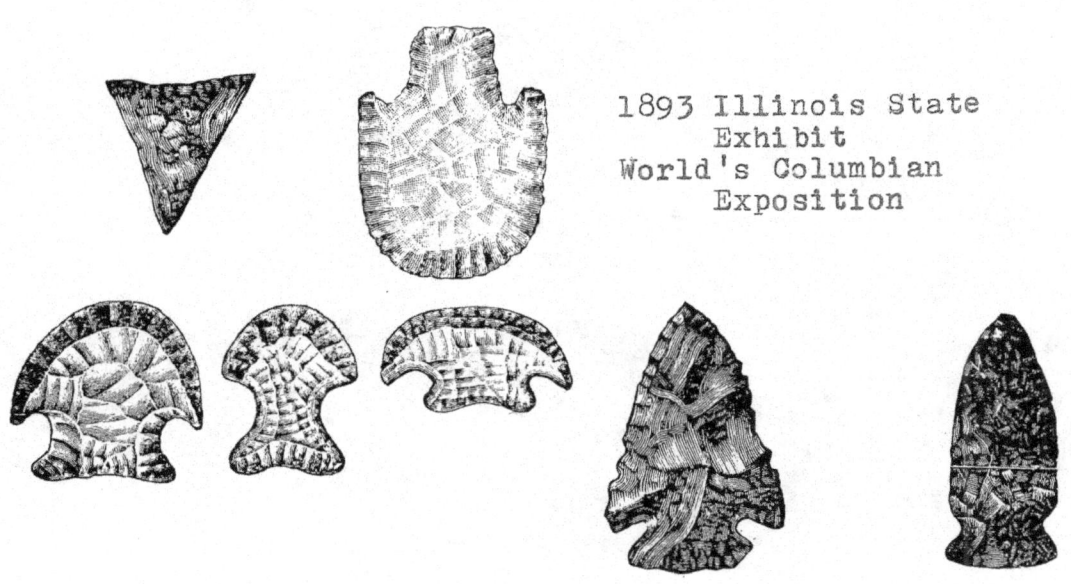

1893 Illinois State Exhibit World's Columbian Exposition

Pakoisheecan (c.1780-c.1840)

Pakoisheecan was a Kickapoo chief during the French and Indian war with the British. It was he who led the attack on the British Ft. Harrison on the Wabash, in 1794.

Pakoisheecan was known as Blackberry Flower among the settlers. Pakoisheecan led the attack by night by crawling along on the ground, pulling himself along with knives. He made his way unseen to the blockhouse and stuffed dry grass in the cracks between the logs. Striking his flint, he lit the dry grass. This burning blockhouse went to the ground even though those within tried furiously to prevent it.

Pakoisheecan's band then rushed the fort but they failed to enter it. Pakoisheecan later told his story to Mrs. Mary A. Dagney Peoria when he was there again in 1821 to settle the treaty.

Pakoisheecan's band stayed in Illinois along the Embarrass or Vermilion until 1832-33. Their new home was in Brown and Jackson Counties, Kansas.

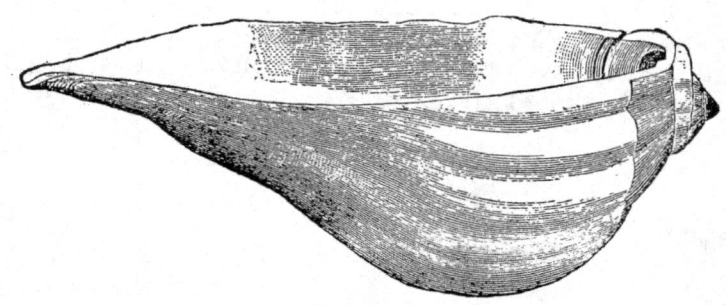
Shell Vessel.

1893 Illinois State Exhibit
World's Columbian Exposition

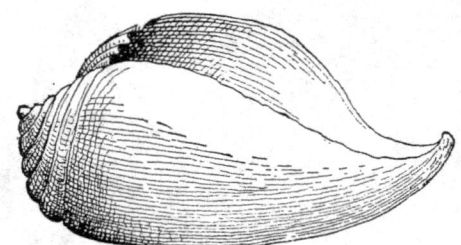
Mound Shell.

Baptiste Peoria (c.1793-1873)

Baptist Peoria was born around 1793 to a French Canadian Baptiste and a member of the Peoria along the Des Plaines River. He was reported to be a tall man and an excellent horseman. He knew the French and English languages as well as several dialects of the Potawatomi, Shawnee, Delaware, Miami, Illinois and Kickapoos. The ability with languages enabled him to be an interpreter on many occasions. From 1821 to 1838 he worked for the United States in helping with the moving of the tribes from Indiana and Illinois, to the west of the Missouri. Many of the early settlers around the Illinois, Kaskaskia, and Wabash Rivers were quite familiar with the figure of Baptiste.

Early in his life, he represented the Peorias in the treaty of Edwardsville in 1818. After 1838, he still generally assisted the government until he was elected head chief of the Miami and Illinois in 1867. It was through his efforts that he consolidated the old Illini confederacy of the Miamis, Kaskaskias, and others into the Confederated Tribes. He accompanied them to the new lands. There he died on September 13, 1873. He left a widow Mary Dagney Baptiste. The county seat of Paoli of Miami County, Kansas is named for him.

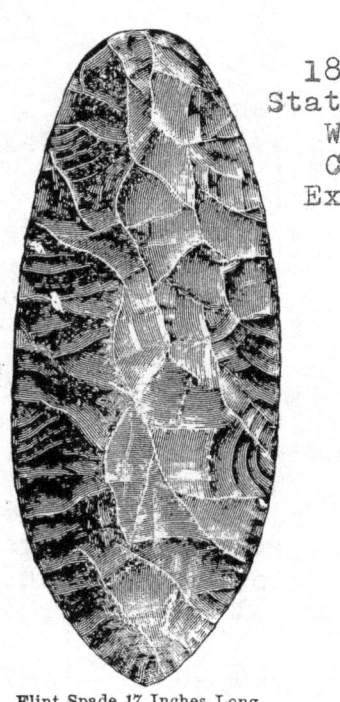

Flint Spade 17 Inches Long.

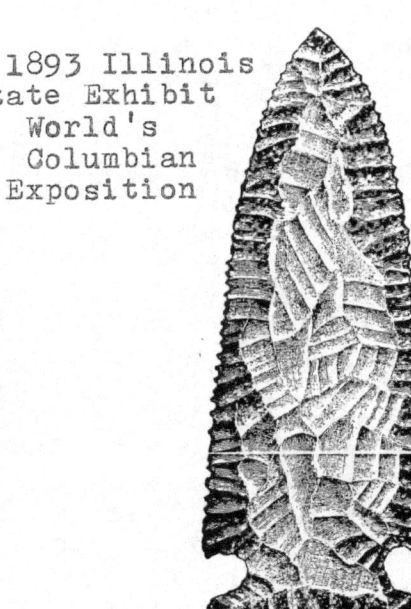

1893 Illinois State Exhibit World's Columbian Exposition

Spear Head.

Pontiac (1720-1769)

Pontiac was born in the northwest part of Ohio around 1720. He grew up around Ft. Detroit. He was an Ottawa which was one of the many branches of the Algonguian. "... He was of middle height, with a figure of remarkable symmetry. His complexion was unusually dark, and his features, though void of regularity, were expressive of boldness and vigor...." (INDIAN HISTORY FOR YOUNG FOLKS.)

A traveler who visited Pontiac's country in 1760 found Pontiac to be a very strong majestic leader who was greatly honored and revered by his people. Pontiac had always been told when he was young man by his father that when he was older that he'd be caught between the French and English. And indeed, Pontiac was.

As Pontiac grew older, many of his Ottawa friends wanted to trade with the English but his father did not. Once when the Chippewa called a war council, Pontiac attended in place of his sick father. The council decided to help the English against the French which Pontiac did not like at all. By the time he returned home, his father had died. Others who did not care for Pontiac's stand attacked his village. Pontiac proved what a good leader he was and was made chief of the Ottawa.

During the French and English war, Pontiac was not happy at all. It was reported that often he would paint his face black to let all who saw him that he was sad. Pontiac approached the English several times but found them to be less kind than the French.

By 1763 Pontiac led forces which captured the British forts of Michilimackinac, Green Bay, and Sandusky and one other. It was only Detroit and Fort Pitt which he failed take.

In early 1764 Pontiac went to Ft. de Chartres to ask the French Commandant Neyon de Villiers to help against the British. De Villiers told Pontiac that he could not since the British and French made peace. Both the men finally became disgusted with each other.

In August of 1764 Pontiac met George Croghan the Commissioner appointed by Sir William Johnson. Pontiac and most of his chiefs spoke with Croghan at Detroit. Pontiac made his stand quite clear to Croghan by saying:

"Father, we have all smoked out of this pipe of peace. It is your children's pipe; and as the war is over, and the Great Spirit and Giver of Light, who has made the earth and everything therein, has brought us all together this day for our mutual good, I declare to all nations that I have settled my peace before I came here, and now deliver my pipe to be sent to Sir William Johnson, that he may know I have made peace, and taken the King of England for my father, in the presence of all the nations now go to visit him, they may smoke out of it with him in peace. Fathers, we are obliged to you for lighting up our old council-fire for us, and desiring us to return to it; but we are now settled on the Miami River, not far from hence. Whenever you want us, you will find us there.

"Our people love liquor, and if we dwelt near you in our village of Detroit, our warriors would be always drunk, and quarrels would arise between us and you." (LIVES OF FAMOUS INDIAN CHIEFS.)

Pontiac and his men kept peace for over a year before he met Sir Johnson again on the Mohawk River. For the next three years Pontiac lived in different parts of Illinois and Indiana.

In April of 1769 Pontiac went to visit St. Ange de Villiers in St. Louis once again. De Villiers and Pierre Chouteau entertained Pontiac but unfortunately Pontiac had heard of a large gathering of the Illinois at Cahokia. They warned him not to go but Pontiac left dressed in his French officer uniform which he had worn since 1765. Pontiac discovered that the group was trading and drinking with English dealers. Pontiac, of course, took no time telling them what he thought.

After Pontiac left, an English trader by the name of Williamson was determined to make an end of Pontiac. Williamson happened on a strolling member of the Kaskaskia band and bribed him with a barrel of whiskey. The assassin followed Pontiac and murdered him in a nearby woods.

De Villiers took the body and buried it near the fort. It was not long before the revenge was taken out on the Illinois who were not to blame for the murder at all.

Grooved Hammer Stones.

A Hafted Spade.

Alexander Robinson or Che-che-pin-qua
(1789-1872)

Robinson was born at Mackinaw, a son of a Scottish trader Robinson and an Ottawa. He lived around Ft. Dearborn early in the 1800's. He especially became prominent as an interpreter and mediator during councils and treaties. On September 28, 1826 he married Catherine Chevalier, daughter of Francois and Mary Ann Chevalier of St. Joseph, Michigan.

In 1827 he and others were responsible for keeping the Potawatomi from joining the Winnebagos. Robinson served as one of the chief counselors during the Chicago Treaty of 1833.

On June 9, 1830 Robinson was licensed to keep a tavern in Chicago. From there he continued to live on his property on the Des Plaines River acquired in 1829 treaty of Prairie du Chien. When his people moved to Kansas, he did not go with them. He died at his home near Chicago in 1872. He and his family were buried near the house. The house stood until it burned in 1955. Robinson's grand daughter had been living in it at that time.

A large Mound in the American Bottom, Madison County, Ill.

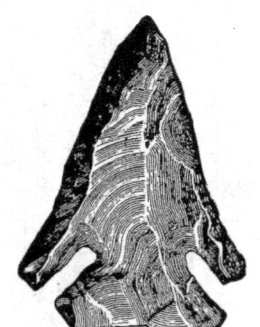

Beveled Edge Flint.

Notched Hoe.

Shaubenee (1775-1859)

Shaubenee was born near the Maumee River in Ohio in 1775. His father was an Ottawa and his mother a Seneca. Around 1800 Shaubenee hunted in the Potawatomi country along the Illinois River. There Shaubenee met chief Spotka and his wife. They decided to give him their daughter Wiomex Okono in marriage. Spotka died around 1815 and consequently Shaubenee was made chief of the village. By the fall of 1837 Shaubenee's village numbered 130 and his own immediate family consisted of 25.

Sometime during 1807 Shaubenee was down on the Wabash. There he met Tecumseh. He was quite impressed with the leader and it was not long before Shaubenee and Billy Caldwell accompanied Tecumseh all over Illinois, visiting the tribes along the Illinois, Fox, and Rock Rivers.

Shaubenee did fight with Tecumseh's forces in the War of 1812 and he was in the field with Tecumseh when the latter waskilled in the Battle of Thames on October 5, 1813. Shortly Shaubenee reluctantly pledged his allegiance to the United States. He returned to his village and remained there for a number of years till 1837.

Gordon S. Hubbard who worked for the American Fur Company at Chicago remarked that he first met Shaubenee in 1818 and was acquainted with him until he died. Hubbard stated that he was impressed "with the nobility of (Shaubenee's) character. Physically he was as a fine a specimen of a man as he ever saw--tall, well-proportioned, strong and active, with a face expressing great strength of mind, and goodness of heart." (LIVES OF FAMOUS INDIAN CHIEFS.) Shaubenee was not much of a orator but whenever he talked, others listened.

Bill Caldwell gave Shaubenee a citation in 1816 which commended him for his war efforts. It read:

"This is to certify that the bearer of this name, Chamblee, was a faithful companion to me during the late war with the United States. The bearer joined the late celebrated warrior, Tecumseh, of the Shawnee Nation in the year 1807 on the Wabash River and remained with the above warrior from the commencement of the hostilities with the United States until our defeat at Morarian Town on the Thames, October 5, 1813. I also have been witness to his intrepidity and courageous warrior (conduct) on many occasions and he showed a great deal of humanity to those unfortunate sons of Mars who fell into his hands. Amhurstburg, August 1, 1816. B. Caldwell, Captain I.D."

It was Shaubenee and Billy Caldwell a few years later in 1827 who calmed Big Foot and persuaded him not to wage war with the Winnebagos. Big Foot, however, did hold Shaubenee prisoner in his camp until Caldwell got him released.

In 1829 Shaubenee and his people were granted land near Dekalb, Illinois. The place became known as Shabbona's Grove.

He lived there with his people in peace until another individual wanted the land. Thus by 1837 Shaubenee and his village were ordered to move to a new reservation in western Missouri. At that time around 130 moved to new homes there but it was not long before some other tribes in Missouri began terrorizing Shaubenee and his people. As a result Shaubenee lost his eldest son and a nephew. This action forced Shaubenee to return to Illinois in 1840 to save his own life. Only Shaubenee's immediate family returned with him to his old home. There he found strangers living there and was ordered to leave by the new owner. A few of Shaubenee's old friends realized his plight and bought him a tract of land of 20 acres of timber on Mazon Creek south of Morris, Illinois. There they built a double log cabin for Shaubenee and his family. Pypeogee and Pyps were his son and nephew he lost.

    Shaubenee lived through many changes in early Illinois. Lincoln and Douglas had already begun their famous debates by 1858. It was in Ottawa, Illinois in August of that year where Douglas made a statement which upset Shaubenee deeply. Douglas had shouted that he was "in favor of confining citizenship to the white men of European descent, instead of conferring it upon Negroes, Indians, and other inferior races." (BROKEN PEACE PIPES.) Shaubenee was there to hear that statement and he realized then that white men would give his people little consideration.

    Shaubenee and his people were reluctant to learn white man's ways, lived in their wigwams, and used the double cabin for storage. Shaubenee died July 27 (17), 1859, and was buried in Morris where a burial monument was not placed until forty years later. Shaubenee's second wife Pokanoka and a grandchild drowned in Grundy County in 1864. After his death, the rest of his family moved west.

Modwe Quah, Daughter of Shabbona Chief.

Published by C. P. Hallam.

Chief Shabbona

Mrs. Josephine Marshno, Great grand-daughter of Shabbona Chief.

Shick Shack or Sha-kah
(c.1785-c.1845)

Shick Shack was a Potawatomi chief who came to the Sangamon River bottom with his group of forty men and their wives and children sometime after the War of 1812 and before 1819. Archibald Job who settled with his family in 1819 at Sylvan Grove reported that the chief's village of twenty-five to thirty deerskin lodges was on the south side of the Sangamon twenty-five miles above its new mouth and a dozen or more miles west of New Salem.

Shick Shack was described to be erect, muscular, and active, about five feet nine inches in height, with black eyes, and black hair. He was an inveterate smoker, but detested liquor. He did not allow any liquor drinking in his camp. For daily activity, he and his people worked at hunting, fishing, trapping, and planting. They enjoyed horse and foot racing, ball playing, and pitching quoits.

Shick Shack had two wives Lo-lo, a Winnebago and Mah-qua-la, a Kickapoo. They both kept their hair neatly braided, wore calico and linsey clothing, and made elaborate beaded moccasins of deer or elk skin for their feet. Mah-qua-la had three daughters by him and Lo-lo had one son Goomah or Gomo. They had both separate lodges but shared all the chores and cooking for the seven of them.

Shick Shack and his people were uncomfortable with all the settlers constantly increasing in numbers in their beloved territory. The last buffalo of the Illinois prairie had long disappeared since 1816 and the elk bands had also vanished since 1818. The one sign of civilization that convinced Shick Shack that the Indian of Illinois was doomed and he should move on was the appearance of the first steam boat on the Illinois River in 1827.

Not long after that, Shick Shack received word that the Winnebago was waging war in the Fever River area. Philip Hash, a settler near by, reported that Shick Shack appeared at his cabin and told each family member "good-bye." Hash, the next day, went to the village area and was surprised to see that everything was gone. He saw the moving trail go across the Sangamon and directly north.

On the first week of May, 1832, Shick Shack and a few of his men encountered some of their former friends of Sangamon County at Dixon's Ferry on Rock River. Those friends were serving as volunteers in the Black Hawk War. The soldiers entertained the braves briefly, for Shick Shack the next day bade the soldiers farewell and headed for Wisconsin.

It is quite probable that Shick Shack and his followers were part of the exodus to Iowa, then later to a reservation west of Fort Leavenworth, Kansas. Shick Shack was likely buried along the Kaw River in one of the many burial grounds.

Tecumseh (1768-1813)

Tecumseh was born in 1768 in Old Piqua, a Shawnee town on the Mad River of Ohio. When he was around seven, his father Puckeshinwa was murdered by some settlers. Soon after his father's death, his mother left with another daughter for Missouri. He was adopted by Blackfish, a subchief but was raised mostly by older sister Tecumapease and an older brother Cheeseekau. His sister taught him the Shawnee golden rule which was: "Do not kill or injure your neighbor, for it is not he that you injure. You injure yourself. But do good to him and therefore add to his days of happiness as you add to your own." ("Tecumseh":Tucker) His older brother taught him to hunt and once when they were in southern Illinois, Tecumseh broke his thighbone. Because of an incorrect set, Tecumseh's leg healed with a slight bow. Nevertheless, he was around five feet nine inches tall, powerful, and reportedly handsome.

Tecumseh also had two foster brothers whom Blackfish had captured. One was Stephen Ruddell who wrote a biography of Tecumseh's boyhood and Richard Sparks who became a Captain under General Anthony Wayne.

Tecumseh was not aroused to hostile feelings until 1780 when George Rogers Clark destroyed the Shawnee towns and forced his people north. Later Tecumseh was more disillusioned by the brutal slaying of Cornstalk by an American mob. The massacre of ninety-six praying Christian Delawares at Gnaddenhutten, Ohio in 1782 did not lessen any of Tecumseh's growing bitterness.

It was once on an occasion with Ruddell that Tecumseh took a stand against senseless torture. He became very upset when some of his people were punishing a settler prisoner. Suddenly Tecumseh became very angry and told them that they were no better than their enemies. Never again did his fellow Shawnees torture another in his presence.

By September of 1792 Tecumseh was chosen to be leader for the Shawnee. For some years Tecumseh continued to build his reputation as an orator and on many occasions, he would be asked to arbitrate between the tribes and the settlers. Once in 1804 Tecumseh was called from his home in Indiana to a council being held in Chillicothe, Ohio. This council attracted a large gathering of both sides. When Tecumseh rose to speak, his foster brother Stephen Ruddell was the interpreter. Tecumseh spoke in his own Algonquian dialect but he had so much emotional force behind his speech that even the settlers knew what he was saying. Colonel John McDonald who attended the session commented later that: "When Tecumseh rose to speak...he appeared one of the most dignified men I ever beheld. While this orator of nature was speaking, the vast crowd preserved the most profound silence ...he dispelled, as if by magic, the apprehensions of the whites. The settlers returned to their deserted farms and business was resumed throughout that region." ("Tecumseh": Tucker.)

A few years earlier Tecumseh had married Manete who was of mixed parentage. She bore him his only son Pugeshashenwa around 1796.

By 1807 Tecumseh was trying to create a confederation of tribes to thwart the movement of settlers west. From that year to 1812 Tecumseh made innumerable visits in Illinois territory and down along the Mississippi, trying to convince his fellow people to unite.

Tecumseh helped the British take Ft. Wayne and Ft. Meigs. However, after the taking of Ft. Meigs, some of the warriors stormed old Ft. Miami where the prisoners were being held. A message was sent to Tecumseh who had already crossed the river. He was quite angry when he was told of the slaughter. He rode back in haste and stormed his own warriors. They were so stunned at their leader that they stopped. Tecumseh realized then that his men were not yet adept to civilized warfare.

Tecumseh was not receiving much aid from Colonel Henry A. Procter. Tecumseh denounced him for not taking a stand. By this time, Tecumseh led a band of three thousand warriors, the largest ever gathered together. There were numerous subchiefs ahead of divisions but they only followed Tecumseh because he was bold enough to dominate them and because of his influence among the British.

By October 1813 the battle was fought on the Thames. Tecumseh was at the head of the line when he was killed. How and by whom he was cut down, no one knows yet to this day.

Tecumseh
1768-1813

Topennebee (c.1799-c.1846)

Topennebee was a principal Potawatomi village chief of southern Michigan as early as 1821. His sister Kawkeeme had married a Burnet and had at least five children by 1821-John, James, Abraham, Rebecca and Nancy.

In the 1826 treaty with the Potawatomi, Topennebee signed as village chief. Abraham, his nephew, received three sections of land on the Wabash. Nancy, Rebecca, James and a grand-nephew William each received one section of land.

Topennebee, Jr. was a student at Carey Mission School on St. Joseph River. This was in 1826 under the direction of Rev. Isaac McCoy.

Topennebee, Sr. signed various treaties from 1828 through 1833. As late as 1846, he ceded the lands in Missouri and then moved to Kansas.

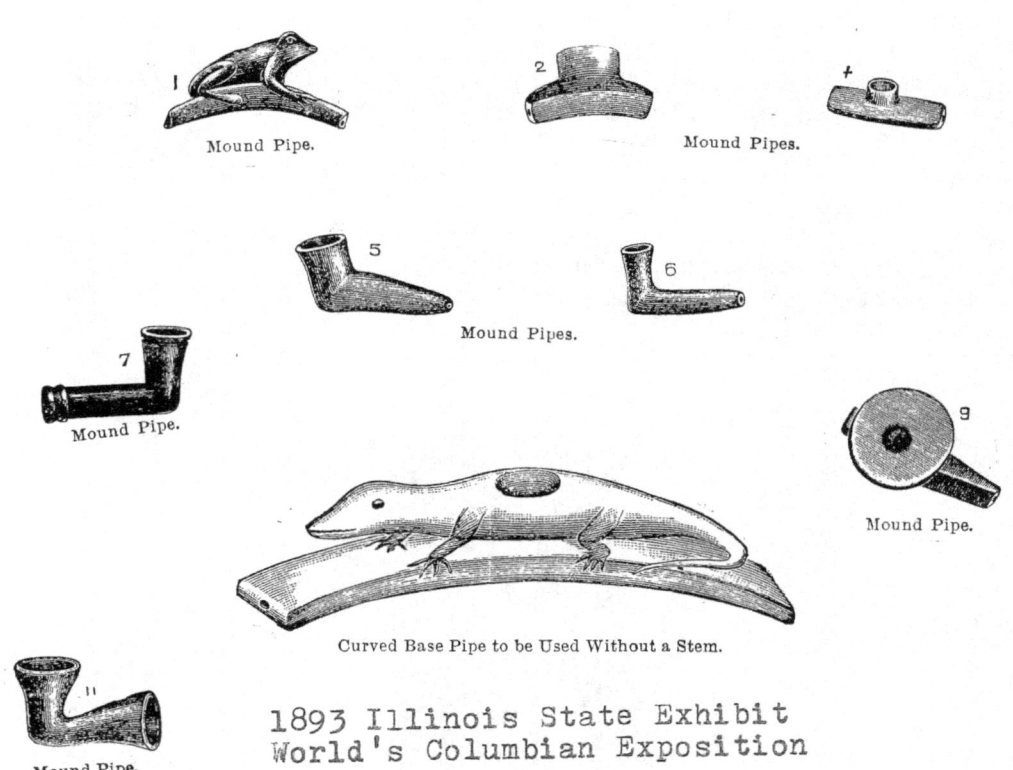

1893 Illinois State Exhibit
World's Columbian Exposition

Wabunsee or Wauponehsee
(c.1780-1848)

Wabunsee was a principal chief of the prairie band of Potawatomis who lived on the Kankakee River. He first became notorious when in October 1811, he jumped abroad one of Gov. Harrison's supply boats which were moving up the Wabash. Gov. Harrison officially reported that Wabunsee successfully killed the pilot and left the boat before anyone could react.

A year later he was one who participated in the Ft. Dearborn scrimmish. Even though he fought, he protected his friends the Kinzies in their own home. He and another also vainly tried to protect their friend Capt. William Wells from being murdered.

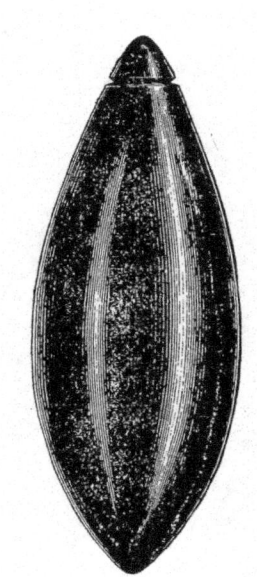

1893 Illinois State
Exhibit
World's Columbian
Exposition

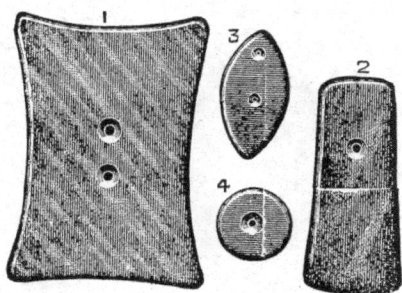

Perforated Pendant.

Wakieshiek (1794-1841)

Wakieshiek or White Cloud was a Winnebago prophet who had a village on a site later known as Prophetstown. His mother was a Winnebago and his father was a Sauk. Wakieshiek was a medicine man and advisor to Black Hawk who mentioned Wakieshiek often in his autobiography.

Wakieshiek remained behind in Illinois when Black Hawk and his people were made to move to Iowa in the fall of 1831. Sometime in the spring of 1832 Black Hawk and his people came back to Illinois to visit Wakieshiek and take food from their own cornfields. Unfortunatly there were communication foul-ups between Makieshiek and Black Hawk. Settlers became upset and as a consequence, the war began. The first act of the Illinois volunteers was to completely destroy Wakieshiek's village on May 10, 1832.

Wakieshiek was imprisoned with Black Hawk even though some American authorities praised him for his graciousness and sense of humanity. George Catlin in his writings alluded that the "Prophet" Wakieshiek and Nah-pope were the true instigators of the war. However, it was later found that one of Black Hawk's chiefs Nah-pope was indeed the one who deceived Black Hawk into believing that the Prophet had invited Black Hawk to come to the Prophet's village to plant corn and that Black Hawk's people would be protected.

White Cloud

Winnemac or Winnemeg
(c.1767-1812)

Winnemac was a Potawatomi chief who lived along the St. Joseph River and spent much time visiting people at Ft. Dearborn. He was a friend of Tecumseh. During negotiations with Governor Harrison at Ft. Wayne, he was one of many there besides Tecumseh. While the Governor and Tecumseh were talking, Winnemac was lying on the ground nearby with a loaded pistol beaded at the Governor. Tecumseh became upset with Harrison and a Captain G.R. Floyd drew his dirk or dagger. Winnemac immediately responded by cocking his gun. The atmosphere calmed and discussion continued.

During August 1812, after the fall of Detroit, Winnemac approached his friend John Kinzie at Ft. Dearborn. He told them of the Potawatomis and others attacking the settlers. Captain Heald ignored Kinzie's warnings and followed his orders of evacuation. Before Heald's troupe from the fort reached safety to Ft. Wayne, most of the party were killed. Captain Wells likewise was lost despite the efforts of Winnemac and Waubansee trying to save him.

Later that winter, Winnemac, four of his braves and Captain Elliot captured Shawnee James Logan. Logan, however, tried to escape and he along with Winnemac were killed in the incident.

Copper Ear Buttons.

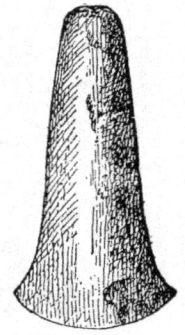

Copper Axe.

1893 Illinois State Exhibit
World's Columbian Exposition

Anecdotal Stories of Early Indians
of Illinois and Early Newspaper Accounts
Chapter 5

The following chapter contains various accounts found about Indians in Illinois. The source containing the item is stated before the story.

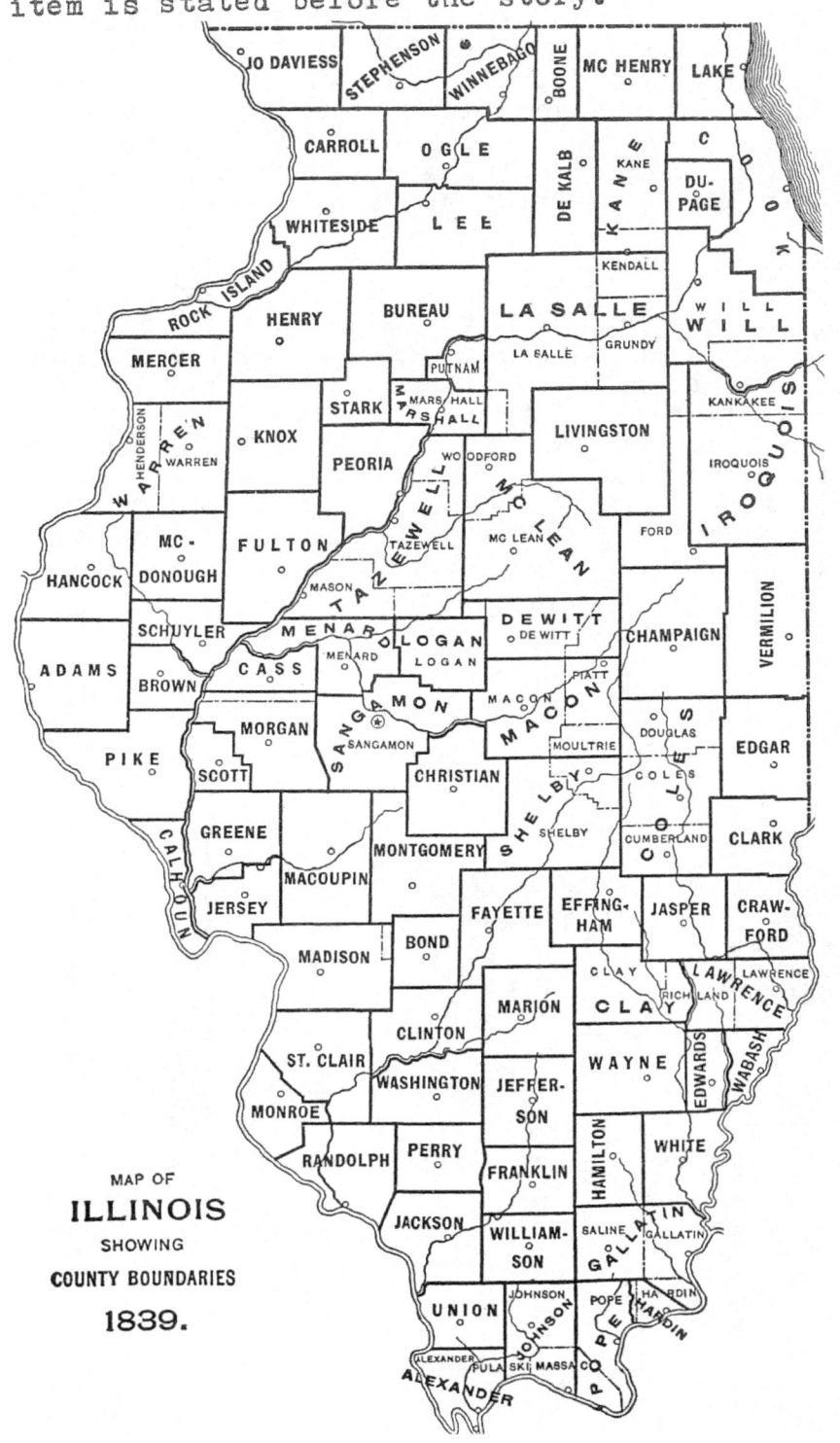

MAP OF
ILLINOIS
SHOWING
COUNTY BOUNDARIES
1839.

"An Indian on Lying"
<u>Southern Illinoisan</u>, newspaper
Shawneetown, Illinois
March 3, 1854

The Cattaraugus WHIG states that a suit was recently brought before a magistrate in the village of Randolph, and during its progress, an Indian was brought forth to testify. His blank, expressionless face, and the general unmeaningless of his whole demeanor gave rise to a serious doubt in the mind of the "court" as to the admissibility of his testimony. Accordingly he was asked what the consequence would be if he should tell a falsehood while under oath. The countenance of the Indian brightened a little as he replied in a solemn tone, "Well, if I tell a lie, guess I be put in jail--great while may be. Bimeby, I die--and then I ketch it again!" The witness was permitted to proceed.

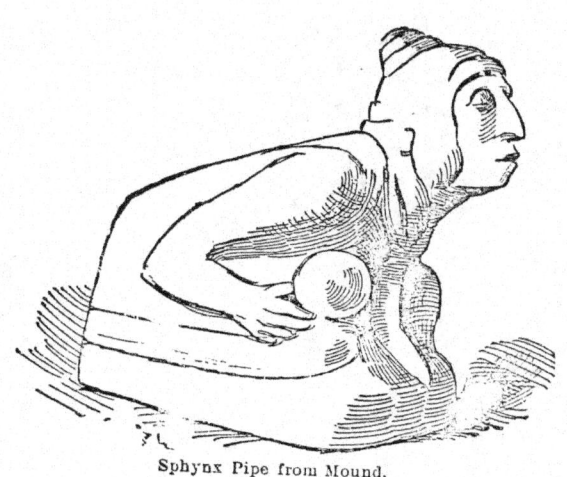

Sphynx Pipe from Mound.

Found in Macoupin County, Illinois

"Uncle Sam"
Western Intelligencer, newspaper
Oct. 9, 1817   Kaskaskia, Illinois

   This expression which originated during the war, from the initials "U.S." on the soldiers' knapsacks, has come into general use. The Indians at the west, from hearing it often used, have imbided the idea that it is actually the name of the President--and while at Sacket's Harbor considerable number of Indians and squaws, crowded around the President, wishing, as they expressed it, to shake hands with Uncle Sam.

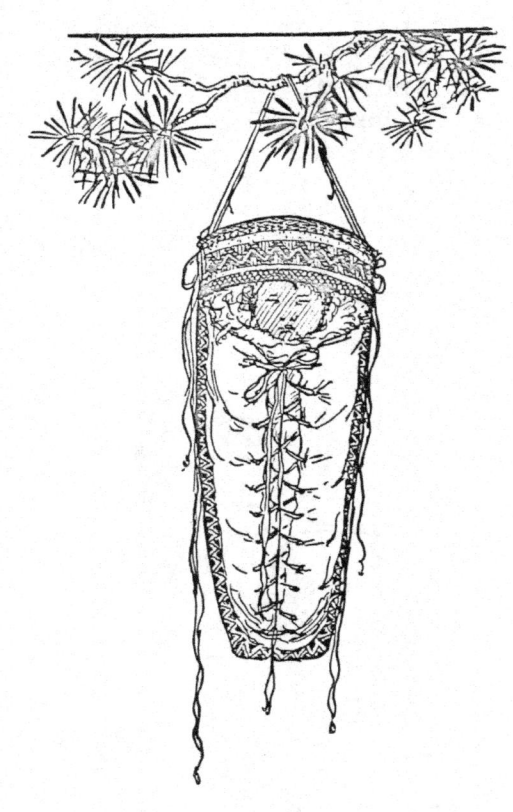

Chief Walker and His Daughter
HISTORY OF TAZEWELL COUNTY, ILLINOIS
Chicago: Chapman & Co., 1879
Pages 265-266

"Mr. Joshua Wagenseller tells us an amusing story connected with the Indians who camped on Dillon Creek. An Indian, familiar to many of the early settlers, by name of Chief Walker, often came to Pekin. On one occasion he offered a barrel full of dollars to any young white man who would marry his daughter. Six young men, from Pekin, thought they would go out and see the young Indian and perchance could strike a bargain with Chief Walker. A barrel of silver dollars was an inducement to take most anything in the shape of a woman for a wife. The boys all posted off to Chief Walker's wigwam. On arriving the old chief met them and led them into his cabin to see the daughter. The boys filed in, took seats around the room and saw the object of their visit sitting silently therein. The boys sat and gazed upon the maiden for a few moments, not a word was spoken, supreme silence reigned. The situation began to grown more embarassing, the boys looked at one another, at the Chief and then at the girl. Soon one of them sneaked out, another followed, and one by one they all slipped away, leaving the Chief and his loved daughter alone. Each one of the wife hunters told the others,'"any of you can have her and the dollars, I don't want her."' So Chief Walker failed to marry off his daughter, and none of the boys got the proffered barrel of dollars."

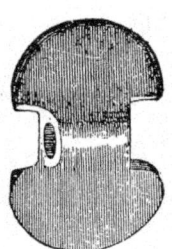

Ceremonial Stone.

1893 Illinois State Exhibit
World's Columbian Exposition

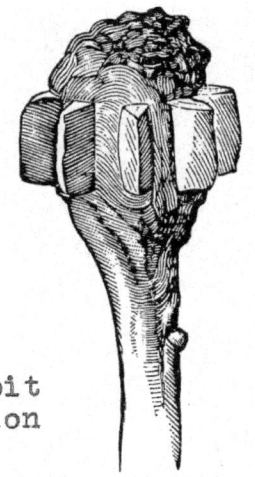

Flints in a War Club.

Western Intelligencer, newspaper
Kaskaskia, Illinois   June 12, 1816

By information received from St. Louis, we learn that treaties of peace were concluded on Saturday the first instant, between the United States and the eight bands of Sious or Sacs who reside above Prairie du Chien...

It must certainly be highly gratifying to those who have witnessed the high toned menaces which those miscreants have been in the habit of dealing out against our frontier settlers, to see them KISS THE ROD AND BOW SUBMISSION TO OUR AUTHORITY, and acknowledge the inquity with which they have acted towards us. Vice and treachery seldom fails to meet its just earned punishment.

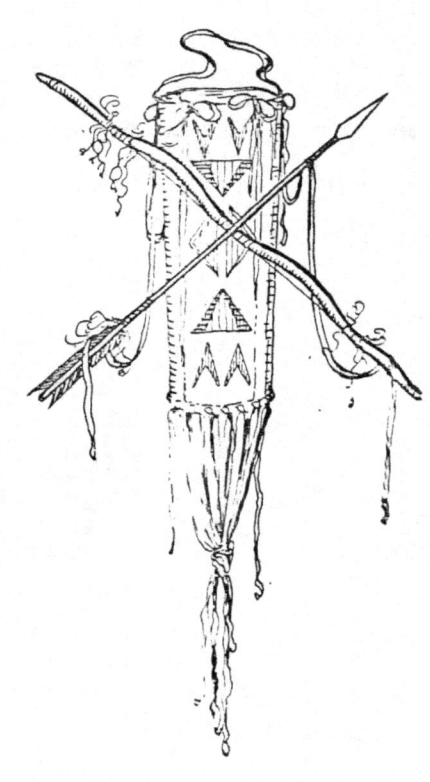

```
        Western Intelligencer, newspaper
          Kaskaskia, Illinois  June 25, 1816
```

Indian News at Rock River

```
     ....The Indian chiefs pressed him (Brig. General
Smith) to desist, declaring that they could not be
responsible for the conduct of their young warriors, who
disapprobated the building of a fort in their neighborhood.
The general treated them civilly but went on with the work,
....
```

Flint Tool.

```
    1893 Illinois State
         Exhibit
  World's Columbian Exposition
```

Perforated Ceremonial Stone Object.

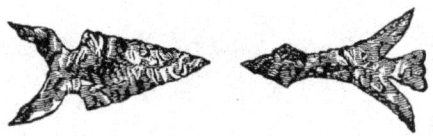

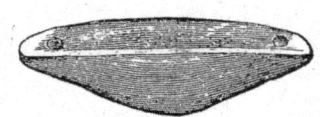

"Indian Treasure Near Moweaqua"
SHELBYVILLE DAILY UNION, newspaper
September 3, 1928

It seemed that a story originated from the first owner Michael Schneider, later changed to Snyder, of a farm a mile west of Moweaqua, Illinois. Snyder's story passed down to later owner James Gregory. The tale involved a band of Indians who had buried considerable treasure there. The legend was strengthened later when several Indians came through and camped there. One Indian came later alone and Snyder understood that the Idnian had a rough map. The Indian left without saying anything to Snyder. This incident must have been sixty to seventy years ago.

During the spring of 1927 James Gregory, Jr. plowed up a strange shaped rock which had an arrow engraved on it. This spring another rock with an arrow turned up. The owner doesn't know whether the Indians left them as guides to a cache.

About two years ago Wiley Auld near Shelbyville unearthed an Indian mound while digging gravel. He found a skeleton of an Indian and some fragments of pottery by it. Other mounds have been found in the county.

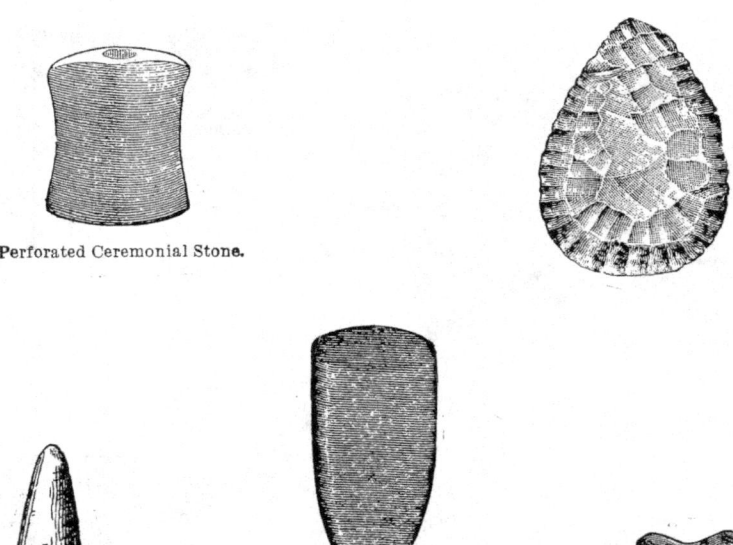

1893 Illinois State Exhibit
World's Columbian Exposition

Western Intelligencer, newspaper
Kaskaskia, Illinois   August 21, 1816

Since our last, 400 Indians, men, women, and children of the Pottawatomie, Kickapoo and Sackie nations, arrived in this town. We understand they have been invited to a council by the Commissioners to adjust the differences existant relative to lands lying between the rivers Illinois and Mississippi, ceded to the United States several years ago, by Sackies and Foxes.

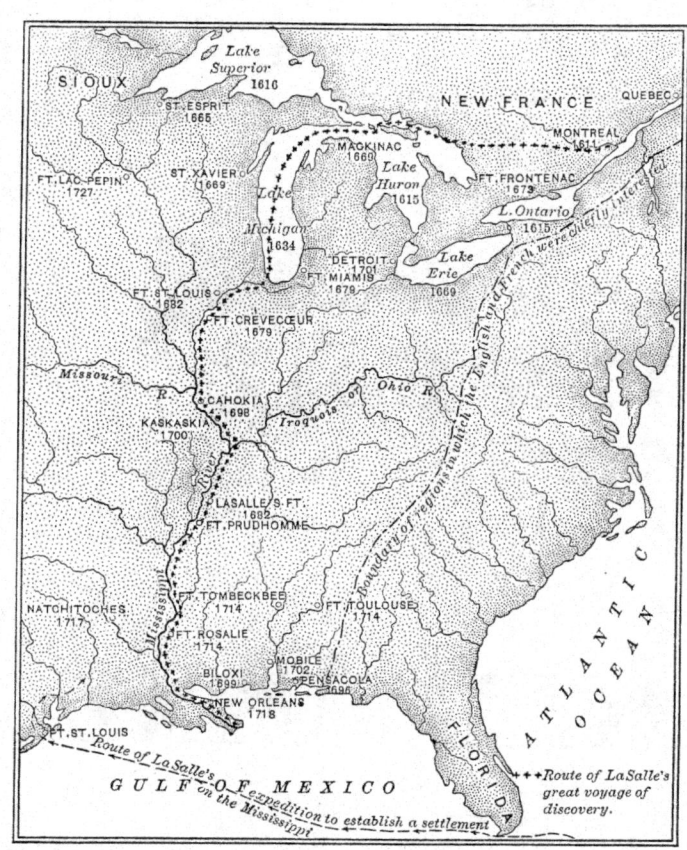

MAP OF LA SALLE'S EXPLORATIONS

Western Intelligencer, newspaper
Kaskaskia, Illinois   May 29, 1816

Six Chickasaw Indians passed through this town on Monday, on their way to Washington City. We may calculate from the success of the Cherokee missioners that they will get the balance of the Creek lands.--We wish to God the Creeks had our negociators in their power--no language can convey the indignation felt at the scandalous trafficing in this case.

From Rock River, same date

A Treaty of peace and amity haveing been concluded at this place, on the 13th instant with the Sacs of Rock River, and its vicinity, who so long repelled every pacific overture of our government....

A Dwelling House of the Iroquois

A Piece of Wampum

Shelby County History, 1900
Ash Grove Township
Shelby County, Illinois

Along the streams was a favorite hunting-ground for the Indian, and as late as 1827 Indian camps still remained. In the winter of 1826 and 1827 the Indians had quite a large camp of ninety or one hundred lodges, on the west side of West Four Mile Branch, on what is known as the William M. Wilson (then 1900) place. The Indians camped there were a part of three tribes: the Kickapoos, Pottawatomies and Delawares, under a chief by the name of Turkey. These Indians were very friendly, and considered honest by the early settlers. This camp was a lively place, particularly on Sunday, made more so by the presence of a great many white people, who would come from the settlements for miles around to spend the day. The camp was kept lively by horse-racing, shooting, foot-racing, jumping and the trying of the muscles of Indians in various ways. In the spring of 1827 the Indians left their hunting-grounds in this part of the country, and were not seen here any more after the year 1828.

FRENCH MISSIONARIES TO THE INDIANS
From an old print

Chief Mashena and the Esquire, 1833
Illinois Sesquicentennial of Christian County, 1880

At one time near Campbell's Point a number of (Kickapoos) had some difficulty with Jake Gragg, who it seems got the better of them. They fled across the South Fork to Esquire Miller's imploring his protection, as 'Jake was after them with a sack full of sticks.' They looked upon the Esquire as a kind of legal protector.

Mashena, the chief, and some of his tribe had a fight with William Wallis, east of Taylorville, using clubs and stones pretty freely. He had the copper-colored tribe arrested and taken before Esquire Campbell. They were fined five dollars and costs. Mashena paid the fine and asked for a receipt, whereupon the following colloquy ensued:

Esquire-- Indian, you don't want any receipt; it is entered on my docket and never can come up against you again.

Mashena--I pays you the money; will you give me a receipt.

Esquire--I tell you that you don't want any, for it's settled on the docket.

Mashena--White man say Indian steal, Esquire say me steal. I say me no steal, but me pay um; now give Indian receipt.

Esquire--Since you insist on it, if you will give me a good reason for wanting it, I'll give you one.

Mashena--Well, when me die me spec' to go the Great Spirit's home. Werry well, when me gets to the gate Peter says: 'Go away, Indian, you steal.' 'Werry well, what if I does, don't I pay 'um?' Peter says, 'Show um receipt,' and if I don't have um I **shall be forced** to go back and look through hell to find Esquire Campbell, to prove Indian pay um.

Barbarity of Rangers
Centennial History of Madison County
Recollections of Capt. Abel Moore in 1835

Buried in the same cemetery is an Indian girl, who was captured by Abraham Pruitt during one of the campaigns of the War of 1812. The Indians had been pursued to the Winnebago Swamps and Pruitt heard firing in a distant part of the swamp and went in search of the cause thereof. On nearing the spot he found David Carter and another man shooting at the child, about six years old, who was mired in the mud, and so closely were the Indians pursued that they had to leave her there. Mr. Pruitt called them cowards and ordered them to cease firing at the helpless child. Mr. Pruitt then, noble-hearted man that he was, went in and rescued the child from the swamp. He placed her on the horse behind him and brought her home with him and raised her to the age of about sixteen when she died. She was of a very mild disposition.

NOTE: The following comment was added by the turn of the century historian. "The feeling of the people towards the aborigines was reflected in a law passed by the territorial legislature in 1814, which offered a reward of fifty dollars for each Indian taken or killed in any white settlement, and of one hundred dollars for any warrior, squaw, or child, taken prisoner or killed in their own territory."

A VIEW OF DETROIT IN 1705

Centennial History of Madison County
Recollections of Major Frank Moore

Murder of Price and Son on 20th June, 1811
in Madison County

The boy rode out to my father's house between the forks of Wood River, to give the alarm. All the neighbors went in pursuit of the Indians. Among them were my father, Abel Moore, Solomon Pruitt, William Montgomery, James Pruitt, John Vickery, a Mr. Dobbs and several others. They went to the spring and found Mr. Price dead, as the boy had stated. They pursued the Indians by following the trail through the grass. They followed it two or three miles above the mouth of Piasa Creek. There they killed one Indian. The other Indians made their escape by crossing the creek into the brush, and night coming on prevented further pursuit. Every man, woman and child took an active part in the resulting Indian war. After the Price murder and its penalty the Indian would shoot at every white man he saw, and vice versa. The white people found it necessary to build a fort and also to organize a company of Rangers. My father was chosen captain and served in that capacity all through the War of 1812. A number of hard battles were fought over at Portage des Sioux, in St. Charles County, Missouri.

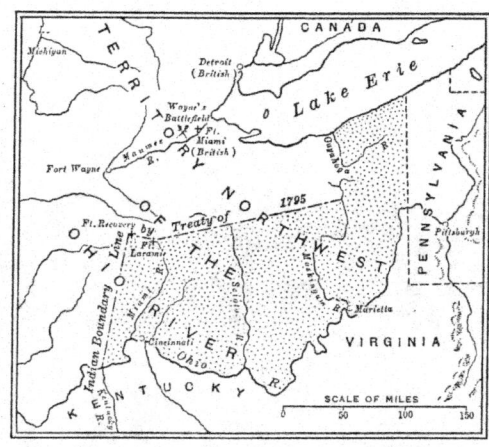

THE NORTHWEST TERRITORY AFTER WAYNE'S
VICTORY

The part given up by the Indians is shaded; that kept
by the Indians is white

Cities of Refuge
Western Intelligencer, newspaper
Kaskaskia, Illinois
August 28, 1816

Indian agent Col. R. J. Meig's comments about a new book

Although the institution of the Great Corn Dance, their ablutions, and cities of refuge, bear strong resemblance to the Jewish customs and laws, yet they by no means prove that the American Indians are descended from the Jews; they only prove that the religion of nature corresponds with the religion of the Jews, communicated to them by Moses by divine command....

TYPES OF INDIAN DWELLINGS,—THE PUEBLO, THE TEPEE, AND THE LONG HOUSE

A View of the Indian
by Rev. James B. Finley,
an early Methodist minister

...Indeed, I do not believe that there are a people on the earth, that are more capable of appreciating a friend, or a kind act done toward them or theirs, than Indians. Better neighbors, and a more honest people, I never lived among. They are particularly so to the stranger, or to the sick or distressed. They will divide the last mouthful, and give almost the last comfort they have, to relieve the suffering. This I have often witnessed.

Anecdote of the Indian Hunter Skills
Rev. James B. Finley

An Indian, upon his return home to his hut, one day, discovered that his venison, which had been hung up to dry, had been stolen. After going some distance in pursuit of the thief, he met a party of travelers, of whom he inquired whether they had seen a little, old, white man, with a short gun, and accompanied by a small dog, with a bob-tail. They applied in the affirmative, and asked the Indian how he was able to give such a minute description of the theft. He answered, "I know he is a little man by his having made a pile of stones in order to reach the venison, from the height I hung it standing on the ground. I know he is an old man by his short steps, which I have traced over the dead leaves in the woods. I know he is a white man by his turning out his toes when he walks, which an Indian never does. I know his gun is short by the mark which the muzzle made upon the bark of a tree against which it leaned. I know the dog is small by his tracks, and that he has a bob-tail I discovered by the mark of it in the dust, where he was sitting at the time his master took down the meat."

MAP OF PORTAGES IN NEW FRANCE AND THE ILLINOIS COUNTRY
The rivers and lakes, with their portages, were the highways for the missionaries, fur traders, and explorers

Recollection of Elisha Fortner
Holland Township, Shelby County

Elisha Fortner, one of the first settlers of this township came to Shelby County in 1829, and first located in the Sand Creek settlement. In 1834 he came down into what is now Holland Township. His widow tells of being frightened by a painted Indian who, because of some grievance, took this plan of revenge: the Indian sat grimly on his horse, within speaking, in front of the cabin. Mrs. Fortner had securely fastened the door, and trembling, watched his motions through a crack between the logs. Actions of this kind appeared a little threatening, but the settlers paid no attention and were not molested. It is almost the unanimous expression of the early settlers, that the Indians were the best of neighbors. As a general thing, they were polite and friendly.

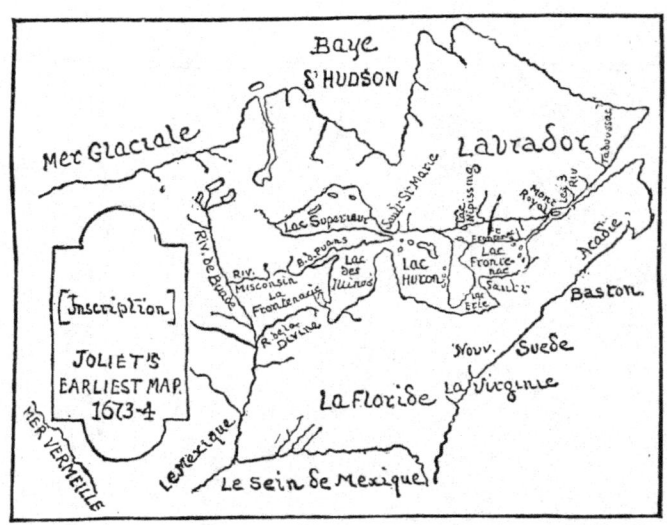

JOLIET'S MAP OF NEW FRANCE (FROM WINSOR'S "CARTIER TO FRONTENAC")

"War with Black Hawk"
Article from SPOKESMAN-REVIEW, Spokane,
                                Washington
Appeared in EVENING TELEGRAPH, Dixon, Illinois
                March 21, 1900

   I never saw Black Hawk to know him. The Indian infantry
was well-armed but had very little ammunition. They were also
well-armed with spears and bows and arrows. To illustrate how
expert an Indian may become with a bow I will relate a little
incident that I saw. An Indian had his bow in his left hand
and quiver of arrow on his back. A small bird flew up about
twelve feet away. He took an arrow from the quiver, placed
it in the bow and shot the bird, which/within six feet from
where it started.   fell

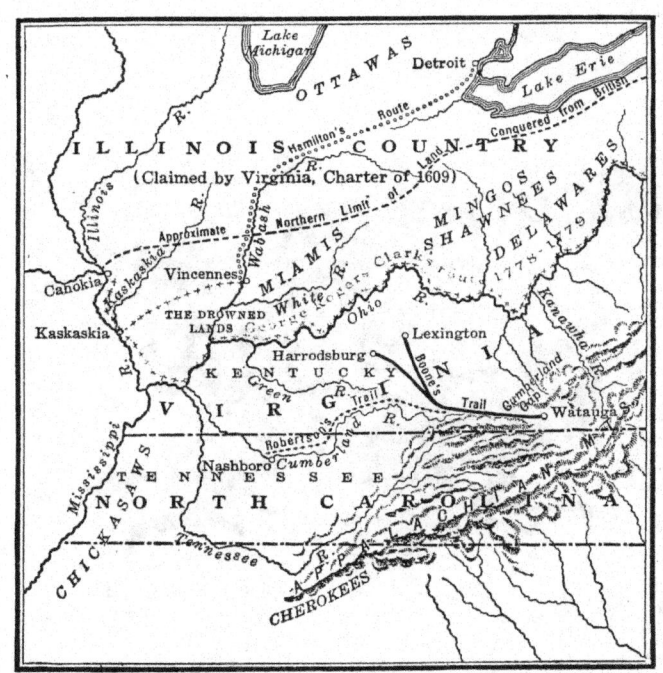

THE REVOLUTIONARY WAR IN THE WEST

"Find Remains of Ancient American"--
"Believed to be Ancester of Indian"
Galena, Illinois
SHELBYVILLE DEMOCRAT, Newspaper
Shelbyville, Illinois October 25, 1926

Abstract

University of Chicago: A skelton was found in a flexed position, arms folded across breast. It was found three feet below the surface, along 1100 foot ridge on a farm. Professor Fay Cooper-Cole directed the expedition.

Professor believed this Illinois find a link between prehistoric America and Ohio Mounds. A large collection of relics have already been in the hands of amateurs of the area: arrow heads, hammer heads, pottery, cooper beads, bear-tooth necklaces, pipes and copper ornaments.

"...The type of civilization revealed is not high in the opinion of Professor Cole, who said that no writing has been uncovered in mounds in any part of the United States."

This reproduction is from an original painting by James A. Wuellner, uncle of Kent Wuellner, St. Mary's School, Alton.

COMBINED HISTORY OF SHELBY AND
MOULTRIE COUNTY
Dry Point Township
Cold Spring Township

In the eastern part of the township (Dry Point), along the Kaskaskia, settlements were made at a later date; the first being by Jeremiah Banning, who came from Virginia in 1828 and settled on Section 35, Range 10. The Indians had just vacated their wigwams, which were on a lake on what is known as the Ferrell (1900) place, taking their departure from the happy hunting grounds before the approach of the pale face.

Letter of George P. Hall dated July 17, 1912
published in the SHELBYVILLE UNION newspaper

My grandfather's name was Samuel Hall, and he with his family and a number of relatives moved from Fayetteville, N.C., to Hopkinsville, Ky. in 1814, and in 1816 came to Illinois, finally settling in Shelby County in 1817. He took up his residence on the east side of Mitchell Creek near what is now Cowden. The country was at that time inhabited by the Delaware and Kickapoo Indians who were friendly to the few white settlers who at that time were scattered throughout the dense wilderness.

My grandfather had a rather large family, consisting of about an equal number of boys and girls; one son, Samuel, was said to have been the first white child born in Dry Point Township.

But the bit of history that I wish to bring out is what I have heard related at my father's fireside. My grandfather's oldest son was named Jahu, and his second son was John-my father. Jahu was fifteen, and John was thirteen when their father settled in Shelby County. Forest, prairie, and stream abounded with all kinds of game, and the boys soon became expert hunters. Their companions were the Indian boys and such few whites as lived near enough to be able to join them. I remember the names of some of their Indian companions. One was White Buffalo, one was Tend It, who was mistaken in the darkness for an enemy and killed by a friendly Kickapoo, and another was He Looks Like a Catfish. If the latter's name indicated his personal appearance, I don't imagine that he was the subject or cause of much rivalry among the dusky belles.

HISTORY OF MACON COUNTY, ILLINOIS
1880

The first white men who settled in this county were the brothers Lorton, from St. Joe, Michigan. They were Indian traders, and built a trading house twelve miles north-east of Decatur in 1816. As has been said, the Indians were at that time numerous, and the Lortons carried on a thriving trade until 1825-26, when the Indians ceased to visit this part of the country except in very small companies....

...Until 1825-26 from 200 to 500 Indians would, at certain seasons of the year, camp in the vicinity of the trading-house of the Lortons....

HISTORY OF FAYETTE COUNTY, ILLINOIS
1878

The Kickapoos had a populous village about one hundred miles north of Vandalia, and the territory comprised within the present limits of Fayette County, was a portion of their hunting grounds. They are spoken of by the early settlers as being peaceably disposed, and anxious to live on terms of friendship with the white neighbors. In the early part of 1815, however, a party of five or six hunters were killed by them. The cause of the massacre is unknown. This led to the establishment by the Rangers of the war of 1812 of a Fort on Shoal Creek, called Hill's Fort, now incorporated within the limits of Bond County. Several sanguinary engagements occurred after its erection.

They (the Kickapoos) had a village much smaller than the former, near where the Vandalia Railroad crosses Owl Creek, near the Bond County line; and another on the bluffs on the Kaskaskia River, about two miles south of Vandalia, now known as the Bunyard Farm. This, however, was not a permanent settlement. They frequently moved their quarters, up or down the river, for several miles. In 1845 a half-breed descendant of the tribe came from Wisconsin to visit the graves of his fathers. He professed to be able to give the exact location of the villages, from a rough chart or map engraven upon a powder-horn. He related a tradition among his tribe of the existence of a silver mine near the junction of Hickory Creek with the Okaw....

Many of the old settlers are full of anecdote and narrative of the early times, and remember distinctly the few scattering tribes which visited the country on hunting expeditions. They were principally the Kickapoo tribe. During the summers of 1819, '20 and '21, large bands of these Indians would come into the county to fish and hunt, and sometimes raise a small patch of corn. A part of the Sauks tribe also visited the county in 1820 and '21, frequently in numbers of from three to five hundred.

There still exists an Indian burial ground on the farm of B. Ward Thompson, four miles south of Vandalia, on section 29 of the same township....

HISTORY OF HARDIN COUNTY, ILLINOIS
1939

Prehistory of Hardin County
by Judge Hall

On the north edge of Hardin County, and which at one time was within its limits, are yet to be seen the wreckage of the Pounds walls. These walls extending east and west from the gateway were really one wall almost a quarter of a mile of length. Oldest men whom I questioned in my boyhood days agreed that this wall was six feet thick; but some believed that this wall and the one around Old Stone Fort on the same mountain trend were originally eight feet high, while others believed they were as much as ten or even twelve feet high, especially near the gateways and at the ends.

These were at first believed to be Indian forts; for the wreckage of eight or ten have been discovered in our Ozark ranges. Some Philadelphia scholars came to Shawneetown in pioneer days and proceeded to make a thorough examination of the Pounds. Their verdict was that those structures were pounds built for corralling animals. One mark that they relied upon for their conclusion was the site of an old buffalo wallow, which may yet be seen just below the only spring on the Pounds. An old buffalo trail and a wallow is to be seen at Old Stone Fort, as well as in other places where similar enclosures were built. Evidences are rather conclusive that these pounds were built by Mound Builders to entrap buffalo, deer, and perhaps wild sheep and goats. A number of gaps in bluffs near the center of our county were also closed by high rock walls, no doubt for the same purposes of entrapping animals when they annually came to our mountains for winter shelter and deergrass provender.

HISTORY OF CLARK COUNTY, ILLINOIS
1907
Edited by Hon. H. C. Bell

Considerable trouble was given the people of York in those early times by the Indians, who had enlisted under the flag of Great Britain in the War of 1812, and who were slow to find out that the war had closed with the defeat of those for whom they had fought. William Hogue, who had come to York in 1816, was a great hunter--the Nimrod of that part of the county--and he was known to have shot and killed two Indians. The first was killed just across the river from York, after he had first shot at and missed Hogue, and the other was killed as he was skulking up on Hogue's little son, who had started home on horseback with a deer he had killed. Hogue was following behind his son, and seeing the Indian skulking from tree to tree along the way the son was going, and manifestly intending to kill him and secure the horse and deer as soon as he got out of the sight and hearing of his father, fired and killed the Indian to save the boy.

This figurine of Archange, wife of Antoine Ouilmette, is now on display at the Illinois State Museum.

Chapter VI

This chapter lists several individuals of the early Illinois country from 1642 to 1861. Following the names are the titles of sources which contained them. In many instances, the individuals can be placed at some definite period of time.

The writer believes that if ONE finds this helpful in his search for family heritage, then the inclusion of this has been warranted. These names are taken from 43 different sources.

AA

Aapennawbee (Potawatomi) Treaty with the Ottawa, August 29, 1821 at Chicago, Illinois

Abeenabee (Potawatomi) Treaty with the Potawatomi, September 20, 1828 at St. Joseph, Michigan

Abeeshah (Potawatomi) Treaty with the Potawatomi, October 26, 1832 at Camp Tippecanoe, Indiana

Abeetaiquezick (Potawatomi) Treaty with the Potawatomi, September 20, 1828 at St. Joseph, Michigan

Abeetuquezuck (Potawatomi) Treaty with the Potawatomi, September 20, 1828 at St. Joseph, Michigan

Accault, Michael or Ako or Aco (French and Indian) Married Aramepinchicue, a Kaskaskia. Had sons Pierre and Michael. Accompanied Father Hennepin. FRENCH FOUNDATIONS, 1680-1693. FROM QUEBEC TO NEW ORLEANS. PIONEER PRIESTS OF NORTH AMERICA 1642-1710.

Achemukquee (Potawatomi) Treaty with the Potawatomi, October 16, 1826. Student at the Carey Mission School.

Achiswewah or Bears Head (Peoria) Void agreement Illinois and Wabash Land Company, 1773

Ackkushewa (Potawatomi) Treaty with the Potawatomi, October 16, 1826 at Wabash on the Mississippi

Ahbenab (Potawatomi) Treaty with the Chippewa, September 26, 1833 at Chicago, Illinois

Ahbetekezhic (Potawatomi) Treaty with the Potawatomi, October 26, 1832 at Camp Tippecanoe, Indiana. Treaty with the Chippewa, September 26, 1833 at Chicago, Illinois

Ahcahomah (Potawatomi) Treaty with the Chippewa, September 26, 1833 at Chicago, Illinois

Ahnowawausa (Potawatomi) Treaty with the Potawatomi, October 16, 1826

Ahnuckquetta (Kickapoo) The cloud or black thunder. Treaty with the Kickapoo, 1832

Ahqueewee (Potawatomi) Treaty with the Chippewa, September 26, 1833 at Chicago, Illinois

Abbott, Madn. F. Treaty with the Chippewa, September 26, 1833 at Chicago, Illinois

Ahsagamishcum (Potawatomi) Treaty with the Chippewa, September 26, 1833 at Chicago, Illinois

Ahtake (Potawatomi) Treaty with the Chippewa, September 26, 1833 at Chicago, Illinois

Ahyou way (Potawatomi) Treaty with the Potawatomi, October 26, 1832 at Camp Tippecanoe, Indiana

Akaketa or Ploughman (Eel River) Treaty with the Eel River, etc., August 7, 1803 at Vincennes, Indiana

Allen, Joseph (Potawatomi) Treaty with the Potawatomi, September 20, 1828 at St. Joseph, Michigan

Allen, Lazette (Potawatomi) Treaty with the Potawatomi, October 26, 1832 at Camp Tippecanoe, Indiana

Allen, Mrs. or Cheebeequai (Potawatomi) Treaty with the Chippewa, September 26, 1833 at Chicago, Illinois

Amantancha or Louis de Ste. Foy (Huron) Interpreter of 1632. Pioneer Priests of North America, 1642-1710

Ameckkose (Potawatomi) Treaty with the Ottawa, August 29, 1821 at Chicago, Illinois

Amsden, Amos (Potawatomi) Treaty with the Chippewa, September 26, 1833 at Chicago, Illinois

Amyot, Daniel Joseph (French-Indian) Son of Mathieu Amyot called Villeneuve. French Foundations, 1680-1693

Anckoaw (Kickapoo) Treaty with the Kickapoo, July 30, 1819 at Edwardsville, Illinois

Andakamigowinimi (Algonquin chief) Pioneer Priests of North America, 1642-1710

Anderson (Delaware) Treaty with the Delawares, etc., September 30, 1809 at Ft. Wayne, Indiana

Anderson, John (Mixed) Treaty with the Chippewa, September 26, 1833 at Chicago, Illinois

Anderson, John W. (Mixed) Treaty with the Chippewa, September 26, 1833 at Chicago, Illinois

Ankwiskkaw (Kickapoo) Treaty with the Kickapoo, July 30, 1819 at Edwardsville, Illinois

Annownssau (Potawatomi) Student at Carey Mission School. Treaty with the Potawatomi, October 16, 1826 at Wabash, Indiana

Ancy, Joseph and Dufour (Indian slaves) Illinois on Eve of Seven Years War 1747-1755

Antilla, Antoine (French-Indian) Treaty with the Chippewa, September 26, 1833 at Chicago, Illinois

Antoine (Potawatomi) Student at Carey Mission School. Treaty with the Potawatomi, October 16, 1826 at Wabash, Indiana

Apicanis (Algonquin) Pioneer Priests of North America, 1642-1710

Appanoose (Fox chief) Died 1845. Indian Place Names in Illinois by Vogel

Aramepinchicue (Kaskaskia) Married Michael Accault, Daughter of Chief Rouensa. Also known as Maria Rouensa. From Quebec to New Orleans

Armand-Jean (Algonquin) Indian student at LeJeune's first school. Pioneer Priests of North America, 1642-1710

Arndt, A.H. Treaty with the Chippewa, September 26, 1833 at Chicago, Illinois

Arnwaiskie, Theotis (Potawatomi) Married May 20, 1826 to Daniel Bourassa. Inhabitants of Chicago, 1825-1831

Ash, Abraham (Delaware) Treaty with the Delaware, etc., September 30, 1809 at Ft. Wayne, Indiana

Ash, Betsey (Mixed) student at Carey Mission School. Treaty with the Potawatomi, October 16, 1826 at Wabash, Indiana

Ashkum or Ashkeewee (Potawatomi chief) One of his sons and two of his daughters baptized by Fr. Ben. Marie Petit. Treaty with the Potawatomi, October 26, 1832 at Camp Tippecanoe, Indiana; Treaty with the Ottawa, August 29, 1821 at Chicago, Illinois; Indian Place Names in Illinois; Treaty with the Potawatomi, September 20, 1828 at St. Joseph, Michigan; Treaty with the Potawatomi, October 27, 1832 at Camp Tippecanoe, Indiana; Treaty with the Potawatomi, October 16, 1826 at Wabash, Indiana; Treaty with the Potawatomi, December 16, 1834 at Potawatomi Mills, Indiana; Treaty with the Potawatomi, August 5, 1836 at Yellow River, Indiana; Treaty with the Potawatomi, September 23, 1836 at Chippewaynaung, Indiana

Atchinson, Silas. Treaty with the Potawatomi, October 26, 1832 at Camp Tippecanoe, Indiana

Atchweemuckquee (Potawatomi) Treaty with the Ottawa, August 29, 1821 at Chicago, Illinois

Aubbenaubbee (Potawatomi chief) Treaty with the Potawatomi, October 26, 1832 at Camp Tippecanoe, Indiana; Treaty with the Potawatomi, October 26, 1832 (second treaty); Treaty with the Potawatomi, September 20, 1828 at St. Joseph, Michigan; Treaty with the Potawatomi, October 27, 1832 at Camp Tippecanoe, Indiana; Treaty with the Potawatomi, October 16, 1826 at Wabash, Indiana

Auntake (Potawatomi) Treaty with the Potawatomi, October 26, 1832 at Camp Tippecanoe, Indiana

Aunt, J.E. Treaty with the Potawatomi, October 27, 1832 at Camp Tippecanoe, Indiana

Aupaumut, Henrick (Mohegan chief) Treaty with the Delwares, etc., September 30, 1809 at Ft. Wayne, Indiana

Autawconum. Daughter of the Crane. Treaty with the Potawatomi, October 26, 1832 at Camp Tippecanoe, Indiana; Treaty with the Potawatomi, October 27, 1832 at Camp Tippecanoe, Indiana

Autiss (Potawatomi) Treaty with the Potawatomi, September 20, 1828 at St. Joseph, Michigan

Aveline, James. Treaty with the Potawatomi, October 27, 1832 at Camp Tippecanoe, Indiana

Awbetone (Potawatomi) Treaty with the Ottawa, August 29, 1821 at Chicago, Illinois

Awnkote (Sac chief) on the Fox River. Treaty with the Chippewa, July 29, 1829 at Prairie Du Chien, Michigan; Treaty with the Chippewa, September 26, 1833 at Chicago, Illinois

Awrawmapingeaw or Whale (Kaskaskia) Treaty with the Peoria, etc., September 25, 1818 at Edwardsville, Illinois

Awwatshee (Kickapoo) Treaty with the Kickapoo, July 30, 1819 at Edwardsville, Illinois

Bailey, David (Mixed) Treaty with the Chippewa, September 26, 1833 at Chicago, Illinois

Bailey, Isaac G. (Mixed) Treaty with the Chippewa, September 26, 1833 at Chicago, Illinois

Bailey, Marie Lefevre or Monee or Tousequa. Wife to Joseph Bailey. Marie (1783-1866) and Joseph had children Esther, Rosene, Eleanor, Sophia, Hortense and Therese. Treaty with the Potawatomi, October 26, 1832 at Camp Tippecanoe, Indiana; Treaty with the Potawatomi, October 26, 1832 at Camp Tippecanoe, Indiana (second); Treaty with the Chippewa, September 26, 1833 at Chicago, Illinois; Treaty with the Potawatomi, October 16, 1826 at Wabash, Indiana

Baldwin, Ebenezer. Treaty with the Peoria, etc., September 25, 1818 at Edwardsville, Illinois

Baldwin, John. Treaty with the Potawatomi, October 26, 1832 at Camp Tippecanoe, Indiana; Treaty with the Chippewa, September 26, 1833 at Chicago, Illinois

Barnerd, James. Treaty with the Ottawa, August 29, 1821 at Chicago, Illinois

Barnett, Harison. Treaty with the Potawatomi, October 26, 1832 at Camp Tippecanoe, Indiana

Barnett, Louis. Treaty with the Potawatomi, October 26, 1832 at Camp Tippecanoe, Indiana; French Foundations; Treaty with the Potawatomi, October 27, 1832 at Camp Tippecanoe, Indiana

Barnett, Moses. Treaty with the Potawatomi, October 26, 1832 at Camp Tippecanoe, Indiana

Barron, Joseph (Part Miami) related to principle chief of Miamis; interpreter. died 31 July 1843 at Logansport, Indiana. Treaty with the Potawatomi, October 26, 1832 at Camp Tippecanoe, Indiana; Illinois and Indiana Indians; Treaty with the Potawatomi, August 5, 1836, at Yellow River, Indiana; Treaty with the Potawatomi, September 23, 1836 at Chippewaynaung, Indiana; Treaty with the Eel River, etc., August 7, 1803 at Vincennes, Indiana; Treaty with the Sauk and Foxes, November 3, 1804 at St. Louis, Missouri; Treaty with the Delawares, etc., September 30, 1809 at Ft. Wayne, Indiana; Treaty with the Kickapoo, December 9, 1809 at Ft. Wayne, Indiana

Barron, Peter (Mixed) Treaty with the Potawatomi, October 26, 1832 at Camp Tippecanoe, Indiana; Treaty with the Potawatomi, September 23, 1836 at Chippewaynaung, Indiana

Barton, J. L. Treaty with the Kickapoo, July 30, 1819 at Edwardsville, Illinois

Batticy or Baptist Peoria (French-Indian) Treaty with the Peoria, etc., September 25, 1818 at Edwardsville, Illinois

Bear (Kaskaskia) Chief of 1698. From Quebec to New Orleans by J. H. Schlarman.

Beaubien, Charles (Mixed Ottawa) Son of J.B. Beaubien and Mannabenaqua, an Ottawa. Treaty with the Ottawa, August 29, 1821 at Chicago, Illinois.

Beaubien, John Baptist. Husband to Mannabenaqua, an Ottawa. Treaty with the Potawatomi, October 26, 1832 at Camp Tippecanoe, Indiana; Treaty with the Chippewa, September 26, 1833 at Chicago, Illinois; Treaty with the Ottawa, August 29, 1821 at Chicago, Illinois.

Beaubien, Josette (French and Potawatomi) Second wife of John Baptist Beaubien and daughter of Francois La Framboise, Sr. and Shawwenoqua. Inhabitants of Chicago, 1825-1831; Treaty with the Chippewa, September 26, 1833 at Chicago, Illinois; Treaty with the Potawatomi, November 15, 1861 at Kansas River, Kansas.

Beaubien, Mark (French and Ottawa) Treaty with the Chippewa, September 26, 1833 at Chicago, Illinois.

Beaubien, Medart B. (French and Ottawa) Son of J. B. Beaubien and Mannabenaqua, an Ottawa, his first wife. Inhabitants of Chicago, 1825-1831; Treaty with the Potawatomi, October 26, 1832 at Camp Tippecanoe, Indiana; Treaty with the Chippewa, September 26, 1833 at Chicago, Illinois.

Beajean, Antoine. Killed by the Iroquois 1693. In 1755 a Beaujeu was 2nd commander of Ft. Contrecoeur. French Foundations, 1680-1693.

Beaver (Delaware) Treaty with the Delaware, Etc., September 30, 1809 at Ft. Wayne, Indiana.

Beeson, Jacob. Treaty with the Chippewa, September 26, 1833 at Chicago, Illinois.

Beeyawyo (Potawatomi) Treaty with the Potawatomi, October 26, 1832 at Camp Tippecanoe, Indiana; Treaty with the Potawatomi, October 27, 1832 at Camp Tippecanoe, Indian.

Bellair, Peter. Treaty with the Chippewa, September 26, 1833 at Chicago, Illinois.

Benac or Benack (Potawatomi chief) Treaty with the Potawatomi, October 26, 1832 at Camp Tippecanoe, Indiana; Treaty with the Potawatomi, October 27, 1832 at Camp Tippecanoe, Indiana.

Benack, Mary Ann (Potawatomi) Wife of Edward McCartney. Sister or daughter to Benac or Osheakkebe. Treaty with the Potawatomi, October 26, 1832 at Camp Tippecanoe, Indiana; Treaty with the Ottawa, August 29, 1821 at Chicago, Illinois.

Bendegakewa (Ottawa) Treaty with the Ottawa, August 24, 1816 at St. Louis, Missouri.

Benton, Jesse, Jr. Treaty with the Chippewa, July 29, 1829 at Prairie Du Chien, Michigan.

Beresford, Robert. Treaty with the Chippewa, September 26, 1833 at Chicago, Illinois.

Berry, James W. Treaty with the Chippewa, September 26, 1833 at Chicago, Illinois.

Bertrand, John B. Sr. Treaty with the Chippewa, September 26, 1833 at Chicago, Illinois.

Bertrand, Joseph, Jr. Treaty with the Chippewa, September 26, 1833 at Chicago, Illinois.

Bertrand, Joseph, Sr. Treaty with the Potawatomi, October 26, 1832 at Camp Tippecanoe, Indiana; Treaty with the Chippewa, September 26, 1833 at Chicago, Illinois.

Bertrand, Madeline (Potawatomi) Wife of Joseph. Had children Joseph, Jr., Benjamin, Laurent, Theresa and Amable. Descendants Leon Bertrand, B H Bertrand, St. Luke Bertrand and Julia Ann Bertrand. Treaty with the Potawatomi, October 26, 1832 at Camp Tippecanoe, Indiana; Treaty with the Chippewa, September 26, 1833 at Chicago, Illinois; Treaty with the Ottawa, August 29, 1821 at Chicago, Illinois; Treaty with the Potawatomi, September 20, 1828 at St. Joseph, Michigan; Treaty with the Potawatomi, November 15, 1861 at Kansas River, Kansas; Treaty with the Potawatomi, October 16, 1826 at Wabash, Indiana.

Besiah (Potawatomi chief) Treaty with the Potawatomi, October 26, 1832 at Camp Tippecanoe, Indiana; Treaty with the Potawatomi, October 27, 1832 at Camp Tippecanoe, Indiana.

Besion, Francis. Treaty with the Potawatomi, October 26, 1832 at Camp Tippecanoe, Indiana; Treaty with the Chippewa, September 26, 1833 at Chicago, Illinois.

Biddle, Agate. Had children. Treaty with the Chippewa, September 26, 1833 at Chicago, Illinois.

Birkhead, George (Chippewa by descent) Treaty with the Christian Indians, March 3, 1823 at St. Mary's, Ohio.

Black Dog (Wea) Treaty with the Eel River, etc., August 7, 1803 at Vincennes, Indiana.

Black Kettle (Iroquois chief) Chief of 1692. Pioneer Layman of North America by Rev. Campbell.

Black Partridge (Potawatomi) Also known as Mucketepoke. Treaty with the Potawatomi, July 18, 1815 at St. Louis, Missouri; Treaty with the Ottawa, August 24, 1816 at St. Louis, Missouri.

Blackstone, John. Treaty with the Chippewa, September 26, 1833 at Chicago, Illinois.

Blodgett, Tyler K. Treaty with the Chippewa, September 26, 1833 at Chicago, Illinois.

Bogardus, J. L. Treaty with the Chippewa, July 29, 1829, at Prairie Du Chien, Michigan.

Bogue, Robert. Treaty with the Peoria, etc., September 25, 1818 at Edwardsville, Illinois.

Boilvin, N. Deceased by 1833. Treaty with the Chippewa, September 26, 1833 at Chicago, Illinois.

Boismenu, Nicholas. Heads of families 1783 at the Cahokias; Treaty with the Chippewa, September 26, 1833 at Chicago, Illinois.

Bolen, Hypolite (Delaware interpreter) Kaskaskia Records 1778-1790, Va. Series, Vol. II; Treaty with the Sauk & Foxes, November 3, 1804 at St. Louis, Missouri.

Bomassen (Chief) English captured him at Pemquid in the 1690's. Pioneer Priests of North America 1642-1710. Vol. III by Rev. Campbell.

Bona, Augustus. Treaty with the Chippewa, September 26, 1833 at Chicago, Illinois.

Borisau, Joe. Treaty with the Potawatomi, October 26, 1832 at Camp Tippecanoe, Indiana.

Bourassa, Daniel. Married a Potawatomi. Had children Joseph, Mark, Jude, Therese, Stephen, Gabriel, Alexander, James, Elai, Jerome, M.D., Lazarus and Achan. Treaty with the Chippewa, September 26, 1833 at Chicago, Illinois; Treaty with the Potawatomi, October 16, 1826 at Wabash, Indiana.

Bourbonnais, Calish. (Potawatomi) Wife of Francois Bourbonnais, Sr. Had children Washington, etal. Grand daughter Mawteno, daughter of Francois, Jr. Descendants Frank and Bescue Bourbonnais. Inhabitants of Chicago, 1825-1831; Treaty with the Potawatomi, October 26, 1832 at Camp Tippecanoe, Indiana; Treaty with the Potawatomi, November 15, 1861 at Kansas River, Kansas; Illinois on the Eve of Seven Years War, 1747-1755.

Bourdon, Joseph. Son of late Michael Bourdon and Marianne Le Fleure. Married Marie an Indian (Potawatomi?) of Prairie Du Chien. Recorded May 27, 1801. Children aged in 1801 were Charlie, 11; Rosalie, 7; Ulalie, 5; Marriages of St. Clair, County, Illinois 1791-1807.

Bourie, David. Treaty with the Chippewa, September 26, 1833 at Chicago, Illinois.

Bourie, John B. (Interpreter) Treaty with the Potawatomi, October 26, 1832 at Camp Tippecanoe, Indiana; Treaty with the Chippewa, September 26, 1833 at Chicago, Illinois; Treaty with the Potawatomi, September 20, 1828 at St. Joseph, Michigan; Treaty with the Potawatomi, October 27, 1832 at Camp Tippecanoe, Indiana; Treaty with the Potawatomi, October 16, 1826, at Wabash, Indiana.

Boutcher, Francois. Wife Waussequa. Had children. Treaty with the Chippewa, September 26, 1833 at Chicago, Illinois; Treaty with the Christian Indians, 3 March 1823 at St. Mary's, Ohio.

Boyd, Joshua. Children Robert and Therese. Treaty with the Chippewa, September 26, 1833 at Chicago, Illinois.

Bozarth, Lot. Treaty with the Potawatomi, October 26, 1832 at Camp Tippecanoe, Indiana.

Brady, S. P. Treaty with the Chippewa, September 26, 1833 at Chicago, Illinois.

Brady, Thom. Heads of Families 1783 of the Cahokias.

Brevoofield, Richard. Treaty with the Peoria, etc., September 25, 1818 at Edwardsville, Illinois.

Britain, Calvin. Treaty with the Chippewa, September 26, 1833 at Chicago, Illinois; Treaty with the Potawatomi, September 20, 1828 at St. Joseph, Michigan.

Brooks, Andrew. Treaty with the Kickapoo, August 30, 1819 at Ft. Harrison, Indiana.

Brooks, George. Treaty with the Chippewa, September 26, 1833 at Chicago, Illinois.

Brouillet, Michael. Treaty with the Kickapoo, August 30, 1819 at Ft. Harrison, Indiana; Treaty with the Piankashaw, December 30, 1805 at Vincennes, Indiana.

Browning, Naomi G. Student at Carey Mission School, 1826. Treaty with the Potawatomi, October 16, 1826 at Wabash, Indiana.

Bruner, Mary Ann. Treaty with the Potawatomi, October 26, 1832 at Camp Tippecanoe, Indiana; Treaty with the Potawatomi, Ocotober 27, 1832 at Camp Tippecanoe, Indiana.

Brush, E. A. Treaty with the Winnebago, August 25, 1828 at Green Bay, Michigan.

Buckmaster, N. Treaty with the Kickapoo, July 30, 1819 at Edwardsville, Illinois.

Bucknett, N. Treaty with the Peoria, et., September 25, 1818 at Edwardsville, Illinois.

Bukongehelas (Delaware) Treaty with the Delawares, etc., June 7, 1803 at Vincennes, Indiana.

Bullett, William. Treaty with the Piankashaw, December 30, 1805 at Vincennes, Indiana.

Burbonnais, Francis, Jr. Treaty with the Chippewa, September 26, 1833 at Chicago, Illinois.

Burbonnais, Francis, Sr. Treaty with the Chippewa, September 26, 1833 at Chicago, Illinois.

Burnett, James, Louison, Jacob, Abraham, Rebecca, John, and Nancy. Children of Kawkeeme, sister of Topnibe, principal chief of the Potawatomi nation. Also had a daughter Martha and a grandson, William. Isaac. Treaty with the Potawatomi, October 26, 1832 at Camp Tippecanoe, Indiana; Treaty with the Chippewa, September 26, 1833 at Chicago, Illinois; Treaty with the Ottawa, August 29, 1821 at Chicago, Illinois; Treaty with the Potawatomi, November 15, 1861 at Kansas River, Kansas; Treaty with the Potawatomi, June 17, 1846 at Council Bluffs, Missouri; Treaty with the Potawatomi, October 27, 1832 at Camp Tippecanoe, Indiana; Treaty with the Potawatomi, October 2, 1818 at St. Mary's, Ohio.

Buzann, Jesse. Treaty with the Potawatomi, October 26, 1832 at Camp Tippecanoe, Indiana.

Cabenaw (Ottawa) Treaty with the Ottawa, August 24, 1816, St. Louis, Missouri.

Cacake (Ottawa) Treaty with the Ottawa, August 24, 1816 at St. Louis, Missouri.

Cadieux, Michael. Treaty with the Potawatomi, October 27, 1832 at Camp Tippecanoe, Indiana.

Cadue, Perre. Treaty with the Potawatomi, October 27, 1832 at Camp Tippecanoe, Indiana.

Campbell, G.W. Treaty with the Chippewa, September 26, 1833 at Chicago, Illinois.

Campbell, James B. Treaty with the Chippewa, September 26, 1833 at Chicago, Illinois; Treaty with the Potawatomi, October 26, 1832 at Camp Tippecanoe, Indiana.

Captain Heald. Treaty with the Potawatomi, October 26, 1832 at Camp Tippecanoe, Indiana.

Carbonca. Treaty with the Potawatomi, October 26, 1832 at Camp Tippecanoe, Indiana.

Cashshakee (Ottawa) Treaty with the Ottawa, August 24, 1816 at St. Louis, Missouri.

Cawwesaut. Treaty with the Potawatomi, October 26, 1832 at Camp Tippecanoe, Indiana; Treaty with the Chippewa, September 26, 1833 at Chicago, Illinois.

Cekutay. Treaty with the Chippewa, September 26, 1833 at Chicago, Illinois.

Cenagewine. Treaty with the Potawatomi October 26, 1832 at Camp Tippecanoe, Indiana; Treaty with the Chippewa, September 26, 1833 at Chicago, Illinois.

Cetahquah. Treaty with the Chippewa, September 26, 1833 at Chicago, Illinois.

Chabert, Isadore. Dau of Richard Chabert. Treaty with the Potawatomi, September 20, 1828 at St. Joseph, Michigan; Treaty with the Chippewa, September 26, 1833 at Chicago, Illinois.

Chacapma. Treaty with the Potawatomi, October 2, 1818 at St. Mary's, Ohio.

Chahwee. Treaty with the Potawatomi, October 26, 1832 at Camp Tippecanoe, Indiana.

Chaketeah. Treaty with the Chippewa, September 26, 1833 at Chicago, Illinois.

Chamblee or Shabbona. Treaty with the Ottawa, August 24, 1816 at St. Louis, Missouri.

Chalipeaux, Pierre. Children of. Treaty with the Chippewa, September 26, 1833 at Chicago, Illinois.

Chandonai, John Bt. Son of Chippewaqua. Treaty with the Chippewa, September 26, 1833 at Chicago, Illinois; Treaty with the Ottawa, August 29, 1821 at Chicago, Illinois; Treaty with the Potawatomi, October 27, 1832 at Camp Tippecanoe, Indiana.

Chandler, Theresa or Toeakqui, a Potawatomi. Had daughter Betsy Fisher. Treaty with the Ottawa, August 29, 1821 at Chicago, Illinois; Treaty with the Chippewa, September 26, 1833 at Chicago, Illinois.

Chapeau, Jacques. Children of. Treaty with the Chippewa, September 26, 1833 at Chicago, Illinois.

Chapin, Adolphus. Treaty with the Chippewa, September 26, 1833 at Chicago, Illinois.

Chapman, C.H. Treaty with the Chippewa, September 26, 1833 at Chicago, Illinois.

Charette, Antoine, Joseph, Louis, Chalot, and Margaret. Children of Equameeg. Treaty with the Christian Indians, March 3, 1823 at St. Mary's, Ohio.

Chatalie, Mary (Potawatomi) Daughter of Chief Neebosh. Treaty with the Potawatomi, October 2, 1818 at St. Mary's, Ohio.

Chaukenozwoh. Student at the Carey Mission School. Treaty with the Potawatomi, October 16, 1826 at Wabash, Indiana.

Chaunier, Joseph. Treaty with the Chippewa, September 26, 1833 at Chicago, Illinois.

Chawcawbeme (Potawatomi) Treaty with the Potawatomi, July 18, 1815 at St. Louis, Missouri.

Chebah (Potawatomi) Treaty with the Potawatomi, October 27, 1832 at Camp Tippecanoe, Indiana.

Chebanse (Potawatomi chief) Indian Place Names in Illinois, by Vogel; Treaty with the Ottawa, August 29, 1821, Chicago.

Checalk (Potawatomi) Treaty with the Potawatomi, October 2, 1818 at St. Mary's, Ohio.

Chechalkose (Potawatomi chief) Treaty with the Potawatomi, October 26, 1832 at Camp Tippecanoe, Indiana; Treaty with the Chippewa, July 29, 1829 at Prairie Du Chien, Michigan; Treaty with the Potawatomi, October 26, 1832 at Camp Tippecanoe, Indiana; Treaty with the Potawatomi, September 20, 1828 at St. Joseph, Michigan; Treaty with the Potawatomi, October 27, 1832 at Camp Tippecanoe, Indiana; Treaty with the Potawatomi, October 16, 1826 at Wabash, Indiana; Treaty with the Potawatomi, September 23, 1836 at Chippewaynaung, Indiana.

Checo (Potawatomi) Treaty with the Potawatomi, October 26, 1832 at Camp Tippecanoe, Indiana.

Cheebaas (Potawatomi) Treaty with the Potawatomi, October 2, 1818 at St. Mary's, Ohio.

Cheegwamackgwago (Potawatomi) Treaty with the Ottawa, August 29, 1821 at Chicago, Illinois.

Cheekeh. Student at Carey Mission School. Treaty with the Potawatomi, October 16, 1826 at Wabash, Indiana.

Chekase (Potawatomi chief) Treaty with the Potawatomi, October 26, 1832 at Camp Tippecanoe, Indiana; Treaty with the Potawatomi, October 27, 1832 at Camp Tippecanoe, Indiana.

Chekawme. Treaty with the Potawatomi, September 23, 1836 at Chippewaynaung, Indiana.

Chekinaka (Ottawa) Treaty with the Ottawa, August 24, 1816 at St. Louis, Missouri.

Cheman. Treaty with the Potawatomi, October 26, 1832 at Camp Tippecanoe, Indiana.

Chepeecoquah. Treaty with the Chippewa, September 26, 1833 at Chicago, Illinois.

Chequamkako. Brother to Toisas and Memotway. Treaty with the Potawatomi, October 26, 1832 at Camp Tippecanoe, Ind.; Treaty with the Potawatomi, October 27, 1832; Treaty with the Potawatomi, December 16, 1834 at Potawatomi Mills, Indiana.

Chequimimo. (Potawatomi) Treaty with the Delawares, etc., September 30, 1809 at Ft. Wayne, Indiana.

Cheshawgun. Treaty with the Potawatomi, October 27, 1832 at Camp Tippecanoe, Indiana.

Chevalier, Jean B., Josette and Angelique. Treaty with the Potawatomi, October 26, 1832 at Camp Tippecanoe, Indiana; Treaty with the Chippewa, September 26, 1833 at Chicago, Illinois.

Chevallier, Charles, Francois, and Joseph. 1790 Illinois Militia.

Chevallier, Louis. Treaty with the Chippewa, September 26, 1833 at Chicago, Illinois.

Chewago. Treaty with the Potawatomi, October 2, 1818 at St. Mary's, Ohio.

Chicag. Treaty with the Potawatomi, October 26, 1832 at Camp Tippecanoe, Indiana.

Chicagou (Mitchigamias chief of 1730's). From Quebec to New Orleans.

Chickkose. Treaty with the Potawatomi, October 26, 1832 at Camp Tippecanoe, Indiana.

Chikawketch. Student at Carey Mission School. Treaty with the Potawatomi, October 16, 1826 at Wabash, Indiana.

Chisinkebah. Treaty with the Chippewa, September 26, 1833 at Chicago, Illinois.

Chobare, Francoise. Treaty with the Chippewa, September 26, 1833 at Chicago, Illinois.

Chobare, Isadore. Treaty with the Chippewa, September 26, 1833 at Chicago, Illinois.

Chouamasee. Treaty with the Potawatomi, October 27, 1832 at Camp Tippecanoe, Indiana.

Chouteau, Auguste (Interpreter) Kaskaskia Records 1778-1790. Vol. II Va. Series; Black Hawk biography; Treaty with the Potawatomi, July 18, 1815 at St. Louis, Mo.; Treaty with the Ottawa, August 24, 1816 at St. Louis, Mo.; Treaty with the Peoria, Etc., September 25, 1818 at Edwardsville, Illinois; Treaty with the Potawatomi, October 2, 1818 at St. Mary's, Ohio; Treaty with the Kickapoo, July 30, 1819 at Edwardsville, Illinois.

Chouteau, C. Treaty with the Chippewa, July 29, 1829 at Prairie Du Chien, Michigan; Treaty with the Winnebago, August 25, 1828 at Green Bay, Michigan.

Chouteau, P. Treaty with the Sauk and Foxes, November 3, 1804 at St. Louis, Missouri.

Chovanin. Treaty with the Potawatomi, October 26, 1832 at Camp Tippecanoe, Indiana.

Cicott, E. O. (Interpreter) Treaty with the Potawatomi, October 26, 1832 at Camp Tippecanoe, Indiana; Treaty with the Potawatomi, October 27, 1832 at Camp Tippecanoe, Indiana; Treaty with the Potawatomi, August 5, 1836 at Yellow River, Indiana.

Cicot, George. Husband to Meshawketoquay and chief of the Potawatomis. Deceased by October 1832. Treaty with the Christian Indians, March 3, 1823 at St. Mary's, Ohio; Treaty with the Potawatomi, September 20, 1828 at St. Joseph, Michigan; Treaty with the Potawatomi, October 16, 1826 at Wabash, Indiana; Treaty with the Potawatomi, October 26, 1832 at Camp Tippecanoe, Indiana.

Cicott, Nancy and Amelia. Children of Jean B. Cicot, son of Pesayquot, sister to Peerish. Treaty with the Potawatomi, October 26, 1832 at Camp Tippecanoe, Indiana; Treaty with the Ottawa, August 29, 1821 at Chicago, Illinois.

Cicott, Z. Treaty with the Chippewa, September 26, 1833 at Chicago, Illinois.

Cigne, Le. War chief of LePied Froid's Miami band. Illinois on the Eve of Seven Years War 1747-1755.

Clampet, Nathan. Treaty with the Kickapoo, July 30, 1819 at Edwardsville, Illinois.

Clark, John K. Children of. Treaty with the Chippewa, September 26, 1833 at Chicago, Illinois.

Clark, O. L. Treaty with the Potawatomi, October 16, 1826 Wabash, Indiana.

Clark, Timothy B. Treaty with the Potawatomi, October 26, 1832 at Camp Tippecanoe, Indiana.

Clements, Richard. Student at the Carey Mission School. Treaty with the Potawatomi, October 16, 1826, at Wabash, Indiana.

Cleveland, Henry. Treaty with the Chippewa, September 26, 1833 at Chicago, Illinois.

Cloutier, John Bt. Children of. Treaty with the Chippewa, September 26, 1833 at Chicago, Illinois.

Clyburn, Archibald. Treaty with the Chippewa, September 26, 1833 at Chicago, Illinois.

Colerick, D.H. Treaty with the Potawatomi, October 27, 1832 at Camp Tippecanoe, Indiana.

Commoyo. Treaty with the Potawatomi, October 26, 1832 at Camp Tippecanoe, Indiana.

Comoza (Potawatomi band chief) Treaty with the Potawatomi, October 26, 1832 at Camp Tippecanoe, Indiana; Treaty with the Potawatomi, September 20, 1828 at St. Joseph, Michigan.

Comparret, Francis. Treaty with the Potawatomi October 27, 1832 at Camp Tippecanoe, Indiana.

Comparet, Jean B. Treaty with the Potawatomi, September 20, 1828 at St. Joseph, Michigan.

Conengee (Potawatomi) Treaty with the Delawares, etc., September 30, 1809 at Ft. Wayne, Indiana.

Conge (Potawatomi) Treaty with the Potawatomi, October 2, 1818 at St. Mary's, Ohio.

Conner, Henry. Interpreter. Received section of land in 1826. Treaty with the Chippewa, September 26, 1833 at Chicago, Illinois; Treaty with the Ottawa, August 9, 1821 at Chicago, Illinois; Treaty with the Potawatomi, October 16, 1826 at Wabash, Indiana.

Conner, James. Treaty with the Potawatomi, October 26, 1832 at Camp Tippecanoe, Indiana; Treaty with the Chippewa, September 26, 1833 at Chicago, Illinois; Treaty with the

Potawatomi, October 16, 1826 at Wabash, Indiana; Treaty with the Potawatomi, October 27, 1832 at Camp Tippecanoe, Indiana.

Conner, John. Treaty with the Delawares, Etc., September 30, 1809 at Ft. Wayne, Indiana; Treaty with the Potawatomi, October 2, 1818 at St. Mary's, Ohio.

Conner, Richard J. Treaty with the Chippewa, September 26, 1833 at Chicago, Illinois.

Conner, Susan. Wife of Thomas and daughter to Pimeqeeshigoqua. Had children. Treaty with the Christian Indians, Marych 3, 1823 at St. Mary's, Ohio.

Conner, William (Interpreter) Received section of land in 1826. Treaty with the Potawatomi, October 26, 1832 at Camp Tippecanoe, Indiana; Treaty with the Potawatomi, October 16, 1826 at Wabash, Indiana; Treaty with the Potawatomi, October 2, 1818 at St. Mary's, Ohio.

Conway, Joseph. Treaty with the Peoria, etc., September 25, 1818 at Edwardsville, Illinois.

Coquahwah. Treaty with the Potawatomi, August 5, 1836 at Yellow River, Indiana.

Coquillard, Alexis. Treaty with the Potawatomi, September 20, 1828 at St. Joseph, Michigan; Treaty with the Potawatomi, October 27, 1832 at Camp Tippecanoe, Indiana.

Corbly, Jacob. Student at Carey Mission School. Treaty with the Potawatomi, October 16, 1826 at Wabash, Indiana.

Countreman, Nancy, Sally and Betsey. Children of Endoga. Also Frederick H. Treaty with the Potawatomi, October 26, 1832 at Camp Tippecanoe, Indiana; Treaty with the Chippewa, September 26, 1833 at Chicago, Illinois; Treaty with the Potawatomi, Octber 26, 1832 at Camp Tippecanoe, Indiana.

Couroway. (Kaskaskia chief) Void agreement of Illinois and Wabash Land Company, 1773.

Corbonno, Pierre. Children of. Treaty with the Chippewa, September 26, 1833 at Chicago, Illinois.

Covill, Thomas R. Treaty with the Chippewa, September 26, 1833 at Chicago, Illinois.

Cowen, James. Treaty with the Chippewa, September 26, 1833 at Chicago, Illinois.

Cowwesaut (Ottawa) Treaty with the Ottawa, August 24, 1816 at St. Louis, Missouri.

Craig, James W. Treaty with the Chippewa, Septeber 26, 1833 at Chicago, Illinois.

Crawford, George. Treaty with the Potawatomi, October 26, 1832 at Camp Tippecanoe, Indiana.

Crume, Marks (Commissioner) Treaty with the Potawatomi, October 26, 1832 at Camp Tippecanoe, Indiana; Treaty with the Potawatomi, October 27, 1832 at Camp Tippecanoe, Indiana.

Cunnepepy. Treaty with the Ottawa, August 24, 1816 at St. Louis, Missouri.

Curtis, Horatio N. Treaty with the Chippewa, September 26, 1833 at Chicago, Illinois.

Curtis, Joseph. Treaty with the Chippewa, September 26, 1833 at Chicago, Illinois.

Cuthewekasaw or Black Hoof (Shawnee) Treaty with the Delawares, June 7, 1803 at Vincennes, Indiana.

Davis, John. Treaty with the Potawatomi, October 26, 1832 at Camp Tippecanoe, Indiana.

Daze, Joseph. Son of Chippewaqua. Treaty with the Ottawa, August 29, 1821 at Chicago, Illinois.

Daze, Paul-Charles. French Foundations 1680-1693.

De Broyeux, Jean. French Foundations 1680-1693.

De Carrie, Sabrevoir. Wife Hopoekaw, a Winnebago. Descendants used name Decorah, one of which was Big Canoe. Indian Place Names in Illinois, by Vogel.

De Coigne, Louis Jefferson (Kaskaskia) Treaty with the Peoria, Etc., September 25, 1818 at Edwardsville, Ill.

De Jean, Francis. Treaty with the Potawatomi, October 26, 1832 at Camp Tippecanoe, Indiana.

Delamay, D. Treaty with the Sauk and Foxes, November 3, 1804 at St. Louis, Missouri.

Demoiselle, La. (Chief at Great Miami River) Illinois on the Eve of the Seven Years War 1747-1755.

Dew, John. Treaty with the Kickapoo, July 30, 1819 at Edwardsville, Illinois.

Dick, Charles. Student at Carey Mission School. Treaty with the Potawatomi, October 16, 1826 at Wabash, Indiana.

Dingley, Isabella. Wife of Daniel Dingley and daughter of Pimegeezhigogua. Had children. Treaty with the Christian Indians, March 3, 1823 at St. Mary's, Ohio.

Dixon, John. Treaty with the Chippewa, September 26, 1833 at Chicago, Illinois.

Dodge, H. Treaty with the Chippewa, July 29, 1829 at Prairie Du Chien, Michigan.

Doer, Joseph. Treaty with the Kickapoo, July 30, 1819 at Edwardsville, Illinois.

Dole, George W. Treaty with the Chippewa, September 26, 1833 at Chicago, Illinois.

Dorsey, J.D. Treaty with the Potawatomi, October 16, 1826 at Wabash, Indiana.

Douglass, Issac A. Treaty with the Kickapoo, July 30, 1819 at Edwardsville, Illinois.

Douglass, John T. Treaty with the Potawatomi, October 26, 1832 at Camp Tippecanoe, Indiana.

Douglass, Joesph. Treaty with the Potawatomi, October 26, 1832 at Camp Tippecanoe, Indiana.

Downing, Rufus. Treaty with the Chippewa, September 26, 1833 at Chicago, Illinois.

Downing, Stephen. Treaty with the Chippewa, September 26, 1833 at Chicago, Illinois.

Drouillard, Andrew. Treaty with the Chippewa, September 26, 1833 at Chicago, Illinois.

Druillard, Louis. Treaty with the Chippewa, September 26, 1833 at Chicago, Illinois; Treaty with the Potawatomi, October 26, 1832 at Camp Tippecanoe, Indiana.

Dubois. Of Vincennes. Treaty with the Piankashaw, December 30, 1805 at Vincennes, Indiana.

Ducharme, Charles. Probable descendant of Dominique Ducharme (1779) French-Canadian Trader. 1790 Illinois militia. Heads of families 1783 of the Cahokias. Also Betsy and Jacque Ducharme.

Ducharme, John B. and Medlin. Treaty with the Potawatomi, October 26, 1832 at Camp Tippecanoe, Indiana; Treaty with the Chippewa, September 26, 1833 at Chicago, Illinois.

Ducoigne (Kaskaskia) Treaty with the Eel River, Etc., August 7, 1803 at Vincennes, Indiana.

Ducoigne, Jean Baptiste Louis (Kaskaskia chief circa 1789) Kaskaskia Records 1778-1790 Va. Series Vol. II; Treaty with the Kaskaskia, August 13, 1803 at Vincennes, Indiana.

Dumais, Eustache and Francois. Brothers. Also spelled Dumay. French Foundations 1680-1693.

Dupuis, Louis. Treaty with the Potawatomi, October 27, 1832 at Camp Tippecanoe, Indiana.

Duquindre, Francois. Treaty with the Potawatomi, October 16, 1826 at Wabash, Indiana.

Duquindre, Ursula. Treaty with the Potawatomi, October 26, 1832 at Camp Tippecanoe, Indiana; Treaty with the Potawatomi, October 27, 1832 at Camp Tippecanoe, Indiana.

Duret, John B. Treaty with the Potawatomi, October 26, 1832 at Camp Tippecanoe, Indiana.

Dutrist, Jean B. Husband to Sahnemoquay. Had children. Treaty with the Potawatomi, September 20, 1828 at St. Joseph, Michigan.

Duverney, Pierre. Husband to Minedemoeyah. Had children. Treaty with the Chippewa, September 26, 1833 at Chicago, Illinois.

Eldridge, Job B. Treaty with the Potawatomi, September 23, 1836 at Chippewaynaung, Indiana.

Ellice, Samuel. Treaty with the Chippewa, September 26, 1833 at Chicago, Illinois.

Elliott, James. Treaty with the Potawatomi, October 26, 1832 at Camp Tippecanoe, Indiana.

Emmell, Oliver. Treaty with the Chippewa, September 26, 1833 at Chicago, Illinois.

Enslen, Henry. Treaty with the Chippewa, September 26, 1833 at Chicago, Illinois.

Epic, Le Pore.(First chief of La Demoiselle's band) Illinois on the Eve of the Seven Years War 1747-1755.

Eppesause (Ottawa) Treaty with the Ottawa, August 29, 1821 at Chicago, Illinois.

Ermatinger, George. (Shawnee descent) Had children. Treaty with the Christian Indians, March 3, 1823 at St. Mary's, Ohio.

Eshcam. Treaty with the Potawatomi, October 2, 1818 at St. Mary's, Ohio.

Eshawinikiwah or Hand and Target (Chief of the Peoriahs). Void Agreement Illinois and Wabash Land Company, 1773.

Eskawbeywis. Treaty with the Chippewa, July 29, 1829 at Prairie Du Chien, Michigan.

Etowanacote. Treaty with the Potawatomi, October 26, 1832 at Camp Tippecanoe, Indiana; Treaty with the Chippewa, September 26, 1833 at Chicago, Illinois.

Evans, Foreman. Treaty with the Chippewa, September 26, 1833 at Chicago, Illinois.

Evans, Montgomery. Treaty with the Chippewa, September 26, 1833 at Chicago, Illinois.

Everts, Gustavus A. Treaty with the Potawatomi, October 27, 1832 at Camp Tippecanoe, Indiana.

Ewing, C.W. Treaty with the Potawatomi, September 20, 1828 at St. Joseph, Michigan; Treaty with the Potawatomi, October 16, 1826 at Wabash, Indiana.

Ewing, G. W. Treaty with the Potawatomi, October 26, 1832 at Camp Tippecanoe, Indiana.

Ewing, Harriet. Treaty with the Chippewa, September 26, 1833 at Chicago, Illinois.

Ewing, W. G. Treaty with the Potawatomi, October 26, 1832 at Camp Tippecanoe, Indiana.

Felix, Frances. Treaty with the Chippewa, September 26, 1833 at Chicago, Illinois.

Ferry, Caroline. Treaty with the Chippewa, September 26, 1833 at Chicago, Illinois.

Fontaine, Felix. Treaty with the Chippewa, September 26, 1833 at Chicago, Illinois.

Forsyth, Jane C. Treaty with the Chippewa, September 26, 1833 at Chicago, Illinois.

Forsyth, John. Treaty with the Potawatomi, October 26, 1832 at Camp Tippecanoe, Indiana.

Forsyth, Robert A. Sr. (Maumee) Deceased by 1828. Had son Robert Jr. and others. Treaty with the Chippewa, September 26, 1833 at Chicago, Illinois; Treaty with the Potawatomi, September 20, 1828 at St. Joseph, Michigan; Treaty with the Winnebago, August 25, 1828 at Green Bay, Michigan; Treaty with the Potawatomi, October 27, 1832 at Camp Tippecanoe, Indiana.

Forsyth, Thomas. Treaty with the Potawatomi, October 26, 1832 at Camp Tippecanoe, Indiana; Treaty with the Chippewa, July 29, 1829 at Prairie Du Chien, Michigan; Treaty with the Potawatomi, October 26, 1832 at Camp Tippecanoe, Indiana; Treaty with the Chippewa, September 26, 1833 at Chicago, Illinois; Treaty with the Potawatomi, September 20, 1828 at St. Joseph, Michigan; Autobiography of Black Hawk.

Foster, James. Treaty with the Potawatomi, October 16, 1826 at Wabash, Indiana.

Francis, Abraham. Treaty with the Chippewa, September 26, 1833 at Chicago, Illinois.

Francois (Potawatomi) Treaty with the Ottawa, August 29, 1821 at Chicago, Illinois.
French, William. Treaty with the Chippewa, September 26, 1833 at Chicago, Illinois.
Froid, Le Pied (Great chief of the Miami 1749) Illinois on the Eve of the Seven Years War.
Fry, Benjamin. Treaty with the Chippewa, September 26, 1833 at Chicago, Illinois.

Gaither, John. Treaty with the Peoria, Etc., September 25, 1818 at Edwardsville, Illinois.
Galloway, James. Treaty with the Chippewa, September 26, 1833 at Chicago, Illinois.
Gamblin, Anthony. Husband to Assapo. Treaty with the Potawatomi, October 26, 1832 at Camp Tippecanoe, Indiana; Treaty with the Potawatomi, September 20, 1828 at St. Joseph, Michigan.
Garagonthié (Iroquois chief of 1690's friendly to French). Pioneer Laymen of North America. Rev. Campbell.
Gentry, Richard. Treaty with the Chippewa, July 29, 1829 at Prairie Du Chien, Michigan.
Getocquar. Treaty with the Potawatomi, October 26, 1832 at Camp Tippecanoe, Indiana.
Ghebause. Treaty with the Potawatomi, October 16, 1826 at Wabash, Indiana; Treaty with the Potawatomi, October 27, 1832 at Camp Tippecanoe, Indiana.
Gibenashwish. Treaty with the Potawatomi, October 27, 1832 at Camp Tippecanoe, Indiana.
Godfroy, Gabriel. Treaty with the Chippewa, September 26, 1833 at Chicago, Illinois; Treaty with the Potawatomi, September 20, 1828 at St. Joseph, Michigan; Treaty with the Potawatomi, October 2, 1818 at St. Mary's, Ohio.
Godfroy, Jno. B. Treaty with the Potawatomi, September 20, 1828 at St. Joseph, Michigan.
Godfroy, J. J. Treaty with the Potawatomi, October 27, 1832 at Camp Tippecanoe, Indiana.
Godfroy, Peter. Treaty with the Potawatomi, October 27, 1832 at Camp Tippecanoe, Indiana.
Godfroy, Samuel. Treaty with the Chippewa, September 26, 1833 at Chicago, Illinois.
Godfroy, T. P. Treaty with the Potawatomi, October 27, 1832 at Camp Tippecanoe, Indiana.
Gomo. Autobiography of Black Hawk.
Gratiot, Henry. Treaty with the Chippewa, September 26, 1833 at Chicago, Illinois; Treaty with the Winnebago, August 25, 1828 at Green Bay, Michigan; Treaty with the Chippewa, July 29, 1829 at Prairie Du Chien, Michigan; Autobiography of Black Hawk.
Gray, Martha. Treaty with the Chippewa, September 26, 1833 at Chicago, Illinois.
Green, John. Treaty with the Chippewa, September 26, 1833 at Chicago, Illinois.
Green, Thomas K. Treaty with the Chippewa, September 26, 1833 at Chicago, Illinois.

Griffith, Polly. Daughter of Nebosh. Some Griffiths also residents of early Kaskaskia. Treaty with the Potawatomi, October 26, 1832 at Camp Tippecanoe, Indiana.

Grignon, Bernard, Louis, and son Paul. Paul, Sr. and Amable. Robert and Perish. Catish and Elizabeth. Ursal and Charlotte. Louise and Rachel. George and Agate Polier. Treaty with the Chippewa, September 26, 1833 at Chicago, Illinois.

Gros Bled or Big Corn. Treaty with the Eel River, Etc., August 7, 1803 at Vincennes, Indiana.

Guion, Charles. Deceased by 1833. Treaty with the Chippewa, September 26, 1833 at Chicago, Illinois.

Hahshequarhiqua or The Bear. Treaty with the Sauk and Foxes, November 3, 1804 at St. Louis, Missouri; Autobiography of Black Hawk.

Hall, Margaret. Children James, William, David and Sarah. Grandchildren Margaret Ellen and Montgomery and Finly Miller. Also Rachel and Sylvia Hall. Treaty with the Chippewa, September 26, 1833 at Chicago, Illinois.

Hall, Thomas. Treaty with the Potawatomi, October 26, 1832 at Camp Tippecanoe, Indiana.

Hamblin, John. Treaty with the Chippewa, September 26, 1833 at Chicago, Illinois.

Hamilton, Allen. Treaty with the Potawatomi, October 26, 1832 at Camp Tippecanoe, Indiana; Treaty with the Potawatomi, September 23, 1836 at Chippewaynaung, Indiana.

Hamilton, Richard J. Treaty with the Chippewa, September 26, 1833 at Chicago, Illinois.

Hanna, Samuel. Treaty with the Potawatomi, October 26, 1832 at Camp Tippecanoe, Indiana.

Harcens, Thomas. Treaty with the Kickapoo, July 30, 1819 at Edwardsville, Illinois.

Hardwick, Angelique. Children of. Treaty with the Chippewa, September 26, 1833 at Chicago, Illinois.

Hardwick, Moses. Treaty with the Chippewa, September 26, 1833 at Chicago, Illinois.

Harrington, James. Treaty with the Chippewa, September 26, 1833 at Chicago, Illinois.

Harse, M. Treaty with the Potawatomi, October 26, 1832 at Camp Tippecanoe, Indiana.

Hartzell, Thomas (Interpreter) Treaty with the Potawatomi, October 26, 1832 at Camp Tippecanoe, Indiana; Treaty with the Chippewa, September 26, 1833 at Chicago, Illinois.

Hatch, A.T. Treaty with the Chippewa, September 26, 1833 at Chicago, Illinois.

Haumpeemannekaw or He Who Walks by Day. Treaty with the Winnebago, August 25, 1828 at Green Bay, Michigan.

Haverhill, George. Treaty with the Chippewa, September 26, 1833 at Chicago, Illinois.

Hayrokawkaw or He Without Horns. Treaty with the Winnebago, August 25, 1828 at Green Bay, Michigan.

Hazard, William. Treaty with the Chippewa, September 26, 1833 at Chicago, Illinois.

Heacock, R. E. Treaty with the Chippewa, September 26, 1833 at Chicago, Illinois.

Head, Henry. Treaty with the Kickapoo, July 30, 1819 at Edwardsville, Illinois.

Head, William. Treaty with the Kickapoo, July 30, 1819 at Edwardsville, Illinois.

Hedges, John P. Treaty with the Chippewa, September 26, 1833 at Chicago, Illinois; Treaty with the Potawatomi, September 20, 1828 at St. Joseph, Michigan.

Hedges, Nancy. Treaty with the Chippewa, September 26, 1833 at Chicago, Illinois.

Helm, Margaret. Treaty with the Chippewa, September 26, 1833 at Chicago, Illinois.

Hemenahwah. Treaty with the Chippewa, September 26, 1833 at Chicago, Illinois.

Hickman, James. Treaty with the Potawatomi, October 26, 1832 at Camp Tippecanoe, Indiana.

Hickman, William W. Treaty with the Kickapoo, July 30, 1819 at Edwardsville, Illinois.

Hill, A. Treaty with the Chippewa, July 29, 1829 at Prairie Du Chien, Michigan.

Hinchman, Felix. Treaty with the Potawatomi, October 16, 1826 at Wabash, Indiana.

Hitchcock, Rufus. Treaty with the Chippewa, September 26, 1833 at Chicago, Illinois.

Hockingpomskenn. Treaty with the Delawares, June 7, 1803 at Vincennes, Indiana; Treaty with the Delawares, Etc., September 30, 1809 at Ft. Wayne, Indiana.

Hoffman, Henry B. Treaty with the Potawatomi, October 26, 1832 at Camp Tippecanoe, Indiana.

Hollenbeck, Clark. Treaty with the Chippewa, September 26, 1833 at Chicago, Illinois.

Hollenbeck, George. Treaty with the Chippewa, September 26, 1833 at Chicago, Illinois.

Hootshoapkaw or Four Legs. Treaty with the Winnebago, August 25, 1828 at Green Bay, Michigan. Also Four Legs, Sr.

Hoowauneekaw or Little Elk. Treaty with the Winnebago, August 25, 1828 at Green Bay, Michigan.

Hopkins, Reuben. Treaty with the Kickapoo, July 30, 1819 at Edwardsville, Illinois.

Hopoekaw (Winnebago) Wife to Sabrevoir De Carrie. Indian Place Names in Illinois by Vogel.

Howard, John. Treaty with the Peoria, Etc., September 25, 1818 at Edwardsville, Illinois.

Hubbard, G. S. (Interpreter) Treaty with the Potawatomi, October 26, 1832 at Camp Tippecanoe, Indiana; Treaty with the Potawatomi, October 26, 1832 at Camp Tippecanoe, Indiana; Treaty with the Chippewa, September 26, 1833 at Chicago, Illinois; Treaty with the Potawatomi, September 20, 1828 at St. Joseph, Michigan.

Hull, David. Treaty with the Chippewa, September 26, 1833 at Chicago, Illinois.

Huff, William. Treaty with the Chippewa, September 26, 1833 at Chicago, Illinois; Treaty with the Potawatomi, October 27, 1832 at Camp Tippecanoe, Indiana.

Hull, Isaac. Treaty with the Chippewa, September 26, 1833 at Chicago, Illinois.

Hunt, Alice. Treaty with the Chippewa, September 26, 1833 at Chicago, Illinois.

Hunt, George. Treaty with the Chippewa, September 26, 1833 at Chicago, Illinois.

Hunt, Henry I. Treaty with the Ottawa, August 29, 1821 at Chicago, Illinois.

Hunt, John E. Treaty with the Chippewa, September 26, 1833 at Chicago, Illinois; Treaty with the Potawatomi, October 26, 1832 at Camp Tippecanoe, Indiana.

Hunter, Edward E. Treaty with the Chippewa, September 26, 1833 at Chicago, Illinois.

Hunter, Maria. Treaty with the Chippewa, September 26, 1833 at Chicago, Illinois

Hurst, H. Of Vincennes. Treaty with the Piankashaw, December 30, 1805 at Vincennes, Indiana.

Ignatius. Brother to Sinnowchewone, Ottawa. Treaty with the Ottawa, August 24, 1816 at St. Louis, Missouri.

Iowah (Wabash Potawatomi chief) Treaty with the Potawatomi, December 16, 1834 at Potawatomi Mills, Indiana; Treaty with the Potawatomi, August 5, 1836 at Yellow River, Indiana.

Isaacs, Angelina. Student at Carey Mission School. Treaty with the Potawatomi, October 16, 1826 at Wabash, Indiana.

Isaacs, Harriet. Student at Carey Mission School. Treaty with the Potawatomi, October 16, 1826 at Wabash, Indiana.

Isaacs, Jemina. Student at Carey Mission School. Treaty with the Potawatomi, October 16, 1826 at Wabash, Indiana.

Isaacs, Susanna. Student at Carey Mission School. Treaty with the Potawatomi, October 16, 1826 at Wabash, Indiana.

Jacco. Treaty with the Wea, October 2, 1818 at St. Mary's, Ohio.

Jarro or Jarrot or Hoowanneekaw. Winnebago chief who was named after Major Nicholas Jarrot, a Frenchman. Indian Place Names in Illinois by Vogel; Treaty with the Winnebago, August 25, 1828 at Green Bay, Michigan.

Jeauneau, Solomon and Jacque. Treaty with the Potawatomi, October 26, 1832 at Camp Tippecanoe, Indiana; Treaty with the Potawatomi, October 26, 1832 at Camp Tippecanoe, Indiana; Treaty with the Chippewa, September 26, 1833 at Chicago, Illinois.

Jebause. Treaty with the Potawatomi, September 20, 1828 at St. Joseph, Michigan.

Jekose. Treaty with the Potawatomi, October 16, 1826 at Wabash, Indiana.

Jequaumkogo. Treaty with the Potawatomi, October 16, 1826 at Wabash, Indiana.

Johnson, John. Treaty with the Chippewa, September 26, 1833 at Chicago, Illinois; Treaty with the Piankashaw, December 30, 1805 at Vincennes, Indiana.

Johnson, John W. Treaty with the Chippewa, July 29, 1829 at Prairie Du Chien, Michigan.

Johnson, L. Treaty with the Potawatomi, October 27, 1832 at Camp Tippecanoe, Indiana.

Johnston, Stephen. Deceased. Children received land. Treaty with the Potawatomi, October 16, 1826 at Wabash, Indiana; Treaty with the Delawares, Etc., September 30, 1809 at Ft. Wayne, Indiana; Treaty with the Kickapoo, July 30, 1819 at Edwardsville, Illinois.

Jones, D. G. Treaty with the Potawatomi, September 20, 1828 at St. Joseph, Michigan; Treaty with the Potawatomi, October 16, 1826 at Wabash, Indiana.

Jones, John. John Rice Jones. Henry Jones. William Jones. Treaty with the Chippewa, September 26, 1833 at Chicago, Illinois; 1790 Illinois Militia.

Jones, John. Student at Carey Mission School. Treaty with the Potawatomi October 16, 1826 at Wabash, Indiana.

Jones, John Rice. Of Indiana Territory. Treaty with the Eel River, Etc., August 7, 1803 at Vincennes, Indiana; Treaty with the Piankashaw, December 30, 1805 at Vincennes, Indiana.

Jones, Thomas. Treaty with the Potawatomi, October 27, 1832 at Camp Tippecanoe, Indiana.

Jopenebee. Treaty with the Chippewa, September 26, 1833 at Chicago, Illinois.

Joquiss. Wabash Potawatomi chief. Treaty with the Potawatomi, August 5, 1836 at Yellow River, Indiana.

Josaih. Treaty with the Potawatomi, September 20, 1828 at St. Joseph, Michigan.

Joseph. Treaty with the Chippewa, September 26, 1833 at Chicago, Illinois.

Joweh. Treaty with the Potawatomi, September 23, 1836 at Chippewaynaung, Indiana.

Jowish. Treaty with the Potawatomi, October 2, 1818 at St. Mary's, Ohio.

Juno, Josette and children. Angelique. Treaty with the Chippewa, September 26, 1833 at Chicago, Illinois.

Jutreace, Baptiste (Interpreter) Treaty with the Potawatomi, October 26, 1832 at Camp Tippecanoe, Indiana; Treaty with the Potawatomi, October 16, 1826 at Wabash, Indiana.

Kaahna. Treaty with the Kickapoo, August 30, 1819 at Ft. Harrison, Indiana.

Kachenabee. Treaty with the Potawatomi, October 26, 1832 at Camp Tippecanoe, Indiana.

Kaikawtaimon. Treaty with the Chippewa, September 26, 1833 at Chicago, Illinois.

Kain, John. Treaty with the Peoria, Etc., September 25, 1818 at Edwardsville, Illinois.

Kakautmo. Student at the Carey Mission School. Treaty with the Potawatomi, October 16, 1826 at Wabash, Indiana.

Kankawsawkaw. Treaty with the Winnebago, August 25, 1828 at Green Bay, Michigan.

Kaquitah. Treaty with the Potawatomi, October 26, 1832 at Camp Tippecanoe, Indiana.

Kasha. Treaty with the Potawatomi, October 16, 1826 at Wabash, Indiana.

Katunga or Charly. Treaty with the Eel River, Etc., August 7, 1803 at Vincennes, Indiana; Treaty with the Delaware, Etc., September 30, 1809 at Ft. Wayne, Indiana.

Kauk. Treaty with the Potawatomi, October 16, 1826 at Wabash, Indiana.

Kaukaamake. Treaty with the Potawatomi, October 16, 1826 at Wabash, Indiana.

Kaukaubesheequa. Wife of John Bt. Corbeau. Treaty with the Christian Indians, March 3, 1823 at St. Mary's, Ohio.

Kaukaukshee. Treaty with the Potawatomi, October 16, 1826 at Wabash, Indiana.

Kaureekausawkaw or White Crow. Treaty with the Winnebago, August 25, 1828 at Green Bay, Michigan.

Kaushquaw. Treaty with the Potawatomi, September 20, 1828 at St. Joseph, Michigan.

Kawaysin. Treaty with the Ottawa, August 29, 1821 at Chicago, Illinois.

Kawbsukwe. Treaty with the Chippewa, July 29, 1829 at Prairie Du Chien, Michigan.

Kawgawgayshee. Treaty with the Chippewa, July 29, 1829 at Prairie Du Chien, Michigan.

Kawk. Treaty with the Potawatomi, October 26, 1832 at Camp Tippecanoe, Indiana.

Kawkawbee. Treaty with the Potawatomi, October 27, 1832 at Camp Tippecanoe, Indiana.

Kawkawkkay. Treaty with the Potawatomi, December 16, 1834 at Potawatomi Mills, Indiana; Treaty with the Potawatomi, August 5, 1836 at Yellow River, Indiana.

Kawkawkemoke. Treaty with the Potawatomi, October 27, 1832 at Camp Tippecanoe, Indiana.

Kawkee. Treaty with the Chippewa, July 29, 1829 at Prairie Du Chien, Michigan.

Kawkmocasin. Treaty with the Potawatomi, October 27, 1832 at Camp Tippecanoe, Indiana.

Kawtenose. Treaty with the Potawatomi, September 23, 1836 at Chippewaynaung, Indiana.

Kawwesaut. Treaty with the Potawatomi, September 23, 1836 at Chippewaynaung, Indiana.

Kayneewee. Treaty with the Ottawa, August 29, 1821 at Chicago, Illinois.

Kayrahtshokaw or Clear Weather. Treaty with the Winnebago, August 25, 1828 at Green Bay, Michigan.

Kaywau. Wife to one of the signers of the treaty. Treaty with the Chippewa, July 29, 1829 at Prairie Du Chien, Michigan.

Kechemaquaw. Treaty with the Kickapoo, August 30, 1819 at Ft. Harrison, Indiana.

Kechkanhanund. Treaty with the Delawares, June 7, 1803 at Vincennes, Indiana.

Keeaisoqua. Treaty with the Potawatomi, September 20, 1828 at St. Joseph, Michigan.

Keekeeweenuska. Treaty with the Potawatomi, September 20, 1828 at St. Joseph, Michigan.

Keemawassaw or Little Chief. Treaty with the Peoria, Etc., September 25, 1818 at Edwardsville, Illinois.

Keemawraneaw or Seal. Treaty with the Peoria, Etc., September 25, 1818 at Edwardsville, Illinois.

Keenew. Treaty with the Chippewa, September 26, 1833 at Chicago, Illinois.

Keenotogo. Treaty with the Ottawa, August 29, 1821 at Chicago, Illinois.

Keeotoawbe. Treaty with the Ottawa, August 29, 1821 at Chicago, Illinois.

Keepotaw. Treaty with the Ottawa, August 29, 1821 at Chicago, Illinois.

Keesas or Sun. Treaty with the Delawares, June 7, 1803 at Vincennes, Indiana; Treaty with the Potawatomi, October 2, 1818 at St. Mary's, Ohio.

Keeshammy or Cut Off a Piece. Treaty with the Peoria, Etc., September 25, 1818 at Edwardsville, Illinois.

Keetatta. Treaty with the Kickapoo, July 30, 1819 at Edwardsville, Illinois.

Keetawkeemawwaw or Andrew. (Mitchigamia) Treaty with the Peoria, Etc., September 25, 1818 at Edwardsville, Illinois.

Keetinsa (Cahokian) Treaty with the Kaskaskia, August 13, 1803 at Vincennes, Indiana.

Keetshay. Treaty with the Kickapoo, July 30, 1819 at Edwardsville, Illinois.

Keewawnay (Band chief) Treaty with the Potawatomi, October 26, 1832 at Camp Tippecanoe, Indiana; Treaty with the Potawatomi, October 26, 1832 at Camp Tippecanoe, Indiana; Indian Place Names in Illinois by Vogel.

Kemegubee. Treaty with the Potawatomi, October 26, 1832 at Camp Tippecanoe, Indiana.

Keokuk. Autobiography of Black Hawk.

Kepeaugun. Treaty with the Potawatomi, October 16, 1826 at Wabash, Indiana.

Kercheval, Benjamin B. Indian subagent married to Eliza C., a Potawatomi. Treaty with the Chippewa, September 26, 1833 at Chicago, Illinois; Treaty with the Potawatomi, October 16, 1826 at Wabash, Indiana.

Kercheval, Eliza C. (Potawatomi) Married to Benjamin B. Kercheval. Treaty with the Potawatomi, October 16, 1826 at Wabash, Indiana.

Kercheval, George. Treaty with the Chippewa, September 26, 1833 at Chicago, Illinois.

Kercheval, Maria. Treaty with the Chippewa, September 26, 1833 at Chicago, Illinois.

Keswahbay. Treaty with the Potawatomi, October 27, 1832 at Camp Tippecanoe, Indiana.

Ketchemechinawaw. Treaty with the Ottawa, August 29, 1821 at Chicago, Illinois.

Kewahcato. Treaty with the Potawatomi, October 26, 1832 at Camp Tippecanoe, Indiana.

Kewagoushcum. Treaty with the Ottawa, August 29, 1821 at Chicago, Illinois.

Kewase. Treaty with the Chippewa, September 26, 1833 at Chicago, Illinois.

Kewaune. Treaty with the Potawatomi, October 16, 1826 at Wabash, Indiana; Treaty with the Potawatomi, September 23, 1836 at Chippewaynaung, Indiana.

Kiala (Fox chief of 1721) From Quebec to New Orleans.

Kicounaisa or Fishe (Kaskaskia chief) Void Agreement Illinois and Wabash Land Company, 1773.

Killbuck. Descendants of Capt. Charles Killbuck, a Delaware. Indian Place Names in Illinois by Vogel; Treaty with the Delawares, Etc., September 30, 1809 at Ft. Wayne, Indiana.

King, Nehemiah. Treaty with the Chippewa, September 26, 1833 at Chicago, Illinois.

Kingskedall, Jacob. Of Vincennes. Treaty with the Piankashaw, December 30, 1805 at Vincennes, Indiana.

Kinkash (Band chief) Treaty with the Potawatomi, October 26, 1832 at Camp Tippecanoe, Indiana; Treaty with the Potawatomi, October 27, 1832 at Camp Tippecanoe, Indiana; Treaty with the Potawatomi, December 16, 1834 at Potwatomi Mills, Indiana; Treaty with the Potawatomi, September 23, 1836 at Chippewaynaung, Indiana.

Kinnekose. Treaty with the Potawatomi, September 20, 1828 at St. Joseph, Michigan.

Kintner, F. R. Treaty with the Potawatomi, October 26, 1832 at Camp Tippecanoe, Indiana.

Kintner, James H. Treaty with the Potawatomi, October 26, 1832 at Camp Tippecanoe, Indiana.

Kinzie, James. Treaty with the Chippewa, September 26, 1833 at Chicago, Illinois.

Kinzie, John H. Treaty with the Chippewa, September 26, 1833 at Chicago, Illinois; Treaty with the Winnebago, August 25, 1828 at Green Bay, Michigan; Autobiography of Black Hawk.

Kinzie, Robert A. Treaty with the Chippewa, September 26, 1833 at Chicago, Illinois; Treaty with the Potawatomi, October 26, 1832 at Camp Tippecanoe, Indiana.

Kiracouria (Kaskaskia chief of 1723) From Quebec to New Orleans.

Kisirinanso (Mascouten chief of 1686) Pioneer Layman of North America by Campbell.

Klinger, Nicholas. Treaty with the Chippewa, September 26, 1833 at Chicago, Illinois.

Knaggs, George B. Treaty with the Chippewa, September 26, 1833 at Chicago, Illinois.

Knaggs, George B. Treaty with the Chippewa, September 26, 1833 at Chicago, Illinois.

Knaggs, James. Son of Chesqua who was sister to Chief Okeos of the Huron Potawatomi. Treaty with the Potawatomi, October 16, 1826 at Wabash, Indiana.

Knaggs, William G. or Waseskukson. Son of Chesqua who was sister to Chief Okeos. Treaty with the Chippewa, September 26, 1833 at Chicago, Illinois; Treaty with the Ottawa, August 29, 1821 at Chicago, Illinois.

Knoshania or the Otter. Treaty with the Kickapoo, December 9, 1809 at Ft. Wayne, Indiana.

Koankaw or Chief. Treaty with the Winnebago, August 25, 1828 at Green Bay, Michigan.

Komack. Treaty with the Potawatomi, October 27, 1832 at Camp Tippecanoe, Indiana.

Kondiaronk. Iroquois chief called the Rat of 1686. Pioneer Laymen of North America by Rev. Campbell.

Kongee. Treaty with the Ottawa, August 29, 1821 at Chicago, Illinois.

Konkapot. Student at the Carey Mission School. Treaty with the Potawatomi, October 16, 1826 at Wabash, Indiana.

Koongeepawtaw. Treaty with the Peoria, Etc., September 25, 1818 at Edwardsville, Illinois.

Kryn. The Great Mohawk of 1689 who was killed on June 4 at Salmon River. Pioneer Laymen of North America by Rev. Campbell.

Kuwawnay (Wabash Potawatomi chief) Treaty with the Potawatomi, December 16, 1834 at Potawatomi Mills, Indiana; Treaty with the Potawatomi, August 5, 1836 at Yellow River, Indiana.

La Boussier. Treaty with the Eel River, Etc., August 7, 1803 at Vincennes, Indiana.

Lacroix, Dom. Of Vincennes. Treaty with the Kickapoo, December 9, 1809 at Ft. Wayne, Indiana.

Lacy, O. P. Treaty with the Chippewa, September 26, 1833 at Chicago, Illinois.

LaFerine. Treaty with the Kickapoo, August 30, 1819 at Ft. Harrison, Indiana.

LaFramboise, Claude, Joseph, Alex, and Josette. Children of Shawwenoqua and Francoise LaFramboise, Sr. Inhabitants of Chicago, 1825-1831; Treaty with the Potawatomi, October 26, 1832 at Camp Tippecanoe, Indiana.

LaFramboise, Alexis. Children of. Treaty with the Chippewa, September 26, 1833 at Chicago, Illinois.

LaFramboise, Madaline and son. Treaty with the Chippewa, September 26, 1833 at Chicago, Illinois.

LaFramboise, Therese. Wife of Joesph Lamboise. Treaty with the Chippewa, September 26, 1833 at Chicago, Illinois; Treaty with the Potawatomi, October 26, 1832 at Camp Tippecanoe, Indiana; Treaty with the Potawatomi, November 15, 1861 at Kansas River, Kansas.

LaGrosse Téte. A Piankeshaw chief in 1789. Kaskaskia Records, 1778-1790. Va. Series Vol. II.

Laird, James. Treaty with the Chippewa, September 26, 1833 at Chicago, Illinois.

LaLime, John B. Son of Nokenoqua. Sold his cabin to John Kinzie. Treaty with the Ottawa, August 29, 1821 at Chicago, Illinois.

Lamseet, Peter. Treaty with the Chippewa, September 26, 1833 at Chicago, Illinois.

Lance. Sac chief. Autobiography of Black Hawk.

Lane, Joseph D. Treaty with the Chippewa, September 26, 1833 at Chicago, Illinois.

Laplante, Pierre. Treaty with the Kickapoo, August 30, 1819 at Ft. Harrison, Indiana.

Larose, Alexis. Treaty with the Chippewa, September 26, 1833 at Chicago, Illinois.

Lasselle, Hyacinthe. (Interpreter) Treaty with the Kickapoo, December 9, 1809 at Ft. Wayne, Indiana.

Laughton, Bernadus H. (Interpreter) Treaty with the Chippewa, September 26, 1833 at Chicago, Illinois.

Laughton, David. Husband of Waishkeshaw, a Potawatomi. Had son Joseph. Inhabitants of Chicago, 1825-1831; Treaty with the Potawatomi, October 26, 1832 at Camp Tippecanoe, Indiana; Treaty with the Chippewa, July 29, 1829 at Prairie Du Chien, Michigan.

Lawe, Therese, George, David, Rachel, Rebecca, Maria, Polly, Jane and Appotone. John. Treaty with the Chippewa, September 26, 1833 at Chicago, Illinois.

Layauvois or Laiyurva. Treaty with the Sauk & Foxes, November 3, 1804 at St. Louis, Missouri.

LeBoeuf, Louis. Called LaFlamme. Married Marie Joseph Pelletier also called Antaya at Cahokia 12 July 1791. Marriages of St. Clair Co., Ill.; Treaty with the Potawatomi, September 20, 1828 at St. Joseph, Michigan.

LeBoeuf, Pierre and Philip. Treaty with the Chippewa, September 26, 1833 at Chicago, Illinois.

LeClerc, Jean Bt. Son of Moiqua and husband to Margaret Pechequetachai. Worked for John Kinzie. Inhabitants of Chicago, 1825-1831; Treaty with the Ottawa, August 29, 1821 at Chicago, Illinois; 1790 Illinois Militia; Treaty with the Potawatomi, October 27, 1832 at Camp Tippecanoe, Indiana.

LeClerc, Fanny. A child. Treaty with the Chippewa, September 26, 1833 at Chicago, Illinois.

Leephart, Jacob. Treaty with the Chippewa, September 26, 1833 at Chicago, Illinois.

Legg, Rachel. Treaty with the Chippewa, September 26, 1833 at Chicago, Illinois.

LeGris. Chief of village of Tippecanoe. Son of LeJarret. Illinois on the Eve of the Seven Years War 1747-1755.

Lewis, Joseph B. Treaty with the Kickapoo, July 30, 1819 at Edwardsville, Illinois.

Letendre, Jean. Children of. Treaty with the Chippewa, September 26, 1833 at Chicago, Illinois.

Lisette. Former Indian girl slave of Richard McCarty. Freed before 1780. Kaskaskia Records 1778-1790. Va. Series Vol. II.

Little Eyes. Treaty with the Eel River, Etc., August 7, 1803 at Vincennes, Indiana.

Little Thunder. Treaty with the Kickapoo, July 30, 1819 at Edwardsville, Illinois.

Loranger, Joseph. Treaty with the Chippewa, September 26, 1833 at Chicago, Illinois.

Louison (Potawatomi) Treaty with the Ottawa, August 29, 1821 at Chicago, Illinois.

Macacanaw. Treaty with the Kickapoo, August 30, 1819 at Ft. Harrison, Indiana.

Macatakeshic. Treaty with the Chippewa, September 26, 1833 at Chicago, Illinois.

Macatoshic. Treaty with the Chippewa, September 26, 1833 at Chicago, Illinois.

Macatewaket. Treaty with the Kickapoo, August 30, 1819 at Ft. Harrison, Indiana.

Macatiwaaluna or Chien Noir (Piankashaw) Treaty with the Piankashaw, December 30, 1805 at Vincennes, Indiana.

Macheweskeaway. Treaty with the Ottawa, August 24, 1816 at St. Louis, Missouri.

Machina. Kickapoo chief located on Mackinaw River. Indian Place Names in Illinois, by Vogel.

Mack, Stephen, Jr. Treaty with the Chippewa, September 26, 1833 at Chicago, Illinois.

Mack, Stephen. Husband to Hononegah, a Potawatomi. Children Rosa and Mary. Mack deceased by 1833. Inhabitants of Chicago, 1825-1831; Treaty with the Chippewa, September 26, 1833 at Chicago, Illinois.

Mahcheotahway. Treaty with the Chippewa, September 26, 1833 at Chicago, Illinois.

Mahgoque. Child of. Treaty with the Chippewa, September 26, 1833 at Chicago, Illinois.

Mahkattamawweeyaw or Black Wolf (Tamaroi) Treaty with the Peoria, Etc., September 25, 1818 at Edwardsville, Illinois.

Makouandeby. Illinois chief of the early 18th c. Indian Place Names in Illinois, by Vogel.

Mamantouensa. Chief of the Kaskaskias, 1730's. From Quebec to New Orleans.

Mamentoriensa. Kaskaskia chief of 1723. From Quebec to New Orleans.

Mandawmin. Treaty with the Ottawa, August 29, 1821 at Chicago, Illinois.

Mangesett or Big Foot. Treaty with the Chippewa, September 26, 1833 at Chicago, Illinois.

Manggonssaw (Mitchigamia) Treaty with the Peoria, Etc., September 25, 1818 at Edwardsville, Illinois.

Manitoo. Potawatomi chief of early 19th c. Indian Place Names in Illinois, by Vogel.

Mann, John. Husband to daughter of Antoine Ouimette. Possibly name was Lezett. Treaty with the Chippewa, September 26, 1833 at Chicago, Illinois.

Mann, Mrs. Daughter and grandchildren of Antoine Ouilmet. Treaty with the Chippewa, September 26, 1833 at Chicago, Illinois.

Markle, William. Treaty with the Kickapoo, August 30, 1819 at Ft. Harrison, Illinois.

Marquis, William. Treaty with the Chippewa, September 26, 1833 at Chicago, Illinois.

Marsh, Lowrin. Treaty with the Chippewa, September 26, 1833 at Chicago, Illinois.

Mason, James. Treaty with the Peoria, Etc., September 25, 1818 at Edwardsville, Illinois.

Masquat. Treaty with the Chippewa, September 26, 1833 at Chicago, Illinois.

Matatah. Potawatomi brave under Black Hawk. Autobiography of Black Hawk.

Matchapaggish. Potawatomi. Treaty with the Ottawa, August 29, 1821 at Chicago, Illinois.

Matchaweeyaas. Potawatomi. Treaty with the Ottawa, August 29, 1821 at Chicago, Illinois.

Matchepeenachewish. Treaty with the Ottawa, August 29, 1821 at Chicago, Illinois.

Mattatas. Sac chief. Autobiography of Black Hawk.

Mauksee. Treaty with the Ottawa, August 29, 1821 at Chicago, Illinois.

Maughquayah or John Baptist. Kaskaskia chief. Void Agreement Illinois and Wabash Land Company, 1773.

Maughquinthepe or Black Dog. Peoriah chief. Void Agreement Illinois and Wabash Land Company, 1773.

Mawntoho. Treaty with the Kickapoo, July 30, 1819 at Edwardsville, Illinois.

Mawressaw or Knife. Peoria of late 18th C. Indian Place Names in Illinois by Vogel; Treaty with the Peoria, Etc. September 25, 1818 at Edwardsville, Illinois.

Mawteno. Daughter of Francois Bourbonnais, Jr. Treaty with the Potawatomi, October 26, 1832 at Camp Tippecanoe, Indiana.

May, Margaret. Treaty with the Chippewa, September 26, 1833 at Chicago, Illinois.

Mayee, John Baptiste. Delivered message to President George Washington, 1793. Messages and Papers of the Presidents.

Maysheeweerattaw or Big Horn. Cahokia. Treaty with the Peoria, Etc., September 25, 1818 at Edwardsville, Illinois.

Maytenway. Potawatomi. Treaty with the Ottawa, August 29, 1821 at Chicago, Illinois.

Meamese. Treaty of the Chippewa, September 26, 1833 at Chicago, Illinois.

Mechinquamesha. Sister to Jacco. Treaty with the Wea, October 2, 1818 at St. Mary's, Ohio.

Meegwun. Potawatomi. Treaty with the Ottawa, August 29, 1821 at Chicago, Illinois.

Meekasaw. Treaty with the Kickapoo, July 30, 1819 at Edwardsville, Illinois.

Meeksaymank. Student at Carey Mission School 1826. Treaty with the Ottawat, August 29, 1821 at Chicago, Illinois; Treaty with the Chippewa, July 29, 1829 at Prairie Du Chien, Michigan; Treaty with the Potawatomi, October 16, 1826 at Wabash, Indiana.

Meeteay. Potawatomi. Treaty with the Ottawa, August 29, 1821 at Chicago, Illinois.

Meggesseese. Potawatomi. Treaty with the Ottawa, August 29, 1821 at Chicago, Illinois.

Meiaskwat, Charles. Algonquin chief of 1640's. Pioneer Priests of North America, 1642-1710 by Campbell.

Meinquipaumiah or Leg and Thigh. Cahoquia chief. Void Agreement Illinois and Wabash Land Company, 1773.

Menard, Pierre, Jr. Treaty with the Chippewa, September 26, 1833 at Chicago, Illinois.

Menard, Peter Maumee. Treaty with the Chippewa, September 26, 1833 at Chicago, Illinois.

Menawche. A Potawatomi woman. Treaty with the Ottawa, August 29, 1821 at Chicago, Illinois.

Menukquet. Treaty with the Chippewa, September 26, 1833 at Chicago, Illinois.

Merrick, Tellery. Treaty with the Kickapoo, July 30, 1819 at Edwardsville, Illinois.

Meseekunnoghquoh or Little Turtle. Miami. Treaty with the Delawares, June 7, 1803 at Vincennes, Indiana; Treaty with the Delawares, Etc., September 30, 1809 at Ft. Wayne, Indiana.

Meshimenah. Treaty with the Chippewa, September 26, 1833 at Chicago, Illinois.

Messheketennow. Potawatomi. Treaty with the Ottawa, August 29, 1821 at Chicago, Illinois.

Mestigoit. Algonquin who aided Paul Le Jeune around 1633. Pioneer Priests of North America, 1642-1710 by Campbell.

Methawnasice. Shawnee. Treaty with the Delawares, June 7, 1803 at Vincennes, Indiana.

Mettaywaw. Chippewa. Treaty with the Ottawa, August 29, 1821 at Chicago, Illinois; Treaty with the Chippewa, September 26, 1833 at Chicago, Illinois.

Mette, Jacque. Treaty with the Chippewa, September 26, 1833 at Chicago, Illinois.

Michel. Treaty with the Ottawa, August 29, 1821 at Chicago, Illinois; Treaty with the Chippewa, July 29, 1829 at Prairie Du Chien, Michigan.

Michel. Kaskaskia chief of 1723. From Quebec to New Orleans.

Micolas or Nicholas. Treaty with the Kaskaskia, August 13, 1803 at Vincennes, Indiana.

Mieure, William. Treaty with the Chippewa, September 26, 1833 at Chicago, Illinois.

Miles, George, Jr. Treaty with the Ottawa, August 29, 1821 at Chicago, Illinois.

Miller, Samuel. Treaty with the Chippewa, September 26, 1833 at Chicago, Illinois; Treaty with the Potawatomi, October 26, 1832 at Camp Tippecanoe, Indiana.

Minedemoeyah. Wife to Pierre Duverney. Had children. Treaty with the Chippewa, September 26, 1833 at Chicago, Illinois.

Minie, Charles. Husband to Mechehee. Treaty with the Chippewa, September 26, 1833 at Chicago, Illinois.

Minie, Francis. Treaty with the Chippewa, September 26, 1833 at Chicago, Illinois.

Miranda, Jane. Treaty with the Chippewa, July 29, 1829 at Prairie Du Chien, Michigan.

Miranda, Jean Bt., Rosetta, Thomas. Children of Joseph Miranda, deceased. Treaty with the Chippewa, September 26, 1833 at Chicago, Illinois.

Misquabonoquah. Treaty with the Chippewa, September 26, 1833 at Chicago, Illinois.

Mixemaung. Treaty with the Potawatomi, October 26, 1832 at Camp Tippecanoe, Indiana; Treaty with the Chippewa, September 26, 1833 at Chicago, Illinois.

Moahway. Treaty with the Chippewa, July 29, 1829 at Prairie Du Chien, Michigan; Treaty with the Chippewa, September 26, 1833 at Chicago, Illinois.

Moaputto. Treaty with the Ottawa, August 29, 1821 at Chicago, Illinois.

Mogawgo. Treaty with the Delawares, Etc., September 30, 1809 at Ft. Wayne, Indiana.

Mongaw. Treaty with the Ottawa, August 29, 1821 at Chicago, Illinois.

Monguago. Treaty with the Ottawa, August 29, 1821 at Chicago, Illinois.

Montgomer, R. Treaty with the Ottawa, August 29, 1821 at Chicago, Illinois.

Montouish. Treaty with the Chippewa, September 26, 1833 at Chicago, Illinois.

Mooyawkacke or Mercier. Cahokia. Treaty with the Peoria, Etc., September 25, 1818 at Edwardsville, Illinois.

Moquiah or the Bear Skin. Treaty with the Kickapoo, December 9, 1809 at Ft. Wayne, Indiana.

Moreau, Joseph. Treaty with the Chippewa, September 26, 1833 at Chicago, Illinois.

Mosser. Potawatomi. Treaty with the Delawares, Etc., September 30, 1809 at Ft. Wayne, Indiana.

Mothe, Le. Menominee chief. Illinois on the Eve of the Seven Years War, 1747-1755.

Mouton, Francis. Treaty with the Chippewa, September 26, 1833 at Chicago, Illinois.

Mowais or Little Wolf. Treaty with the Ottawa, August 24, 1816 at St. Louis, Mo.

Mucketepennese or Black Bird. Treaty with the Ottawa, August 24, 1816 at St. Louis, Mo.

Muller, Alexander, Paschal, Margaret and Socra. Children. Treaty with the Chippewa, September 26, 1833 at Chicago, Illinois.

McCarty, Jona. Treaty with the Chippewa, September 26, 1833 at Chicago, Illinois.

McCullough, Solomon. Treaty with the Chippewa, September 26, 1833 at Chicago, Illinois.

McKee, David. Treaty with the Chippewa, September 26, 1833 at Chicago, Illinois.

McKee, John. Treaty with the Peoria, Etc., September 25, 1818 at Edwardsville, Illinois.

McKee, William P. Treaty with the Peoria, Etc., September 25, 1818 at Edwardsville, Illinois; Treaty with the Kickapoo, July 30, 1819 at Edwardsville, Illinois.

McKenzie, Catherine. Deceased. Treaty with the Chippewa, September 26, 1833 at Chicago, Illinois.

McMillan, Franklin. Treaty with the Chippewa, September 26, 1833 at Chicago, Illinois.

Nahbwait. Treaty with the Chippewa, September 26, 1833 at Chicago, Illinois.

Nahchewah. Treaty with the Chippewa, September 26, 1833 at Chicago, Illinois.

Nahchewine. Treaty with the Chippewa, September 26, 1833 at Chicago, Illinois.

Namah or Sturgeon. Sac chief. Autobiography of Black Hawk.

Namequa. Daughter of Black Hawk. Indian Place Names in Illinois by Vogel.

Namash. Treaty with the Chippewa, September 26, 1833 at Chicago, Illinois.

Namatawayshuc. Treaty with the Chippewa, September 26, 1833 at Chicago, Illinois.

Namattsheekeeaw. Treaty with the Kickapoo, July 30, 1819 at Edwardsville, Illinois.

Nanamakee or Thunder. Black Hawk's ancestor. Autobiography of Black Hawk.

Nangesay or Stout. Treaty with the Ottawa, August 24, 1816 at St. Louis, Mo.

Nanousekah. Son of Penamo. Treaty with the Delawares, Etc., September 30, 1809 at Ft. Wayne, Indiana; Treaty with the Potawatomi, October 2, 1818 at St. Mary's, Ohio.

Naper, Joseph. Treaty with the Chippewa, September 26, 1833 at Chicago, Illinois.

Nash, Isaac. Treaty with the Chippewa, September 26, 1833 at Chicago, Illinois.

Navarre, Perre F. Husband to Keshewaquay. Treaty with the Chippewa, September 26, 1833 at Chicago, Illinois; Treaty with the Potawatomi, September 20, 1828 at St. Joseph, Michigan.

Nawbaycaw. Treaty with the Chippewa, September 26, 1833 at Chicago, Illinois.

Naynawwitwaw or Sentinel. Treaty with the Peoria, Etc., September 25, 1818 at Edwardsville, Illinois.

Nayosay. Treaty with the Chippewa, September 26, 1833 at Chicago, Illinois.

Nayoucheemon. Potawatomi. Treaty with the Ottawa, August 29, 1821 at Chicago, Illinois.

Neahmemsieeh. Treaty with the Delawares, June 7, 1803 at Vincennes, Indiana.

Neapope. Sac chief. Autobiography of Black Hawk.

Nebaynocscum. Treaty with the Chippewa, September 26, 1833 at Chicago, Illinois.

Neekawnakoa. Treaty with the Kickapoo, July 30, 1819 at Edwardsville, Illinois.

Negabamat. Algonquin chief of 1640's. Pioneer Priests of North America, 1642-1710 by Campbell.

Neggeneshkek. Treaty with the Potawatomi, July 18, 1815 at St. Louis, Mo.

Nehmehtohah or Standing. Treaty with the Delawares, June 7, 1803 at Vincennes, Indiana.

Nekawnoshkee. Treaty with the Chippewa, September 26, 1833 at Chicago, Illinois.

Neseewawbeetuck. Treaty with the Chippewa, September 26, 1833 at Chicago, Illinois.

Newman, Joseph. Treaty with the Kickapoo, July 30, 1819 at Edwardsville, Illinois.

Nigigwash. Treaty with the Ottawa, August 24, 1816 at St. Louis, Missouri.

Nisnoansee. A child. Treaty with the Chippewa, September 26, 1833 at Chicago, Illinois.

Noel. Algonquin of 1650's. Pioneer Priests of North America, 1642-1710 by Campbell.

Nobel, John and Mark. Treaty with the Chippewa, September 26, 1833 at Chicago, Illinois.

Noire, La Mouche. Piankashaw chief. Illinois on the Eve of the Seven Years War, 1747-1755.

Nokawjegaun. Treaty with the Ottawa, August 29, 1821 at Chicago, Illinois.

Nomite. Sac chief. Autobiography of Black Hawk.

Nonee. Treaty with the Chippewa, September 26, 1833 at Chicago, Illinois; Treaty with the Potawatomi, October 16, 1826 at Wabash, Indiana.

Nonoah or Child at the Breast. Treaty with the Kickapoo, December 9, 1809 at Ft. Wayne, Indiana.

Noshaywequat. Treaty with the Ottawa, August 29, 1821 at Chicago, Illinois.

Nsawwayquet. Treaty with the Chippewa, September 26, 1833 at Chicago, Illinois.

Obwaquaunk. Treaty with the Chippewa, September 26, 1833 at Chicago, Illinois.

Ocheepwaise. Treaty with the Chippewa, September 26, 1833 at Chicago, Illinois.

Ocksinga. Mitchigamian. Treaty with the Kaskaskia, August 13, 1803 at Vincennes, Indiana.

Ogee, Joseph. French-Winnebago married to Madeline, a Potawatomi. Treaty with the Chippewa, September 26, 1833 at Chicago, Illinois; Inhabitants of Chicago, 1825-1831; Treaty with the Winnebago, August 25, 1828 at Green Bay, Michigan.

O'keemase. Treaty with the Chippewa, September 26, 1833 at Chicago, Illinois; Treaty with the Potawatomi, September 23, 1836 at Chippewaynaung, Indiana.

O'kemahwahbasee. Treaty with the Chippewa, September 26, 1833 at Chicago, Illinois.

Onchequaka. Sac chief. Autobiography of Black Hawk.

Ongles, Les Grands. Chief of Wea and brother to Le Jarret. Illinois on the Eve of the Seven Years War, 1747-1755.

Onuckkemeck. Potawatomi. Treaty with the Ottawa, August 29, 1821 at Chicago, Illinois.

Opaho. Treaty with the Ottawa, August 24, 1816 at St. Louis, Missouri.

Osseemeet. Potawatomi. Treaty with the Ottawa, August 29, 1821 at Chicago, Illinois.

Ossmeet. Brother to Five Medals. Treaty with the Delawares, Etc., September 30, 1809 at Ft. Wayne, Indiana.

Ottawonce. Treaty with the Ottawa, August 24, 1816 at St. Louis, Missouri.

Ouilmett, Antoine. Husband to Archangel, a Potawatomi. Had children Copah, Elizabeth or Lezett, Louis, and Mitchel. Lezett, Louis and Mitchel students at Carey Mission School in 1826. Inhabitants of Chicago, 1825-1831; Treaty with the Chippewa, September 26, 1833 at Chicago, Illinois; Treaty with the Potawatomi, October 16, 1826 at Wabash, Indiana.

Outawa. Treaty with the Potawatomi, July 18, 1815 at St. Louis, Missouri; Treaty with the Ottawa, August 24, 1816 at St. Louis, Missouri.

Outchequaka or Sunfish. Treaty with the Sauk and Foxes, November 3, 1804 at St. Louis, Missouri.

Owl. Miami. Treaty with the Delawares, Etc., September 30, 1809 at Ft. Wayne, Indiana.

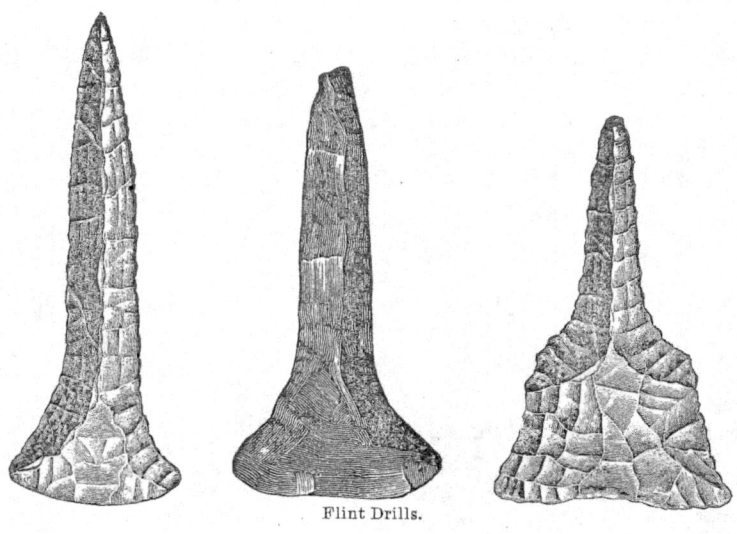

Flint Drills.

Pacakinqua. Treaty with the Kickapoo, August 30, 1819 at Fort Harrison, Indiana.

Pacan. Treaty with the Kickapoo, July 30, 1819 at Edwardsville, Illinois.

Page´, Francois. Treaty with the Chippewa, etc., September 26, 1833 at Chicago, Illinois.

Pa-mob-a-mee. Treaty with the Chippewa, etc., September 26, 1833 at Chicago, Illinois.

Papenegeesawwaw. Treaty with the Peoria, etc., September 25, 1818 at Edwardsville, Illinois.

Parker, Payne C. Treaty with the Chippewa, etc., September 26, 1833 at Chicago, Illinois.

Pasheeto. Treaty with the Kickapoo, July 30, 1819 at Edwardsville, Illinois.

Pashepaho or the Giger. Sac chief. Treaty with the Sauk and Foxes, November 3, 1804 at St. Louis, Missouri. Antoine LeClair´s biography of Black Hawk.

Pashsheweha or cat. Treaty with the Delaware, etc., June 7, 1803 at Vincennes, Indiana.

Pat-e-go-shue. Treaty with the Potawatomi, October 26, 1832 at Camp Tippecanoe, Indiana. Treaty with the Chippewa, etc., September 26, 1833 at Chicago, Illinois.

Paukahummawa or Sun. Sac chief. Antoine LeClair´s biography of Black hawk.

Pauquia or Montour. Treaty with the Piankashaw, December 30, 1805 at Vincennes, Indiana.

Pawkonasheeno. Treaty with the Kickapoo, July 30, 1819 at Edwardsville, Illinois.

Pay-maw-sue. Treaty with the Chippewa, etc., September 26, 1833 at Chicago, Illinois.

Pe-te-no-on. Treaty with the Potawatomi, October 27, 1832 at Tippecanoe, Indiana.

Pe-an-nish. Treaty with the Ottawa, etc., August 29, 1821 at Chicago, Illinois.

Peckoneca. Treaty with the Kickapoo, July 30, 1819 at Edwardsville, Illinois.

Pedagogue. Treaty with the Eel River, etc., August 7, 1803 at Vincennes, Indiana.

Pee-chee-co. Treaty with the Ottawa, etc., August 29, 1821 at Chicago, Illinois.

Peeples, Thornton. Treaty with the Kickapoo, August 30, 1819 at Edwardsville, Illinois.

Pelecheah. Treaty with the Kickapoo, August 30, 1819 at Fort Harrison, Indiana.

Peltier, Antoine. Treaty with the Chippewa, etc., September 26, 1833 at Chicago, Illinois.

Peltier, Charles, deceased. Treaty with the Chippewa, etc., September 26, 1833 at Chicago, Illinois.

Pemasaw or Walker. Treaty with the Ottawa, etc., August 24, 1816 at St. Louis, Missouri.

Pemmeekawwattaw or Henry. Treaty with the Peoria, etc., September 25, 1818 at Edwardsville, Illinois.

Pemoatam. Treaty with the Kickapoo, July 30, 1819 at Edwardsville, Illinois.

Pe-nay-o-cat. Treaty with the Chippewa, etc., September 26, 1833 at Chicago, Illinois.

Pequiah. Treaty with the Wea, October 2, 1818 at St. Mary's, Ohio.

Perry, Elbert. Treaty with the Kickapoo, July 30, 1819 at Edwardsville, Illinois.

Pe-she-ka. Treaty with the Chippewa, etc., September 26, 1833 at Chicago, Illinois.

Petchekekapon. Treaty with the Delawares, etc., September 30, 1809 at Fort Wayne, Indiana.

Petshekosheek. Treaty with the Kickapoo, July 30, 1819 at Edwardsville, Illinois.

Phelps, T.E. Treaty with the Chippewa, etc., September 26, 1833 at Chicago, Illinois.

Pierre, an Algonquin. Interpreter of 1632. Had been schooled in France.

Pish-she-baw-gay. Treaty with the Ottawa, etc., August 29, 1821 at Chicago, Illinois.

Platter, Jacob. Treaty with the Chippewa, etc., September 26, 1833 at Chicago, Illinois.

Polier, Agate. Treaty with the Chippewa, etc., September 26, 1833 at Chicago, Illinois.

Pomeroy, George. Treaty with the Chippewa, etc., September 26, 1833 at Chicago, Illinois.

Porter, Andrew. Treaty with the Chippewa, etc., September 26, 1833 at Chicago, Illinois.

Porter, Samuel Humes. Treaty with the Chippewa, etc., September 26, 1833 at Chicago, Illinois.

Porthier, Joseph. Treaty with the Chippewa, etc., September 26, 1833 at Chicago, Illinois.

Prickett, Abraham. Treaty with the Peoria, etc., September 25, 1818 at Edwardsville, Illinois.

Prickett, Jacob. Treaty with the Peoria, etc., September 25, 1818 at Edwardsville, Illinois. Treaty with the Kickapoo, August 30, 1819 at Fort Harrison, Indiana.

Princesse de Missouris. Visited Paris in 1725 and later married ? Dubois. Lived at Kaskaskia, Illinois.

Pug-gay-gaus. Treaty with the Ottawa, etc., August 29, 1821 at Chicago, Illinois.

Pugh, Jona H. Treaty with the Kickapoo, July 30, 1819 at Edwardsville, Illinois.

Puk-quech-a-min-nee. Treaty with the Chippewa, etc., September 26, 1833 at Chicago, Illinois.

Puk-won. Treaty with the Chippewa, etc., September 26, 1833 at Chicago, Illinois.

Pulliam, R. Treaty with the Peoria, etc., September 25, 1818 at Edwardsville, Illinois.

Puppequor or Gun. Treaty with the Eel River, August 7, 1803 at Vincennes, Indiana.

Pyesa. Black Hawk's father. Antoine LeClair's biography of Blawk Hawk.

Quah-quah-tah. Treaty with the Chippewa, etc., September 26, 1833 at Chicago, Illinois.

Quashquame or Jumping Fish. Treaty with the Sauk and Foxes, November 3, 1804 at St. Louis, Missouri. Antoine LeClair's biography of Black Hawk.

Quay-guee. Treaty with the Ottawa, etc., August 29, 1821 at Chicago, Illinois.

Queckkawpeetaw or Round Seat. Treaty with the Peoria, etc., September 25, 1818 at Edwardsville, Illinois.

Quema or Young Man. Treaty with the Wea, October 2, 1818 at St. Mary's, Ohio.

Quick, Thomas P. Treaty with the Chippewa, etc., September 26, 1833 at Chicago, Illinois.

Quoi-quoi-taw. Treaty with the Ottawa, etc., August 29, 1821 at Chicago, Illinois.

Randle, Edmund. Treaty with the Peoria, etc., Sept. 25, 1818 at Edwardsville. Treaty with the Kickapoo, July 30, 1819 at Edwardsville, Illinois.

Randle, John H. Treaty with the Peoria, etc., September 25, 1818 at Edwardsville, Illinois.

Randle, Josias. Treaty with the Peoria, etc., September 25, 1818 at Edwardsville, Illinois.

Rawmissawnoa or Wind. Treaty with the Peoria, etc., September 25, 1818 at Edwardsville, Illinois.

Read, Ebenezer. Treaty with the Chippewa, etc., September 26, 1833 at Chicago, Illinois.

Reed, Charles. Treaty with the Chippewa, etc., September 26, 1833 at Chicago, Illinois.

Reed, Henry Ossum. Treaty with the Chippewa, etc., September 26, 1833 at Chicago, Illinois.

Remington, Joseph. Treaty with the Kickapoo, July 30, 1819 at Edwardsville, Illinois.

Renard, Joe or Nemahson or A Man on his Feet. Treaty with the Kickapoo, December 9, 1809 at Fort Wayne, Indiana.

Rice, Ica. Treaty with the Potawatomi, October 27, 1832 at Tippecanoe, Indiana. Treaty with the Chippewa, etc., September 26, 1833 at Chicago, Illinois.

Rice, Moses. Treaty with the Potawatomi, October 26, 1832 at Tippecanoe, Indiana. Treaty with the Chippewa, etc., September 26, 1833 at Chicago, Illinois.

Richardson, Samuel L. Treaty with the Kickapoo, August 30, 1819 at Fort Harrison, Indiana.

Richeikeming. Treaty with the Ottawa, etc., August 24, 1816 at St. Louis, Missouri.

Richewille. Treaty with the Delawares, etc., June 7, 1803 at Vincennes, Indiana.

Roach, David. Treaty with the Kickapoo, July 30, 1819 at Edwardsville, Illinois.

Roberts, Edmund. Treaty with the Chippewa, etc., September 26, 1833 at Chicago, Illinois.

Roland, John. Treaty with the Ottawa, etc. August 24, 1816 at St. Louis, Missouri.

Rouensa. Kaskaskia chief of the 1680´s.

Rousseau, Dominique. Treaty with the Chippewa, etc., September 26, 1833 at Chicago, Illinois.

Saconquaneva or Tired Legs. Treaty with the Eel River, etc., August 7, 1803 at Vincennes, Indiana.

Sackanackshut. Treaty with the Delawares, etc., September 30, 1809 at Fort Wayne, Indiana.

Sanatuwa. Potawatomi chief. Antoine LeClair´s biography of Black Hawk.

Sauk-ee. Treaty with the Chippewa, etc., September 26, 1833 at Chicago, Illinois.

Sau-sau-quas-see. Treaty with the Chippewa, etc., September 26, 1833 at Chicago, Illinois.

Sawkeema. Treaty with the Kickapoo, July 30, 1819 at Edwardsville, Illinois.

Saw-ko-nosh. Treaty with the Chippewa, etc., September 26, 1833 at Chicago, Illinois.

Saw-o-tup. Treaty with the Chippewa, etc., September 26, 1833 at Chicago, Illinois.

Say-gaw-koo-nuck. Treaty with the Ottawa, etc., August 29, 1821 at Chicago, Illinois.

Schwarz, John E. Treaty with the Chippewa, etc., September 26, 1833 at Chicago, Illinois.

Sen-e-bau-um. Treaty with the Chippewa, etc., September 26, 1833 at Chicago, Illinois.

Ses-cobe-mesh. Treaty with the Ottawa, etc., August 29, 1821 at Chicago, Illinois.

Sesibahoura. Algonquin chief of 1660´s.

Shaauquebe. Treaty with the Pottawatomi, October 16, 1826 at Wabash, Indiana.

Shab-eh-nay. Village chief new Paw-Paw Grove. Treaty with the Pottawatomi, October 26, 1832 at Camp Tippecanoe, Indiana. Treaty with the Chippewa, etc., July 29, 1829 at Prairie du Chien, Michigan. Treaty with the Chippewa, etc., September 26, 1833 at Chicago, Illinois.

Shab-y-a-tuk. Treaty with the Chippewa, etc., September 26, 1833 at Chicago, Illinois.

Shamana. Treaty with the Wea, Octoear 2, 1818 at St. Mary´s, Ohio.

Shan-na-nees. Treaty with the Chippewa, etc., September 26, 1833 at Chicago, Illinois.

Shaw, John. Treaty with the Delawares, etc., September 1809 at Fort Wayne, Indiana.

Shawanoe. Treaty with the Ottawa, etc., August 24, 1816 at St. Louis, Missouri. Treaty with the Potawatomi, Octobear 2, 1818 at St. Mary´s, Ohio.

Shawapenomo. Treaty with the Delawares, etc., September 30, 1809 at Fort Wayne, Indiana.

Shaw-ko-to. Treaty with the Ottawa, etc., August 29, 1821 at Chicago, Illinois.

Shaw-wah-nuk-wuk. Treaty with the Pottawatomi, October 27, 1832 at Tippecanoe, Indiana. Treaty with the Chippewa, etc., September 26, 1833 at Chicago, Illinois.

Shaw-waw-nas-see. Treaty with the Ottawa, etc., August 29, 1821 at Chicago, Illinois. Treaty with the Potawatomi, October 26, 1832 at Camp Tippecanoe, Indiana. Treaty with the Chippewa, etc., September 26, 1833 at Chicago, Illinois.

Shaw-way-no. Treaty with the Ottawa, etc., August 29, 1821 at Chicago, Illinois.

Shaw-we-mon-e-tay. Treaty with the Chippewa, etc., September 26, 1833 at Chicago, Illinois.

Shaw-wen-ne-me-tay. Treaty with the Ottawa, etc., August 29, 1821 at Chicago, Illinois.

Shay-auk-ke-bee. Treaty with the Ottawa, etc., August 29, 1821 at Chicago, Illinois.

Shay-tee. Treaty with the Pottawatomi, October 26, 1832 at Camp Tippecanoe, Indiana. Treaty with the Chippewa, etc., September 26, 1833 at Chicago, Illinois.

Shee-shaw-gan. Treaty with the Ottawa, etc., August 29, 1821 at Chicago, Illinois.

Shekoan. Treaty with the Kickapoo, July 30, 1819 at Edwardsville, Illinois.

Shellhouse, Lorance. Treaty with the Chippewa, etc., September 26, 1833 at Chicago, Illinois.

Shellhouse, Martin G. Treaty with the Chippewa, etc., September 26, 1833 at Chicago, Illinois.

She-mah-gah. Treaty with the Chippewa, etc., September 26, 1833 at Chicago, Illinois.

Sherman, Benjamin. Treaty with the Chippewa, etc., September 26, 1833 at Chicago, Illinois.

Sheshangomequah or Swallow. Treaty with the Delawares, etc., September 30, 1809 at Fort Wayne, Indiana.

Sheshebungge. Treaty with the Ottawa, etc., August 24, 1816 at St. Louis, Missouri.

Shim-e-nah. Treaty with the Chippewa, etc., September 26, 1833 at Chicago, Illinois.

Shinn, John Jr. Treaty with the Chippewa, etc., September 26, 1833 at Chicago, Illinois.

Shirley, James. Treaty with the Chippewa, etc., September 26, 1833 at Chicago, Illinois.

Shissahecon, brother to Tuthinipee. Treaty with the Delawares, etc., September 30, 1809 at Fort Wayne, Indiana.

Sho-bon-ier. Treaty with the Pottawatomi, October 26, 1832 at Camp Tippecanoe, Indiana. Treaty with the Chippewa, etc., September 26, 1833 at Chicago, Illinois.

Sho-mang. Treaty with the Ottawa, etc., August 29, 1821 at Chicago, Illinois.

Sho-min Jr. Treaty with the Chippewa, etc., September 26, 1833 at Chicago, Illinois.

Sho-min. Treaty with the Potawatomi, October 26, 1832 at Camp Tippecanoe, Indiana. Treaty with the Chippewa, etc., September 26, 1833 at Chicago, Illinois.

Shopinnaw or Pint. Treaty with the Peoria, etc., September 25, 1818 at Edwardsville, Illinois.

Silver Heels. Treaty with the Delawares, etc., September 30, 1809 at Fort Wayne, Indiana.

Sinnowchewone. Treaty with the Ottawa, etc., August 24, 1816 at St. Louis, Missouri.

Smith, Charles. Of Vincennes. Treaty with the Kickapoo, December 9, 1809 at Fort Wayne, Indiana.

Smith, Dan D. Treaty with the Kickapoo, July 30, 1819 at Edwardsville, Illinois.

Smith, Jeduthan. Treaty with the Chippewa, etc., September 26, 1833 at Chicago, Illinois.

Spanquissee. Treaty with the Ottawa, etc., August 24, 1816 at St. Louis, Missouri.

Squah-ke-zic. Treaty with the Chippewa, etc., September 26, 1833 at Chicago, Illinois.

Stephenson, B. Treaty with the Peoria, etc., September 25, 1818 at Edwardsville, Illinois.

Stewart, Catherine. Treaty with the Chippewa, etc., September 26, 1833 at Chicago, Illinois.

Stillman, Henry B. Treaty with the Chippewa, etc., September 26, 1833 at Chicago, Illinois.

Stuart, Robert. Treaty with the Chippewa, etc., September 26, 1833 at Chicago, Illinois.

Sunawchewome. Treaty with the Potawatomi, July 18, 1815 at St. Louis, Missouri.

Swettland, William. Treaty with the Peoria, etc., September 25, 1818 at Edwardsville, Illinois.

Ta-cau-ko. Treaty with the Chippewa, etc., September 26, 1833 at Chicago, Illinois.

Takaonenee. Treaty with the Ottawa, etc., August 24, 1816 at St. Louis, Missouri.

Tatapucky. Potawatomi chief. Antoine LeClair's biography of Black Hawk.

Tawwaning or Trader. Treaty with the Ottawa, etc., August 24, 1816 at St. Louis, Missouri.

Taylor, Charles. Treaty with the Chippewa, etc., September 26, 1833 at Chicago, Illinois.

Tecko. Treaty with the Kickapoo, July 30, 1819 at Edwardsville, Illinois.

Tecumcena. Treaty with the Kickapoo, August 30, 1819 at Fort Harrison, Indiana.

Tecumseh. Antoine LeClair's biography of Black Hawk.

Ten Eyck, Conrad. Treaty with the Ottawa, etc., August 29, 1821 at Chicago, Illinois.

Teta Buxike. Treaty with the Delawares, etc., June 7, 1803 at Vincennes, Indiana.

Tharp, John. Treaty with the Chippewa, etc., September 26, 1833 at Chicago, Illinois.

Thebault, Joseph. Treaty with the Chippewa, etc., September 26, 1833 at Chicago, Illinois.

Thompson, Squire. Treaty with the Chippewa, etc., September 26, 1833 at Chicago, Illinois. Treaty with the Pottawatomi, October 27, 1832 at Tippecanoe, Indiana.

Thompson, William. Married a Potawatomi in Tazewell Co., Illinois.

Tivet. Kaskaskia chief of 1698.

To-to-me. Treaty with the Ottawa, etc., August 29, 1821 at Chicago, Illinois.

Tremble, Marie. Treaty with the Chippewa, etc., September 26, 1833 at Chicago, Illinois.

Trowbridge, C. C. Treaty with the Chippewa, etc., September 26, 1833 at Chicago, Illinois.

Tshee-tshee-chin-be-quay. Treaty with the Chippewa, etc., September 26, 1833 at Chicago, Illinois.

Tsonnontouan. Seneca chief of 1678.

Turner, James C. Treaty with the Kickapoo, August 30, 1819 at Fort Harrison, Indiana.

Tuthinipee. Treaty with the Delawares, etc., June 7, 1803 at Vincennes, Indiana. Treaty with the Potawatomi, October 2, 1818 at St. Mary's, Ohio.

Vasseur, Noel. Treaty with the Potawatomi, October 26, 1832 at Camp Tippecanoe, Indiana. Treaty with the Chippewa, etc., September 26, 1833 at Chicago, Illinois.

Vieux, Jacques. Treaty with the Chippewa, etc., September 26, 1833 at Chicago, Illinois.

Vigo. Treaty with the Sauk and Foxes, November 3, 1804 at St. Louis, Missouri.

Visget, Jacob. Treaty with the Ottawa, etc., August 29, 1821 at Chicago, Illinois.

Wabakinklelia or Gros Bled. Treaty with the Piankashaw, December 30, 1805 at Vincennes, Indiana.

Wa-baw-nee-she. Treaty with the Ottawa, etc., August 29, 1821 at Chicago, Illinois.

Wa-be-no-say. Treaty with the Chippewa, etc., September 26, 1833 at Chicago, Illinois.

Wackshinggaw or Crooked Moon. Treaty with the Peoria, etc., September 25, 1818 at Edwardsville, Illinois.

Wacome. Sauk chief. Antoine LeClair's biography of Black Hawk.

Wagohaw. Treaty with the Kickapoo, August 30, 1819 at Fort Harrison, Indiana.

Wah-be-kai. Treaty with the Chippewa, etc., September 26, 1833 at Chicago, Illinois.

Wah-be-me-mee. Treaty with the Chippewa, etc., September 26, 1833 at Chicago, Illinois.

Wah-bou-seh. Treaty with the Chippewa, etc., September 26, 1833 at Chicago, Illinois.

Wah-mix-i-co. Treaty with the Chippewa, etc., September 26, 1833 at Chicago, Illinois.

Wah-sus-kuk. Treaty with the Chippewa, etc., September 26, 1833 at Chicago, Illinois.

Wai-saw-o-ke-ah-ne-aw. Treaty with the Potawatomi, October 26, 1832 at Camp Tippecanoe, Indiana. Treaty with the Chippewa, etc., September 26, 1833 at Chicago, Illinois.

Wakoah or Fox Hair. Treaty with the Kickapoo, December 9, 1809 at Fort Wayne, Indiana.

Walker, Chief. Potawatomi in Tazewell County, Illinois.

Walker, George E. Treaty with the Potawatomi, October 26, 1832 at Camp Tippecanoe, Indiana. Treaty with the Chippewa, etc., September 26, 1833 at Chicago, Illinois.

Walker, James. Treaty with the Chippewa, etc., September 26, 1833 at Chicago, Illinois.

Walworth, Reuben H. Treaty with the Peoria, etc., September 25, 1818 at Edwardsville, Illinois.

Wannangsea or Five Medals. Treaty with the Delawares, etc., June 7, 1803 at Vincennes, Indiana. Treaty with the Delawares, etc., September 30, 1809 at Fort Wayne, Indiana.

Wapello. Sauk chief. Antoine LeClair's biography of Black Hawk.

Wapemanqua or the Loon. Treaty with the Delawares, etc., September 30, 1809 at Fort Wayne, Indiana.

Wapewy or White Hair. Treaty with the Potawatomi, July 18, 1815 at St. Louis, Missouri.

Wapunsy. Treaty with the Ottawa, etc., August 24, 1816 at St. Louis, Missouri.

Washeone. Treaty with the Potawatomi, October 16, 1826 at Wabash, Indiana. Antoine LeClair's biography of Black Hawk.

Wassawcosangaw or Shine. Treaty with the Peoria, etc., September 25, 1818 at Edwardsville, Illinois.

Watkins, John. Treaty with the Chippewa, etc., September 26, 1833 at Chicago, Illinois.

Watt, James. Treaty with the Peoria, etc., September 25, 1818 at Edwardsville, Illinois. Treaty with the Kickapoo, July 30, 1819 at Edwardsville, Illinois.

Wau-pon-eh-see. Treaty with the Chippewa, etc., July 29, 1829 at Prairie du Chien, Michigan. Treaty with the Chippewa, etc., September 26, 1833 at Chicago, Illinois.

Wau-se-on-o-quet. Treaty with the Chippewa, etc., September 26, 1833 at Chicago, Illinois.

Waw-ba-saye. Treaty with the Ottawa, eetc., August 29, 1821 at Chicago, Illinois.

Wawpackeshaw. Treaty with the Kickapoo, July 30, 1819 at Edwardsville, Illinois.

Wawpamahwhawaw or White Wolf. Treaty with the Peoria, etc., September 25, 1818 at Edwardsville, Illinois.

Wawpeekonyaw. Treaty with the Kickapoo, July 30, 1819 at Edwardsville, Illinois.

Wawpeeshawkawnan or Shield. Treaty with the Peoria, etc., September 25, 1818 at Edwardsville, Illinois.

Waw-seb-baw. Treaty with the Ottawa, etc., August 29, 1821 at Chicago, Illinois.

Waw-we-uck-ke-meck. Treaty with the Ottawa, etc., August 29, 1821 at Chicago, Illinois.

Way-me-go. Treaty with the Ottawa, etc. August 29, 1821 at Chicago, Illinois.

Wecomawkawnaw. Treaty with the Peoria, etc., September 25, 1818 at Edwardsville, Illinois.

Weed, Edmund. Treaty with the Chippewa, etc., September 26, 1833 at Chicago, Illinois.

Weesoetee. Treaty with the Kickapoo, July 30, 1819 at Edwardsville, Illinois.

We-in-co. Treaty with the Chippewa, etc., September 26, 1833 at Chicago, Illinois.

We-is-saw. Treaty with the Chippewa, etc., September 26, 1833 at Chicago, Illinois. Treaty with the Potawatomi, October 27, 1832 at Tippecanoe, Indiana.

Wells, William. Treaty with the Delawares, etc., September 30, 1809 at Fort Wayne, Indiana.

Wenchester, Palemon H. Treaty with the Kickapoo, July 30, 1819 at Edwardsville, Illinois.

Wendell, John I. Treaty with the Chippewa, etc., September 26, 1833 at Chicago, Illinois.

Wendall, Tunis S. Treaty with the Chippewa, etc., September 26, 1833 at Chicago, Illinois.

Whipley, J. Treaty with the Ottawa, etc., August 29, 1821 at Chicago, Illinois.

White Cloud. Antoine LeClair's biography of Black Hawk.

White Elk. Treaty with the Kickapoo, July 30, 1819 at Edwardsville, Illinois.

Whitney, Daniel. Treaty with the Chippewa, etc., September 26, 1833 at Chicago, Illinois.

Williams, John Lee. Treaty with the Kickapoo, July 30, 1819 at Edwardsville, Illinois.

Wilson, John. Treaty with the Peoria, etc., September 25, 1818 at Edwardsville. Treaty with the Kickapoo, July 30, 1819 at Edwardsville, Illinois.

Winnemac. Treaty with the Delawares, etc., June 7, 1803 at Vincennes, Indiana. Treaty with the Delawares, etc., September 30, 1809 at Fort Wayne, Indiana.

Winslow, Dr. E. Treaty with the Chippewa, etc., September 26, 1833 at Chicago, Illinois. Treaty with the Potawatomi, October 27, 1832 at Tippecanoe, Indiana.

Wi-saw/Weesaw. Treaty with the Potawatomi, October 26, 1832 at Camp Tippecanoe, Indiana. Treaty with the Ottawa, etc., August 29, 1821 at Chicago, Illinois. Treaty with the Potawatomi, September 23, 1836 at Chippewaynaung, Indiana.

Wissineeaw or the Eater. Treaty with the Peoria, etc., September 25, 1818 at Edwardsville, Illinois.

Wolcott, Ellen M. Treaty with the Chippewa, etc., September 26, 1833 at Chicago, Illinois.

Wonesee. Treaty with the Ottawa, etc., August 24, 1816 at St. Louis, Missouri.

Woodcox, George B. Treaty with the Chippewa, etc., September 26, 1833 at Chicago, Illinois.

Woodcox, John. Treaty with the Chippewa, etc., September 26, 1833 at Chicago, Illinois.

Wright, John. Treaty with the Chippewa, etc., September 26, 1833 at Chicago, Illinois.

Wy-ne-naig. Treaty with the Ottawa, etc., August 29, 1821 at Chicago, Illinois.

The Young Wyandot. A Miami of Elk Hart. Treaty with the Delawares, etc., September 30, 1809 at Fort Wayne, Indiana.

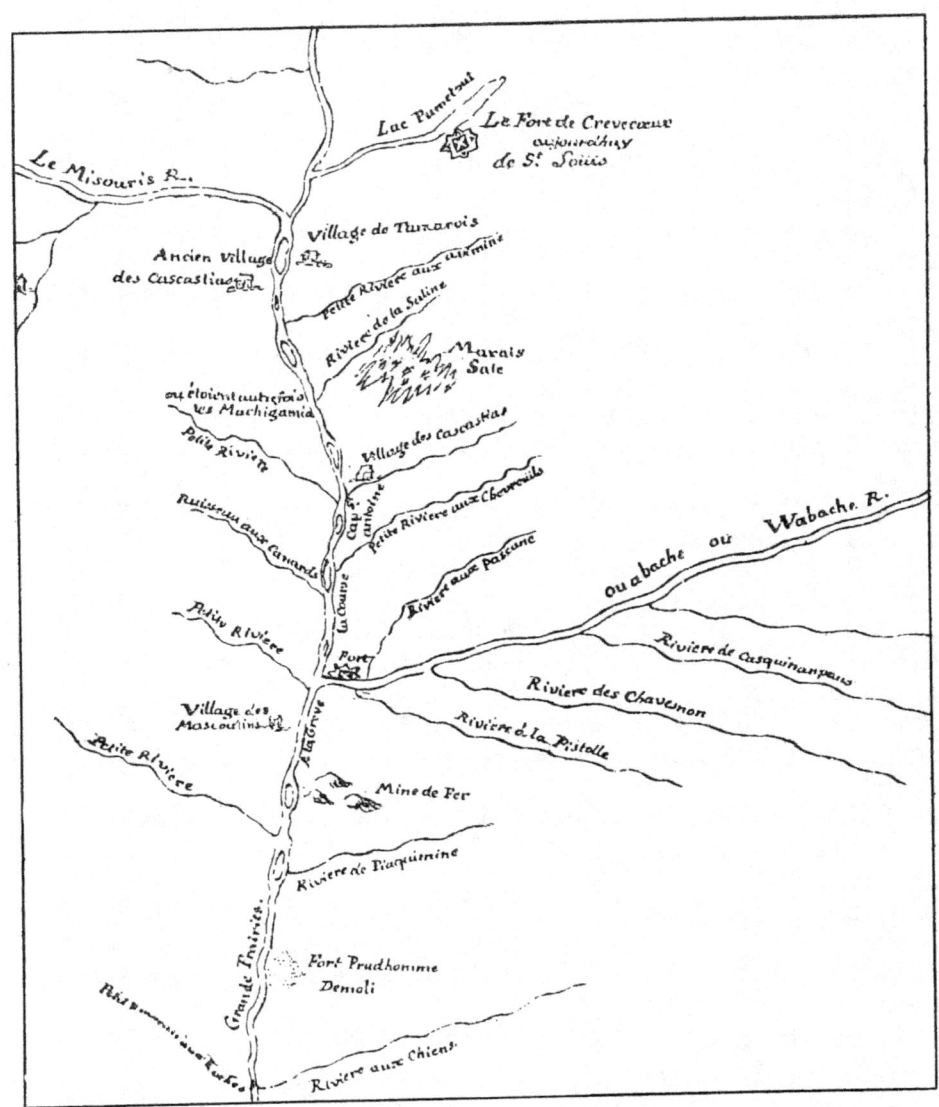

Section of a French map of the Mississippi Valley thought to have been made in 1703 or soon after that. The site designated "Fort" near the Ohio-Mississippi confluence was apparently the Juchereau tannery. The Ohio River is called the "ouabache ou Wabache R."

BIBLIOGRAPHY

Articles

"Archeological Sites to be Excavated." Northwestern University Archeological Program, 1979.

"Barbarity of Rangers." CENTENNIAL HISTORY OF MADISON COUNTY, ILL. 1912.

Bateman, Newton, L.L.D. editor. "History of Winnebago County." HISTORICAL ENCYCLOPEDIA OF ILLINOIS AND HISTORY OF WINNEBAGO COUNTY. Chicago: 1916. Vol. 2.

Belting, Natalia Maree. "The Native American as Myth and Fact." JOURNAL OF THE ILLINOIS STATE HISTORICAL SOCIETY. Vol. LXIX, #2. May, 1976.

Bennett, Milo. "The Building of a State--the Story of Illinois." JOURNAL OF THE ILLINOIS STATE HISTORICAL SOCIETY. Vol. 13. October, 1920.

Blodgett, Henry Williams (1821-1905) of Waukegan. "Recollections of the Potawatomi Chief Aptakisic." January 23, 1893.

Brown, Margaret Kimball. "The Search for the Michigamia Indian Village." OUTDOOR ILLINOIS. Vol XI, #3. March, 1972.

Buckley, Cornelious. "Stephen Mack, First Settler of Winnebago County." THE JOURNAL OF THE ILLINOIS STATE HISTORICAL SOCIETY. Vol. XII. April, 1919.

"Bulletin." WESTERN INTELLIGENCER. Kaskaskia, Illinois. August 21, 1816.

Burchett, Keith A. "Black Partridge at Fort Dearborn." ILLINOIS HISTORY. Vol. 29. November, 1975.

Chandler, Josephine Craven. "The Spoon River Country." JOURNAL OF THE ILLINOIS STATE HISTORICAL SOCIETY. Vol. XIV, #3-4.

"Chief Mashena and the Esquire, 1833." ILLINOIS SESQUICENTENNIAL OF CHRISTIAN COUNTY, ILL. 1880.

"Chief Walker and His Daughter." HISTORY OF TAZEWELL COUNTY, ILL. Chicago: Chapman & Co., 1879.

"Cities of Refuge." WESTERN INTELLIGENCER. Kaskaskia, Illinois. August 28, 1816.

Conway, Thomas G. "Potawatomi Politics." THE JOURNAL OF THE ILLINOIS STATE HISTORICAL SOCIETY. Vol. LXV, #4. Winter, 1972.

Deale, Valentine B. "The History of the Potawatomis Before 1722." ETHNOHISTORY. Vol. V. #4. Fall, 1958.

Custer, Milo. "Kannekuk or Kuanakuk." THE JOURNAL OF THE ILLINOIS STATE HISTORICAL SOCIETY. April, 1918.

Dept. of Illinois Conservation. "Prehistoric Sites." OUTDOOR ILLINOIS. Vol. XI #10. December, 1972.

East, Ernest G. "The Inhabitants of Chicago, 1825-1831." THE JOURNAL OF THE ILLINOIS STATE HISTORICAL SOCIETY, Vol. XXXVII. June, 1944.

Foreman, Grant. "Illinois and Her Indians." PAPERS IN ILLINOIS HISTORY. Springfield, 1939.

Gerwing, Anselm J. O.S.B. "The Chicago Indian Treaty of 1833." JOURNAL OF THE ILLINOIS HISTORICAL SOCIETY. Vol. 57. Summer, 1964.

Edmunds, R. David. "The Illinois River Potawatomi in the War of 1812." THE JOURNAL OF THE ILLINOIS HISTORICAL SOCIETY. Winter, 1969.

"Find Remains of Ancient American." SHELBYVILLE DEMOCRAT. Shelbyville, Illinois. October 25, 1926.

Gilmour, Peter. "Kampsville: International Center." OUTDOOR ILLINOIS. Vol. XIV #3. March, 1975.

Gormer, Peter. "Archeologist Fears His Project May be Relic of the Present." CHICAGO TRIBUNE. April 26, 1979.

Hall, George P. "Letter." SHELBYVILLE UNION. Shelbyville, Illinois. July 17, 1912.

Hauser, Raymond E. "The Illinois Indian Tribe: From Autonomy and Self-sufficiency to Dependency and Depopulation." JOURNAL OF THE ILLINOIS STATE HISTORICAL SOCIETY. Vol. LXIX. #2. May, 1976.

"Indian News at Rock River." WESTERN INTELLIGENCER. Kaskaskia, Ill. June 25, 1816.

"An Indian on Lying." SOUTHERN ILLINOISAN. Shawneetown, Ill. March 3, 1854.

"Indian Treasure Near Moweaqua." SHELBYVILLE DAILY UNION. Shelbyville, Ill. September 3, 1928.

Iseminger, William. "Cahokia Mounds." OUTDOOR ILLINOIS. Vol. XIII. #15. May, 1974.

"John D. Haeger: The American Fur Co. and The Chicago of 1812-1835." JOURNAL OF THE ILLINOIS STATE HISTORICAL SOCIETY. Summer, 1968.

Kelley, John. "1822 Chicago: from Tales of an 1822 Chicagoan." JOURNAL OF THE ILLINOIS STATE HISTORICAL SOCIETY. Oct.-Jan. 1922.

"Kiss the Rod and Bow Submission to our Authority." WESTERN INTELLIGENCER. Kaskaskia, Ill. June 12, 1816.

Kren, Robert. "Grand Illinois Venture." OUTDOOR ILLINOIS. Vol. XV. #3. March, 1976.

McVicker, George G. "A Chapter in the Warfare Against the Indian in Illinois During the Year 1812." JOURNAL OF THE ILLINOIS STATE HISTORICAL SOCIETY. Vol. XXIV.

Mohlerbrock, Robert H. "A New Geography of Williamson County." OUTDOOR ILLINOIS. Vol. XV, #1. January, 1976.

"Murder of Price and Son on 20 June 1811 in Madison Co., Ill." CENTENNIAL HISTORY OF MADISON CO., ILL. 1912.

Pearson, James E. "A New Geography of McHenry County." OUTDOOR ILLINOIS. Vol. XV. #8. 1976.

Platt, Doris. "LaSalle: Hardluck Explorer." AMERICAN HISTORY ILLUSTRATED. Vol. II, #2. May, 1967.

Rademacher, Carol Sims. "Climbing the Genealogical Tree." OUTDOOR ILLINOIS. Vol. XV #1. January, 1976.

Rennick, Percival Graham. "Peoria and Galena Trail." JOURNAL OF THE ILLINOIS STATE HISTORICAL SOCIETY. Vol. XXVII, #4.

Shannon, Dr. Frederick F. "Great Dates and Deeds of the Illinois." JOURNAL OF THE ILLINOIS STATE HISTORICAL SOCIETY. Vol. XVII. April-July, 1924.

Snyder, Dr. J.F. "Shick-Shack in Romance and in Real Life." JOURNAL OF THE ILLINOIS STATE HISTORICAL SOCIETY. Vol. II, #3. October, 1909.

Steen, Charlie R. translator. "An Indian Delegation in France, 1725." JOURNAL OF THE ILLINOIS STATE HISTORICAL SOCIETY. Vol. LXVII, #4. September, 1974.

Stelle, James. "An Indian at His Father's Grave." SOUTHERN ILLINOISAN. Shawneetown. September 2, 1853.

Struever, Stuart. "The Koster Site." OUTDOOR ILLINOIS. Vol. X, #2. February, 1971.

"Treaties." WESTERN INTELLIGENCER. Kaskaskia, Illinois. May 29, 1816.

Tucker, Glenn. "Tecumseh." AMERICAN HISTORY ILLUSTRATED. February, 1972.

"Uncle Sam." WESTERN INTELLIGENCER. Kaskaskia, Ill. October 9, 1817.

Vogel, Virgil. "Black Hawk as a Prisoner of War, 1832." THIS COUNTRY WAS OURS. New York: Harper & Row, 1972.

Vogel, Virgil. "Indian Place Names in Illinois." JOURNAL OF THE ILLINOIS STATE HISTORICAL SOCIETY. 1962. Four parts.

Walters, Alta P. "Shabonee." JOURNAL OF THE ILLINOIS State Historical Society. Vol. XVII, # . October, 1924.

"War with Black Hawk." EVENING TELEGRAPH. Dixon, Ill. March 21, 1900.

Weik, Jesse W. "An Unpublished Chapter in the Early History of Chicago." JOURNAL OF THE ILLINOIS STATE HISTORICAL SOCIETY. Vol. 7, #4. January, 1915.

Books

Adair, James. THE HISTORY OF THE AMERICAN INDIANS. London: Edward & Charles Dilly, Printed 1775.

Alvord, Clarence Walworth, editor. THE ILLINOIS COUNTRY 1673-1818. Springfield, Ill: Illinois Centennial Commission, 1920.

Armstrong, Virginia Irving. I HAVE SPOKEN. New York: Pocket Books, 1972.

Beckwith, Hiram W. THE ILLINOIS AND INDIANA INDIANS. Chicago: Fergus Printing Co., 1884.

Billard, Jules B., editor. THE WORLD OF THE AMERICAN INDIAN. Washington, D.C.: National Georgraphic Society, 1974.

Brandon, William. THE AMERICAN HERITAGE BOOK OF INDIANS. New York: Dell Pub. Co., 1974.

Brevets ILLINOIS HISTORICAL MARKERS & SITES. South Dakota. Brevet Press, Inc., 1976.

Campbell, Rev. T. J. S.J. PIONEER PRIESTS OF NORTH AMERICA. Vol. III. New York: The American Press, 1911.

Campbell, Rev. T. J. S.J. PIONEER LAYMEN OF NORTH AMERICA. Vol. I and II. The American Press, 1916.

Catherwood, Mary Hartwell. HEROES OF THE MIDDLE WEST. THE FRENCH. Boston: Ginn & Co., 1898.

Catlin, George. LETTERS AND NOTES ON THE NORTH AMERICAN INDIANS. Philadelphia: Hazard, 1857. Two volumes.

CENTENNIAL HISTORY OF MADISON CO., ILLINOIS AND ITS PEOPLE: 1812 to 1912. Chicago: Unigraphic, 1912.

Chafee, George D., editor. HISTORIC ENCYCLOPEDIA OF ILLINOIS AND HISTORY OF SHELBY COUNTY. Chicago: Munsell Publ. Co., 1910.

Church, Charles A. HISTORICAL ENCYCLOPEDIA OF ILLINOIS AND HISTORY OF WINNEBAGO COUNTY. Chicago: Munsell Pub. Co., 1916.

Clayton, John. Compiler. THE ILLINOIS FACT BOOK AND HISTORICAL ALMANAC, 1673-1968. Carbondale: Southern Illinois University Press, 1970.

COMBINED HISTORY OF SHELBY AND MOULTRIE COUNTY, ILLINOIS. Philadelphia: Brink, McDonough & Co., 1881.

Drake, Francis S. INDIAN HISTORY FOR YOUNG FOLKS. New York: Harper & Brothers, 1884.

Drennan, Dorothy D. CHRISTIAN COUNTY HISTORY OF 1880. Jacksonville, Ill: Production Press, Inc., 1968.

Edmunds, Walter D. THE MUSKET AND THE CROSS. Boston: Little, Brown & Co., 1968.

Fell, Barry. AMERICA: B.C. ANCIENT SETTLERS IN THE NEW WORLD. New York: Demeter Press Book, 1977.

Finley, Rev. James B. LIFE AMONG THE INDIANS. Cinncinnati: Curts & Jennings, 1857.

Forbes, Jack D., editor. THE INDIAN IN AMERICA'S PAST. New Jersey, 1964.

Gibson, A.M. THE KICKAPOOS: LORDS OF THE MIDDLE BORDER. University of Oklahoma Press, 1963.

HISTORICAL ENCYCLOPEDIA OF ILLINOIS AND LEE CO., ILL. Chicago: Munsell Publ. Co., 1904.

HISTORY OF CLARK COUNTY, ILLINOIS. 1907.

HISTORY OF FAYETTE COUNTY, ILLINOIS. 1878.

HISTORY OF HARDIN COUNTY, ILLINOIS. 1939.

HISTORY OF MACON COUNTY, ILLINOIS. Philadelphia: Brink, McDonough & Co., 1880.

Hodge, Frederick Webb. HANDBOOK OF NORTH AMERICAN INDIANS. NORTH OF MEXICO. Washington: Gov. Printing Office. 1912. Repub. 1968.

Jacobs, Wilbur R. DISPOSSESSING THE AMERICAN INDIAN. New York: Charles Scribner's Sons, 1972.

Kinzie, Mrs. John H. WAU*BUN: THE EARLY DAYS IN THE NORTHWEST. Chicago: Rand, McNally & Co., 1901. Reprint of 1855.

Kogon, Herman and Lloyd Wendt. CHICAGO: A PICTORIAL HISTORY. New York: E.P. Dutton & Co., 1958.

LeClair, Antoine. translator. LIFE OF MAKATAIMESHEKIAKIAK OR BLACK HAWK. Boston: Russell, Odiome & Metcalf, 1834.

Logie, Alfred E. CANADIAN WONDER TALES. Chicago: Row, Peterson & Co., 1925.

Lossing, Benson John. HARPER'S ENCYCLOPEDIA OF U.S. HISTORY. New York: Harper & Brothers, Publ. 1912. Ten volumes.

McKenney, Thomas L. and James Hall. THE INDIAN TRIBES OF NORTH AMERICA. Edinburgh, Eng.: John Grant. Rept. of 1865 edition.

Munro, William Bennett. CRUSADERS OF NEW FRANCE. New Haven: Yale University Press, 1918.

Murie, Claus J. A FIELD GUIDE TO ANIMAL TRACKS. C. 1940.

Naylor, Maria, editor. AUTHENTIC INDIAN DESIGNS. New York: Dover Publications, Inc., 1975.

Northey, Sue. THE AMERICAN INDIAN. San Antonio, Texas. The Naylor Co., 1854.

Parkman, Francis. LASALLE AND THE DISCOVERY OF THE GREAT WEST. Boston: Little, Brown, & Co., 1904.

Pease & Werner, editors. THE FRENCH FOUNDATIONS, 1680-1693. Springfield: Illinois State Historical Society, 1934. Vol. 2.

Peithmann, Irvin M. BROKEN PEACE PIPES. Springfield: Charles C. Thomas, Publ. 1964.

Quimby, George Irving. INDIANLIFE IN THE UPPER GREAT LAKES. Chicago: University of Chicago Press, 1960.

Robinson, Le., A.M. HISTORY OF ILLINOIS. New York: American Book Co., 1909.

Schlarman, J. H. FROM QUEBEC TO NEW ORLEANS. Belleville, Ill.: Buechler Pub. Co., 1929.

Sloane, Eric. THE SPIRITS OF '76. New York: Walker & Co., 1973.

Smith, George W. HISTORY OF ILLINOIS AND HER PEOPLE. Chicago: American Historical Society, 1927. Six volumes.

Thwaites, Reuben Gold and Calvin Noyes Kendall. A HISTORY OF THE UNITED STATES. Boston: Houghton Mifflin Co., 1914.

Thwaites, Reuben Gold. Editor: TRAVELS AND EXPLORATIONS OF THE JESUIT MISSIONARIES IN NEW FRANCE, 1610-1791. Cleveland: The Burrows Brothers Co., 1900,1901.

Timberlake, Henry. MEMOIRS, 1750-1765. Marietta, Ga.: Continental Book Co., 1948. Reprint.

Vogel, Virgil J. THIS COUNTRY WAS OURS: A DOCUMENTARY HISTORY OF THE AMERICAN INDIAN. New York: Harper & Row, Publ., 1972.

Walker, C.B. THE MISSISSIPPI VALLEY. Iowa, 1879.

Washburn, Wilcomb B. RED MAN'S LAND, WHITE MAN'S LAW. New York: Charles Scribner's Sons, 1971.

Whiteford, Andrew Hunter. NORTH AMERICAN ARTS. New York: Golden Press, 1970.

Wood, Norman Barton. LIVES OF FAMOUS INDIAN CHIEFS. Aurora, Ill.: American Indian Hist. Pub. Co., 1857.

Woodburn, Moran and Hill. OUR UNITED STATES. New York: Longmans, Green & Co., 1931.

Documents

Bureau of Indian Affairs. LAWS AND TREATIES. Charles J. Kappler. Washington, D.C. 1904. Various treaties from 1803 to 1861.

"Indian Tribes of North America." BUREAU OF AMERICAN ETHNOLOGY. Bulletin 145. Smithsonian Institution Press, 1952.

Office of Indian Affairs. Various Bulletins from Bureau of Ethnology.

"Report of the Illinois Board of World's Fair Commissioners at the World's Columbian Exposition." May 1-October 30, 1893. Springfield, Illinois: H.W. Rokker, Printe & Binder, 1895.

"A Study of Siouan Cults." Bureau of Interior. Washington, D.C.

State Department. TERRITORIAL PAPERS: TERRITORY NORTHWEST OF THE RIVER OHIO, 1787-1801. Washington, D.C. 1963.

INDEX

Allouez, Father Jean Claude 33
America, B.C. 7
American Fur Co. 63, 69
Amhurstburg 69
Aptakisic 36
Archaic Indian 5,7
Atkinson, Gen. Henry 40,41
Atwater, __ 46
Auld, Wiley 84
Aztecs 9

Bad Axe River 40
Baggatiway 33
Banning, Jeremiah 97
Baptist 28
Battle Ground Creek 32
Battle of Thames 69
Beaubien, Alexander 37,58
Beaubien, Charles 37
Beaubien, Jean Baptiste 37,58
Beubien, Medart 37
Beaubois, Rev. de 59
Beckwith, Hiram 15
Beaubois, Nicholas Ignace 47
Belting, Natalie Maree 17
Bennett, A. Milo 48
Bienville, de Father 59
Big Foot or Maungeezik 38,45,69
Biggs, William 17,31
Blackberry Flower 64
Blackfish 72
Black Hawk or Makataimeshekiakiak 27, 39,40,41,53,56, 76,95
Black Hawk War 46, 58,95
Black Partridge 42,43, 52

Blodgett, Judge Henry W. 36
Boisbriant, M. de 59,60
Bond Co., Ill. 99
Bourbonnais, Calish 44
Bourbonnais, Francois,Jr. 44
Bourbonnais, Francois,Sr. 44
Bourbonnais, Mawteno 44
Bourbonnais, Washington 44
Bourbonnais, Zeffa 44
Bourgmont, Etienne 47
Brandon, William 9,12
British 29,31,51,52,64,66
Brown, Margaret Kimball 25
Brown Co., Kansas 64
Buikstra, Jane 5
Bunyard, ___ 99
Burnet, Abraham 74
Burnet, James 74
Burnet, John 74
Burnet, Nancy 74
Burnet, Rebecca 74
Burnet, William 74

Cahokia Indians 7,8,10,13
Cahokia 67
Cahokia Mounds 50
Caldwell, Billy 38,45,58, 69
Calhoun Co., Ill. 5
Campbell, Esquire 88
Campbell's Point 88
Carey Mission School 63,74
Caromaine, Chief Naw Kaw 29,46
Carter, David 89
Cass, General 61
Catherwood, Mary Hartwell 17,23
Catlin, George 1,33,34,39, 55,56,57,76
Chamblee or Shaubenee 45
Charleston, Ill. 32
Cheeseekau 72
Cherokee 86
Chevalier, Catherine 68

Chevalier, Francois 68
Chevalier, Mary Ann 68
Chicago 29,32,36,38,42,
　48,51,58,61,62,63,69
Chicago Tribune 7
Chicagou, Chief 47,48
Chickasaw 86
Chillicothe, Ohio 72
Chippewa 33,58,66
Chouteau, Pierre 67
Christian Co., Ill. 88
Civil War 29
Clark Co., Ill. 101
Clark, George Rogers 1,
　11,50,72
Clovis or Paleo Indian
　3,5
Coiracoentanen Indians
　23
Confederated Tribes 1867,
　28
Cooper-Cole, Prof. Fay
　96
Cornstalk, Chief 72
Council Bluffs, Iowa 45,
　63
Counties of Illinois 78
Creek 86
Croghan, Col. George 29,
　66

Dagney, Ambroise 49
Dagney, Christmas 28,49
Dagney, Mary Isaacs 49,
　65
Dagney, Mary Shields Cott
　49
Danville, Illinois 29,55
Dearborn 29
Decatur, Illinois 98
Dekalb, Ill. 69
Delaware Ind. 14,15,65,
　72,87,97
Deliette, Sieur 16-23
Des Moines River 39
De Sota, Hernando 13
Des Plaines River, Ill.
　36,65,68
De Tonti, Henri 16,18,
　23
Detroit 67,77
De Villiers, Comm. Neyon
　66

De Villiers, St. Ange 67
Dickson Mounds 8
Dillon Creek 81
Dixon, ___ 62
Dixon, Ill. 95
Dixon's Ferry 71
Dobbs, ___ 90
Douglas 70
Duchess of Orleans 47
Ducoigne, Jean Baptiste
　1,11,14,50
Du Page Co., Ill. 36

Edwards, Gov. 32,42,52
Eel-Rivers Ind. 28
Elliot, Capt. 77
Embarras River 32,64

Fayette Co., Ill. 99
Fayetteville, N.C. 97
Fell, Barry 7
Ferrell, ___ 97
Fever River 71
Finley, James B. 92,93
Florida 13
Floyd, Capt. G.R. 77
Ft. Armstrong 31,56
Ft. Dearborn 36,37,38,42,
　45,58,63,68,75,77
Ft. De Chartres 66
Ft. Detroit 51,66
Ft. Green Bay 66
Ft. Harrison 64
Fort Hill, Ill. 99
Ft. Leavenworth, Kansas
　71
Ft. Meigs 73
Ft. Miami 73
Ft. Michilimackinac 66
Ft. Pimitoui 23,26
Ft. Pitt 66
Ft. St. Louis 16,23,24
Ft. Sandusky 66
Ft. Wayne, Ind. 61,73,77
Fortner, Elisha 94
Fox Ind. 16,27,31,40,
　56,60,85
Fox River, Ill. 62,69
France 59
Franklin, Ben ii
French 9,13,15,28,29,32,33,
　47,59,62,63,64,66

French India Co. 59
Fulton Co., Ill. 8

Gaines, General 40
Galena, Ill. 31,96
Galena Trail 44
Gnaddenhutten, Ohio 72
Gomo 52, 71
Gorner, Peter 7,8
Gragg, Jake 88
Great Corn Dance 91
Great Lakes 11
Gregory, James 84
Gregory, James, Jr. 84
Grundy Co., Ill. 70

Hall, Geo. P. 97
Hall, Jahu 97
Hall, John 97
Hall, Judge 100
Hall, Samuel 97
Hardin Co., Ill. 100
Hardscrabble 37
Harrison, Gen. Wm. H. 50,75,77
Hash, Philip 71
Heald, Capt. 42,77
Helm, Mrs. Linai T. 42
Helm, Lt. Linai 42
He Looks Like a Catfish 97
Helton, Harlin 5
Hickory Creek 99
Historic Indians 12,13
Hogue, William 101
Hononegah 53
  wife of Stephen Mack
Hootshoopkaw 46
Hopewell Indians 8
Hopkinsville, K6. 97
Howard, Benjamin 52
Hubbard, Gordon S. 69

Illinois Indian 1,9,12, 13,14-26,28,29,31,34, 65,67,76,96
Illinois Confederacy 59, 65
Illinoisan, Southern iii

Illinois River 3,7,8,9,12, 15,16,31,42,52,59,65,69, 71,85
India Company 47
Indian Creek 36
Indiana 65
Iowa 57,71,76
Iroquois 16,22,23,26
Isaacs, Mary Ann 49
Iseminger, William 10,11
Jackson, President 36
Jackson Co., Kansas 64
Jefferson Barracks, Mo. 40
Jeneir 54
Jesuits 15,45,47
Jews 91
Job, Archibald 71
Jocco 48
Johnson, Sir William 66,67
Joseph, son of Necanape 47

Kannekuk 32,55
Kankakee Co., Ill. 54
Kankakee River 42,75
Kansas 28,32,36,49,55,56, 58,62,68,74
Kaskaskia, Ill. 14,28,32,50, 59,80,82,83,85,86,91
Kaskaskia River 7,31,65,97, 99
Kaskaskias Indians 13,23, 24,49,65
Kawkeeme 74
Kaw River 36,71
Keokuk 40,56,57
Kickapoo Indians 17,20,28, 31,32,55,64,65,85,87,97, 99
Kickapoo Prophet 55
Kilgore, ___ 44
King Louis XV 47
King Louis 59
Kinzie, John 29,50,75,77
Koster Sites 5,7,8

LeClaire, ___ 57
LaFramboise, Alex 58
LaFramboise, Claude 58
LaFramboise Francois 37,58
LaFramboise, Francois, Jr. 58

LaFramboise, Joseph 58
LaFramboise, Josette 37, 58
Lake Geneva 38
Lake Michigan 42,63
Lake Shelbyville 8
LaLime, Jean 51
LaSalle 16,17,29,47
Later Archaic Ind. 7
Later Mississippian In. 9,10
Late Woodland, Mound Builders 10,11, 12
Leavenworth Co., Kansas 55
LeClaire, Antoine 39
Lenape 14
Levering, Capt. Samuel 52
Lewisburg, Kansas 49
Lincoln 70
Logan, James (Shawnee) 77
Lolo 71
Lorton, ___ 98

Maccanaw 32
McCoy, Rev. Isaac 28,55, 74
McDonald, Col. John 72
McHenry Co., Iowa 41
Mack, Almon 53
Mack, Henry 53
Mack, Hononegah 53
Mack, Mary 53
Mack, Rosa 53
Mack, Stephen Jr. 53
Mackinaw 68
Macon Co., Ill. 98
Macoupin Co., Ill. 79
Madison Co., Ill. 89, 90
Mad River, Ohio 72
Mahquala 71
Makataimeshekiakiak or Black Haw 27,39,40,41
Mamantouensa 59,60
Manete 73
Manitou 15,23
Mann, ___ 63
Mannabenaqua (Beaubien) 37

Manteno, Ill. 44
Marest, Father 24,33
Marie, dau. of Necanape 47
Marquette, Pierre 9,13,16
Mashena, Chief 88
Matson, N. 44
Maumee 61,69
Maungeezik or Big Foot 38
Mayans 12
Mazon Creek 70
Mechinquamesha 49
Mecure de France 47
Mediterranean 3
Meig, Col. R.J. 91
Metea 61
Miami 20,28,29,42,49,65
Miami Co., Kansas 65
Miami River 67
Michigan Territory 36,74
Miller, Esquire 88
Minnemung or Yellow Head
Mississippian Ind. 8,9
Mississippi River 7,12,13,16, 23,36,40,59,73,85
Missouri 70,74
Missouri River 36,65
Mitchell Creek 97
Mitchigamias 13,47,59
Modoc, Ill. 25
Mohawk River 67
Mohcossea 31
Momence, Isadore 54
Montgomery, William 90
Montreal 33,63
Moore, Capt. Abel 89,90
Moore, Major Frank 90
Moran, Pierre or Peerish 54
Morarian Town 69
Morris, Ill. 70
Moses 91
Mouingouenas 13,23,59
Moweaqua, Ill. 84

Nahpope 39,76
Naperville, Ill. 36,37
Nebraska 31
Neescotnemeg 45
Newberry, Carrie Mack 53
New Salem, Ill. 71
Nicanape 47
North Carolina 9
Northey 15

Northwestern Univ. 5

Ogee, John 62
Ogee, Joseph 62
Ogee, L.H. 62
Ogee, Madaline 62
Ohio 69.96
Okaw River 31,99
Okono Wiomex 69
Old Piqua 72
Old Stone Fort 100
Omaha, Neb. 46
Omaha Reservation 29
Ottawa Ind. 20,29,33,37,
  52,58,66,69
Ottawa, Ill. 70
Ouilmette, Antoine 63
Ouilmette, Archange 63
Ouilmette, Copah 63
Ouilmette, Lezett 63
Ouilmette, Louis 63
Ouilmette, Mitchell 63
Owl Creek 99

Pakoisheecan 32,64
Paleo or Clovis Ind.
  3,5
Paoli, Kansas 65
Parkman, Francis 16
Pekin, Ill. 81
Pensacola, Fla. 59
Peoria, Baptiste 28,49,
  65
Peoria, Mary A. Dagney
  64,65
Peoria, Ill. 28,42,52,
  62
Peoria, Lake 42
Peoria Ind. 13,23,59,
  65
Peoria Trail 44
Pepper 52
Piankaskaws 13,28
Piasa 9
Piasa Creek 90
Pierre, son of Nicanape
  47
Pike Co., Ill. 9,10
Platt River 36
Point, DuSable,
  Catharine 51

Pointe DuSable, Jean Baptiste
  51,63
Pokanoka 70
Pontiac 29,66,67
Pontiac, Michigan 53
Popul Vuh 12
Portage des Sioux, Mo.
  90
Porter, George B. 36
Potawatomi 20,28,29,31,32,33,
  34,36,38,42,51,52,53,58,61,
  65,68,74,75,77,85,87
Potherie, Bacqueville de la
  33
Powell, Major James 28
Prairie Du Chien 82
Prayer-stick 55
Price, ___ 90
Procter, Col. Henry A. 73
Prophet 39
Prophetstown 76
Pruitt, Abraham 89
Pruitt, Solomon 90
Puckeshinwa 72
Pugeshashenwa 73
Pyesa, Sac chief 39
Pypeogee 70
Pyps 70

Randolph Co., Ill. 7,25,79
Rennick, Percival Graham
  44
Reynolds, Gov. 31
Robinson, Alexander 45,58,63,
  68
Rochester, Michigan 53
Rockies 9
Rock Island, Ill. 31,46,56
Rock River 27,32,39,40,53,
  56,62,69,71,83,86
Rockton, Ill. 53
Ruddell, Stephen 72

Sacket's Harbor 80
St. Charles, Mo. 51.90
St. Clair Co., Ill. 43
St. Joseph, Mich. 42,61,77,
  98
St. Lawrence 9
St. Louis 67,82
Sand Creek 94

Sangamon River 31,71
Santa Domingo 51
Sauk or Sac Ind. 27,29, 31,39,40,56,76,82,85,86
Schlarman, J.H. 24
Schneider, Michael 84
Schoolcraft, Henry R. 61
Seneca 69
Shabbona's Grove 69
Shaubenee or Chamblee 38,45,69,70
Shawnee 65
Shawnee Prophet 52
Shawneetown, Ill. 32,79, 100
Shawwenoqua 37,58
Shelby Co., Ill. 8,87, 94,97
Shelbyville, Ill. 8,32, 84
Shickshack or Shakah 71
Shoal Creek, Ill. 99
Sinclair, Patrick 51
Siouan Cults, A Study of 3
Sioux 16
Sloane, Eric 2
Smith, Brig. Gen. 83
Smith, Dad Joe 44
Sparks, Richard 72
Spirits of '76 2
Spotka, Chief 69
Starved Rock 23,28
State Museum of Iowa 41
Stelle, James iii
Straits, Bering 3
Strowbridge, Col. 44
Strueve, Stuart 5,8
Stuyvesant Institute, N.Y. 57
Sylvan Grove 71

Tamarois 13,23,59
Tamenund 14
Taporiara 23
Taylorville, Ill. 88
Tazewell Co., Ill. 81
Tecumapease 72

Tecumseh 29,42,45,46,52, 69,72,73,77
Tend It 97
Thomas, Henry 44
Thompson, B.Ward 99
Thwaites 16
Tisné, M. du 59,60
Topennebee 54,74
Treaty of Chicago 1833 33,58,68
Treaty of Edwardsville 1819 31,50,65
Treaty of Ft. Harrison 1819 31
Treaty of Green Bay 1828 29
Treaty of Greenville 1795 28
Treaty of Prairie du Chien 63,68
Treaty of St. Louis 1804 27,49,55
Treaty of Tippecanoe River 33
Treaty of St. Mary's 1818 61
Treaty of Vincennes 1803 14,50
Turkey, Chief 87

Uncle Sam 80
Union 31
University of Chicago 96
University of Illinois 8, 17
Utica, Ill. 16

Vandalia, Ill. 99
Vandalia Railroad 99
Vermilion Co., Ill. 64
Vermilion River 29,31,32, 64
Vickery, John 90
Vincennes River 29
Virginia 9

Wabash River 28,31,49,64, 69,75

Wabunsee 75,77
Wagenseller, Jacob 81
Wakieshiek 76
Walker, C.B. 15
Walker, Chief 81
Wallis, William 88
War of 1812 29,31,32,
 69,71,77,89,90,101
Wasepeotan, Musqua 61
Washington, D.C. 40,56,
 86
Washington, General 28
Wayne, Gen. Anthony 72
Weas 13,28
Wells, Capt. William
 42,75,77
Welsh,____ 63
White Beaver 41
White Buffalo 97
White Cloud 40,76
Williamson, ____ 67
Wilson, William M. 87
Winnebago 3,29,31,38,46,
 58,62,68,71,76
Winnebago Swamps 89
Winnebago War 1827 31
Winnemac, Chief 42,77
Wisconsin 11,71,99
Wood River 90
World of American Indian
 3,5
World's Columbian
 Exposition 2,10

Yellowhead or
 Minnemung 45

ABOUT THE AUTHOR

A central Illinois native, Helen Cox Tregillis was born in Shelby County in 1944. She attended schools in Westervelt and Shelbyville, Illinois. She graduated from Eastern Illinois University, Charleston, with degrees in English, Spanish and guidance. She also attended the University of Minnesota at St. Paul, University of Scranton at Scranton, PA, and St. Francis College at St. Francis, PA.

In 1977 she wrote her first book TALES OF OLD SHELBYVILLE, an anecdotal of Shelbyville, Illinois. Since that time she has authored several more.

She has been a past member of several organizations: Illinois chapter of Colonial Daughters of the Seventeenth Century; the Shelby County Historical and Genealogical Society; Shelbyville Charter chapter of ABWA; and National Trust for Historic Preservation.

Currently she resides in Shelby County, and continues her writing, research and public relations efforts for community celebrations.